LAW AND GENDER INEQUALITY

Law in India is a series aimed at scholars, students, and law professionals, whose engagement with the law, especially in South Asia, reaches beyond standard black letter law towards an understanding of how laws and legal institutions have an impact upon, and in turn are affected by, society as a whole.

Series advisors:
UPENDRA BAXI, RAJEEV DHAVAN, MARC GALANTER
Founding advisor:
Late S. P. SATHE

OTHER BOOKS IN THE SERIES

RINA VERMA WILLIAMS
Postcolonial Politics and Personal Law
Colonial Legal Legacies and the Indian State
(Oxford India Paperbacks)

ROBERT LINGAT
The Classical Law of India
(translated and edited by J.D.M. Derrett)
(Oxford India Paperbacks)

ARVIND SHARMA
Hinduism and Human Rights
A Conceptual Approach

B. SIVARAMAYYA
Matrimonial Property Rights
(Oxford India Paperbacks)

LAW AND GENDER INEQUALITY
❖

The Politics of Women's Rights in India

Flavia Agnes

OXFORD
UNIVERSITY PRESS

OXFORD
UNIVERSITY PRESS

Oxford University Press is a department of the University of Oxford.
It furthers the University's objective of excellence in research, scholarship,
and education by publishing worldwide. Oxford is a registered trademark of
Oxford University Press in the UK and in certain other countries

Published in India by

Oxford University Press
22 Workspace, 2nd Floor, 1/22 Asaf Ali Road, New Delhi 110 002

© Oxford University Press 1999

First published 1999
Oxford India Paperbacks 2001
Ninth impression 2012

ISBN-13: 978-0-19-565524-7
ISBN-10: 0-19-565524-9

Printed in India by Repro India Limited

Dedicated to fifty years of nation building

Acknowledgements

The research that served as the foundation for this book was conducted as my M Phil dissertation with the National Law School, Bangalore. I am grateful to my guides, Professors N.S. Gopalakrishnan and M.P.P. Pillai for their useful suggestions and warm encouragement through the period of this research and to Professor Madhava Menon, Director, National Law School for not only motivating me to take on this work but also for helping me to structure it. To the faculty members and students of the National Law School I would like to express my gratitude for their participation in the various seminars, that I had presented during the course of this research and also for ensuring a lively debate which helped to formulate the study. Without NSG's gentle but constant goading I would never have found the time to complete this work.

Professors Upendra Baxi and B. Sivaramayya made comments on the first draft that have been extremely encouraging. I have tried to incorporate some of their valuable suggestions while working on the final draft.

The research could neither have been embarked upon nor completed in its present state, without the involvement of Madhusree Dutta, my friend and colleague at Majlis. Although not possessing a legal background, nevertheless her political clarity has helped me immensely in sorting out my doubts and confusion. I extend my special thanks to her.

I also extend my warm gratitude to my colleagues Saumya Uma and Veena Gowda for their help in locating source material, helping with the references and for reading through the various drafts and offering some very useful suggestions. Their contribution has enriched this work. I also extend a special thanks to them for taking on a greater burden of litigation work at the Majlis legal centre, while I was engaged in research work. I also thank each one at Majlis for the support and encouragement they extended to me while completing this work.

My thanks to Daisy Rodrigues for her help in entering the data, correcting the various drafts and all other minute editorial help which was required for completing this work in its present form. I must mention the help offered by Savita Krishnan in laboriously cross-checking all the references.

I also thank my daughters, Odile and Audrey for their gentle, unobtrusive emotional support through this venture.

Flavia Agnes
March, 1998

Contents

Abbreviations

ACJ	—	Appellate Case Journal
AIDWA	—	All India Democratic Women's Association
AIMPLB	—	All India Muslim Personal Law Board
AIR	—	All India Reporter
All	—	Allahabad
Anr	—	Another
AP	—	Andhra Pradesh
Art.s.	—	Article/s
BHCR	—	Bombay High Court Reports
BJP	—	Bharatiya Janata Party
BLR	—	Bengal Law Reporter
Bom.LR	—	Bombay Law Reporer
Bom	—	Bombay
Cal	—	Calcutta
Cr.PC	—	Code of Criminal Procedure
Cri.LJ	—	Criminal Law Journal
Cri.MC	—	Criminal Maintenance Cases
CAD	—	Constituent Assembly Debates
Del	—	Delhi
DMC	—	Divorce and Matrimonial Cases
FB	—	Full Bench
Guj	—	Gujarat
HC	—	High Court
HP	—	Himachal Pradesh
IA	—	Indian Appeals
IDA	—	Indian Divorce Act
ILR	—	Indian Law Reports
IPC	—	Indian Penal Code
J	—	Judge
JJ	—	Judges
JT	—	Judgment Today
Kar	—	Karnataka
KLT	—	Kerala Law Times

LAD	—	Legislative Assembly Debates
LC	—	Law Commission
LSD	—	Lok Sabha Debates
MIA	—	Moore's Indian Appeals
Mad	—	Madras
Madh Bh	—	Madhya Bharat
MLJ	—	Madras Law Journal
MP	—	Madhya Pradesh
Nag	—	Nagpur
Ori	—	Orissa
Ors	—	Others
P	—	Page
PP	—	Pages
Pat	—	Patna
PC	—	Privy Council
PD	—	Parliamentary Debates
P&H	—	Punjab and Haryana
PLJ	—	Pakistan Law Journal
PLD	—	Pakistan Law Digest
POC	—	Perry's Oriental Cases
Punj	—	Punjab
Rpt	—	Reprint
Raj	—	Rajasthan
RSD	—	Rajya Sabha Debates
R/w	—	Read with
S/s	—	Section/s
SB	—	Special Bench
SC	—	Supreme Court
SCC	—	Suprme Court Cases
SCR	—	Supreme Court Reporter
CW	—	Supreme Court Weekly
SDA	—	Sudder Diwani Adawlut
TLLS	—	Tagore Law Lecture Series
Tra—Co	—	Travancore and Cochin
UCC	—	Uniform Civil Code
v	—	Versus
WEF	—	With Effect From
WR	—	Weekly Reporter
WP	—	Writ Petition
WRAG	—	Women's Research Action Group

Table of Cases

1

INTRODUCTION—*A Need for Rescrutiny*

1.1 The Dilemma

The issue of women's rights and family law reform has been increasingly entangled within the polemics of identity politics and minority rights. At one level, there is a tendency among social activists to project the demand for an all-encompassing Uniform Civil Code (UCC) as a magic wand which will eliminate the woes and sufferings of Indian women in general and of minority women in particular. At another level, within a communally vitiated political climate, the demand carries an agenda of 'national integration' and 'communal harmony'. The demand is also laden with a moral undertone of abolishing polygamy and other 'barbaric' customs of the minorities and extending to them the egalitarian code of the 'enlightened majority'.

The sharp polarization between the pro-UCC lobby (with women's rights' groups sharing an uneasy alliance with the Hindu fundamentalists) and the anti-UCC lobby symbolized by Muslim fundamentalists, leaves very little space for voicing misgivings about the feasibility of an all-encompassing code, within a culturally diverse pluralistic society.

The secular lobbies demanding the protection of women's rights, place gender as a neutral terrain which is disjunct from the contemporary political events. In this context, it would be relevant to take note of the historical fact that although the plank of social reform has been 'women's welfare' the political manoeuverings at each stage of reform have resulted in bartering away crucial economic rights of women. In the current political context, the binaries within which the demand is located, postulates similar dangers.

It is true that the hardships and sufferings experienced by women of all communities, minority as well as majority, cannot be swept under the carpet nor glossed over with the rhetoric of freedom of religion. But within a complex social, political and economic structure, the demand of gender equality cannot be confined within a linear mould of granting uniform rights to women of all communities. In order to be relevant to women's lives, there is an urgent need to contextualize the proposed reforms within a comprehensive framework, inclusive of political and economic diversities.

The Bar Council Review on Uniform Civil Code articulates this premise as follows:

> The production of a new, progressive code, overnight, sought to be enforced from above, may be seen as a quick solution. Let us however remember, that there are well meaning, genuinely secular-minded intellectuals and social activists who would utter a word of caution and hoist the 'go slow' signal in order to achieve productive social results. This approach is informed by the experience of world history and the knowledge that crude homogenization is not the best solution. This caution must not, however, be equated with acceptance of the status-quo nor treated as a call for inaction.[1]

The current research is guided by a similar concern.

1.2 The Scope of the Research

The study is an attempt to map the issue of gender and law reform upon a broad canvas of history and politics and explore strategies which could safeguard women's rights within a sphere of complex social and political boundaries. While the aim of this research is not to formulate a complex code reflective of this plurality, it is hoped that the thumbnail sketch of the origin and development of family laws in India, along with an exploration of the state interventions at various strategic points in history, will provide the necessary backdrop, against which the demand for gender equality can be reformulated.

The under-currents beneath the rhetoric of women's rights are examined here. Since property and its regulation forms the basis of all civil laws, the legal systems located within feudal and capitalistic patriarchal moulds would necessarily be based upon anti-women stipulations to varying degrees. But within this universe of sexist biases, it is interesting to observe that at particular historical junctures, certain biases of a particular system are either over-emphasized or undermined.

The quote from Manu that a woman must be protected by

her father in childhood, by her husband in youth and by her sons in her old age, and that she is not entitled to freedom is common knowledge. But it is less well-known that Manu laid down comprehensive principles concerning women's separate property approximately two thousand years before the English legal system accepted this in principle, and issued the warning; 'Friends or relations of a woman, who, out of folly or avarice, live upon the property belonging to her, or the wicked ones who deprive her of the enjoyment of her own belongings go to hell'[2], or that Narada dictated that the husband must give one-third of his property to the first wife at his second marriage.[3] These positive dictates are shrouded by an over-emphasis on practices, which are not contained in the *smriti* texts, just as the universally accepted principles of Hindu law—widow immo-lations and infant marriages—are not. These projections which rendered the Hindu society barbaric, provided the moral justi-fication for colonial rule and its reformist scheme. During the corresponding period, undermining the issue of meagre economic rights of English women, within an indissoluble marital bondage under the tenets of feudal Christianity then becomes a political mission.

To cite another example, the Muslim husband's right to polygamy and triple *talaq* is known to the common man in every street corner. But the awareness that Islam introduced the revolutionary concept of contractual marriage and provided the wife with a unique right of *mehr*, as a restraint upon the husband's power of arbitrary divorce and further, that the Muslim law protects female heirs by restraining the male power of testa-mentary succession is confined to academic echelons. In this sphere of selective knowledge, the polygamy of a Muslim male, which would lead to an increase in the Muslim population and threaten Hindu society, would provide the basis for the enactment of a Uniform Civil Code, within a culture of aggressive major-itarianism. This political agenda can then be conveniently crouched under an avowed concern for the protection of Muslim women's rights. The codified Hindu law has to be then held up as a model of reform, glossing over the fact that this codification has not been able to arrest the trend of increasing violence towards and even murder of young Hindu brides in their matrimonial homes, to curb Hindu bigamy nor to protect Hindu wives from poverty and destitution.

Similarly, in the political controversy over the UCC, which is locked within the binaries of Hindu majority and Muslim minority, the claims of other religious minorities to a separate personal law, as a marker of their cultural identity, can be conveniently undermined.

The issue is shrouded with other riddles. Why are Christians, whose parent statute revolutionalized the matrimonial laws of all other communities in India, still saddled with archaic provisions which deny them the basic right of divorce? Why does a numerically insignificant religious community like the Parsis, warrant a separate personal law or, even more pertinently, why does an important secular statute like *the Indian Succession Act* divide the secular Indian population into two basic categories: 'Parsis' and 'non-Parsis'? If this is the norm, then why are the reformist and breakaway religions like the Buddhists, Jains, Sikhs (and also the Arya Samajis, Brahmos and the Prarthana Samajis), who are numerically more significant and whose basic tenets differ from Hinduism, and from each other, clubbed together under legal Hinduism?

How was it possible to codify Hindu law despite strong opposition from the various sects and the *sanathan* religious leaders, while even a stray whisper of opposition suffices to stall minority reforms? Then again, if stalling minority reform is the norm, how was a hastily formulated bill constraining the rights of divorced Muslim women hurriedly enacted despite opposition from secular forces?

Probing the answers to these riddles, which lie not in legal edifices but within political vagaries, is the starting point of this book. To achieve this, it was essential to cross the boundaries of popular presumptions and examine the lesser known aspects of family law. The first task was to examine whether, within the constrained sphere of patriarchal norms, there were spaces within religious laws and customary practices of Hindus and Muslims, which women could negotiate to protect their economic rights. The second task was to explore whether the statutory interventions during colonial and post-colonial periods, which were set within the adversarial adjudicative fora introduced by the British, have led to the widening of this constrained sphere. This political grounding of women's rights is essential for evolving strategies which will effectively safeguard women's rights in a communally vitiated political climate.

1.3 The Scheme of the Chapters

The study is divided into four parts. Part One deals with the pre-colonial and colonial legal systems. Chapters 2 and 3 set out the scriptural mandates and customary practices which governed family relationships of various communities in the pre-colonial societies of ancient India. Within the broad scheme of legal principles, the safeguards provided for securing women's rights form the nucleus. The following two chapters, 4 and 5, examine the transformations brought about within these systems through colonial interventions. Since the present legal system in India was introduced by the British, changes brought about during nearly three centuries of colonial rule in the administrative structure of the courts and in the realm of personal laws, both by statutory reforms, as well as judicial interpretations, are important markers. The politicization of women's rights within the realm of family law is inextricably woven into the history of this period.

Part Two of the study examines the Post-independence developments. The Constitution enacted in 1950, became the touchstone against which women's claims to gender equality were to be tested. In Chapter 6, the Hindu law reforms of the 1950s and the implications of this for women are examined in the context of the constitutional guarantee of equality and non-discrimination. Chapter 7 examines whether, in the subsequent decades, the state adhered to its promise of moving towards uniformity and gender equality, or whether there has been a reverse trend, consolidating communal identities. The implications of two significant judicial decisions which invoked wide media publicity and altered the parameters of the discourse on family law reforms—the Tilhari judgement invalidating triple talaq, and the Supreme Court directive for the enactment of a Uniform Civil Code in the context of conversion and bigamy by Hindu males—are analysed in Chapter 8.

In Part Three, the political questions which shroud reforms within non-Muslim minorities (the Parsis and the Christians) are explored. Since the legal systems governing these communities do not figure prominently in the discourse on the Uniform Civil Code, the legislative history contextualized within the social and political terrains is set out in detail, starkly revealing the intricate links between political issues and women's rights.

The concluding section, Part Four, addresses current debates. The issue of the Uniform Civil Code has dominated the gender discourse during the last decade. The communally vitiated atmosphere has brought two constitutional guarantees—minority rights and gender equality—into direct conflict, which has resulted in a political stalemate. To circumvent this problem, legal scholars and women's organizations have been compelled to reformulate their earlier demand for a compulsory Uniform Civil Code. Various alternative measures, both long-term and interim, are being explored by the legal academia, women's groups, and official fora, as well as the Muslim intelligentsia. These efforts are summarized in the concluding chapters. The relevance and implications of the various formulations and strategies to women's economic rights, both within marriage and after its dissolution, are critically assessed. Some suggestions for strengthening the economic rights of women are made which are, at best, tentative. The objective is to bring the focus of the debate to the central issue, that of arresting the trend of destitution and consequential impoverishment of women.

1.4 Research Methodology

The research is grounded within the contemporary women's movement and addresses itself to the trends and currents within it. The analysis of legal texts is undertaken within the framework of feminist jurisprudence. Although the study is primarily a legal exploration, the legal discourse is located within historical developments and contemporary political events and therefore acquires an interdisciplinary flavour.

The research is based on published material, such as legal texts, law journals, reported and unreported judgements; Constituent Assembly and Parliamentary debates, official documents, drafts and bills prepared by legal academicians, women's groups and the official fora; papers presented during conferences and seminars, informal presentations and discussions at legal workshops, and media reportage.

An examination of the strengths and weaknesses of the model drafts formulated in recent years is an important feature of this research. This will hopefully aid the process of arriving at the level of minimum consensus among the progressive and secular lobbies concerned with women's welfare which is a basic pre-condition for reform in the realm of family laws. Even if the first step of this process is facilitated by this work, the attempt would be well worth while.

Notes

1. Mishra, V.C. (ed.), 'Special Issue on Uniform Civil Code', *Indian Bar Review* XVIII/3–4 (1991) p.vi–vii.
2. Manu's dictate is reaffirmed by later *smritikars* such as Katyayana.
3. Narada's dictate is based on Manu who says: 'To a woman whose husband marries a second wife, let him give an equal sum as a compensation for the supersession, provided no stridhana has been bestowed on her but if she has been allotted let him allot half', (*Manusmriti* III: 52).

PART ONE:

PRE-COLONIAL AND COLONIAL LEGAL STRUCTURES

2

Plurality of Hindu Law and Women's Rights Under it

Introduction

It is generally believed that the 'pristine' Hindu law was particularly harsh towards women and denied them sexual and economic freedom. These two freedoms, in fact, are co-ordinate. The Hindu joint family structure based on male coparcenary, was the institution through which sexual control was effected by denying women the right to own property. In this realm of patriarchal domination, women were treated as chattels and upon marriage dominion over them was transferred from the father to the husband within the confines of perpetual tutelage. In support of this premise, it is emphasized that Manu, the arch law giver of the Hindu religion stipulated: 'A woman must be dependent upon her father in childhood, upon her husband in youth and upon her sons in old age. She should never be free.' The strict sexual control was also effected through ordeals. Sita's ordeal by fire is set out as an example. It is also believed that the modernity ushered in during the colonial rule and post-independence period helped to loosen out this strict sexual control by granting women the right of divorce and property ownership.

While not negating in their entirety the above premises, this chapter sets out to explore whether, within these strict dictates, the Hindu law permitted any space for negotiating women's rights. In addition, whether the Indian society of the pre-colonial era was uniformly governed by a singular set of laws and if not, whether the diversity within customary practices situated women's rights on a varying scale. In order to probe the answers to these queries, the following areas are explored: (i) the diverse sources of Hindu law; (ii) women's right to property under the orthodox scriptural law; (iii) the various regional and local customs which granted women rights; (iv) the heterogeneous characteristics of the Indian society governed by the Hindu law.

2.1 The Diverse Sources of Hindu Law

Plurality of laws and customs and non-state legal structure were the essential characteristics of the ancient Indian communities. The original texts were of Aryan origin but the assimilation between Aryan and non-Aryan tribes led to diverse customs and practices.

The scriptural law, like most ancient legal systems, traces its origin to divine revelations. During the early period, there was no distinction between religion, law and morality. They were cumulatively referred to as *dharma*. The three sources of dharma are *shruti* (the divine revelations or utterances, primarily the *Vedas*), *smriti* (the memorized word—the *dharmasutras* and the *dharmashastras*) and *sadachara* (good custom).[1] Although the Vedas were treated as the fountainhead of Hindu law by jurists, they do not contain positive law (or lawyer's law).[2] Hence the codified laws governing Hindu marriage and family relationships derive their roots from the smritis and *nibandhas* (commentaries and digests).[3]

From about eight century BC to fifth century AD elaborate guidelines governing all aspects of social relations were laid down in the smritis—the dharmasutras and the dharmashastras. The *smritikars* were neither kings, religious heads nor legislators.[4] They were philosophers, social thinkers and teachers. They preached dharma, a code of conduct governing all aspects of life from the spiritual to the temporal. The dharmashastra literature is a complete science and covers all aspects of law, ethics and morality. These were works of encyclopaedic scope and covered a wide range of topics—social obligations and duties of the various castes and of individuals in different stages of life; the rules of governance, principles of punishment and warfare for kings and officials; codes of social behaviour between men and women of different castes, as well as between husbands and wives, fathers and sons and family members within the domestic sphere; rules of exogamy and endogamy, sonship and punishments for sexual improprieties; rituals of birth, death, marriage, worship and sacrifice; the philosophy of karma and rebirth; civil or financial matters like rules of contracts, property devolution and interest rates etc. While some rules were mandatory, others were indicatory and hence were not binding and could be treated as mere guidelines. The religious and moral precepts were *achara* and the legal business or positive law was *vyavahara.*

These were not written texts and the knowledge was passed down by an oral tradition from generation to generation through the institution of Brahminical priesthood or *guru-shishya parampara.* So each generation could have re-interpreted the guidelines incorporating their contemporary contexts. In this tradition, the same smriti could have been evolved by several philosophers and at different historical times. Hence it is not surprising to find contradictory statements regarding a controversial issue attributed to the same smritikar.

The nibandhas which were detailed commentaries upon the earlier smritis, were of a later period (fifth to eighteenth century AD). Here too, the authors had sufficient scope to re-interpret the original precepts as per the social organizations of their times. Many a times, while laying down a new principle, the commentators used the ploy of interpretation or explanation of an old dictum for greater validity.

Despite the claim of divine origin, the smritis were based on local and well-established customs.[5] The general agreement among the smritikars was that the time-honoured and accepted customs have greater validity than the scriptures. Since each smriti was influenced by local customs of its region, the eighty-odd known smritis differed a great deal from each other.

The two distinct and dominant schools, validated under the Anglo-Hindu law (a colonial construction), were *Mitakshara* of Vijnaneshwar (eleventh century) and Dayabhaga of Jimmutavahana (twelfth century). While the latter was the leading authority in Bengal, the former was recognized as an authority in the rest of the British India. But there were also several regional deviations, which were categorized as sub-schools of Mitakshara. Significant among these were Mithila, Benares, Bombay and the Dravida schools.[6]

The smritis regarded marriage as an essential *sanskar.* Marriage was mandatory, to discharge the debt to one's ancestors, the debt of begetting offsprings. It was also essential for performance of religious and spiritual duties. So a wife was not just a *patni* or *grihapatni* but a *dharmapatni.* Since progeny was the most important factor, a husband could procure numerous wives for this purpose and could also appropriate the children born to these wives out of other alliances through the institution of sonship, to fulfil spiritual obligations or for temporal objectives such as property devolution. Children could also be begotten through concubines, slaves and other informal alliances and these children were conferred recognition under a legal premise called *dasiputra*.

Although marriages were deemed indissoluble, under certain exceptional situations, the wife or the husband were permitted to dissolve the matrimonial union. Narada (who relied upon an earlier version of *Manusmriti*) laid down five situations in which a woman could take another husband—her first husband having perished, died naturally, gone abroad, impotent or lost caste.[7] Kautilya's *Arthashastra* also stipulated certain situations in which either the husband or the wife could divorce each other—mutual enmity, apprehension of danger and desertion for justifiable reasons. According to scholars, the stipulation in *Manusmriti* against remarriage of wives and widows appears to be a later insertion.[8]

2.2 Concept of Stridhana in Smritis[9]

The smritis and commentaries, with their roots in a feudal society of agrarian landholdings,[10] prescribed a patriarchal family structure, within which women's right to property was constrained. Under the Mitakshara law, the property of a Hindu male devolved through survivorship jointly upon four generations of male heirs. The ownership was by birth and not by succession. Upon his birth, the male member acquired the right to property.

Although the male members owned property, this ownership cannot be equated with the modern notion of ownership which essentially confers the right of alienation. The basic characteristic of the joint property was its inalienability. The property could not be easily disposed of by way of sale, gift or will. Hence the joint ownership, of males was more notional than actual. The property was managed by the head of the family or *karta* for the benefit of the entire family including its female members. So, in effect, until the property was partitioned, the right of male members was essentially the right of maintenance. Even after partition, the property in the hands of each of the coparcenars, continued to be joint property, held in trust along with his male progeny for the benefit of the next line of descendants.

Since women did not form part of the coparcenary, they did not have even the notional right of joint ownership, hence they could not demand partition. After partition, a sonless widow had the right to inherit the share of her deceased husband.[11] Women had the right to be maintained from the joint property and this right included the right of residence. Since divorce was not commonly prevalent, after marriage, women could not easily be deprived of their right of residence and maintenance in their husband's house.

The husband was bound to maintain the wife despite all her faults including quarrelsome nature, neglect of household, barrenness and adultery, though the scale at which she had to be maintained would go down as per the severity of her faults. He could marry again, but he was under the legal obligation to continue to maintain the first wife. In addition, the wife was entitled to 'supersession fee' an equal share of the property, which the husband gifted to the new wife. Women also had the right to claim marriage expenses from the joint property in their natal house.

In order to partially set off the disability suffered under the notion of joint ownership by male members, the smritikars assigned a special category of property to women they termed as *stridhana*. The first mention of this term is found in the Gautama Dharmasutra. He provided not only for the woman's separate property but also distinct and separate rules for its succession.[12] From this period to the next millennium, the scope of stridhana was gradually expanded to include almost every category of property.

Continuing the tradition set by Gautama, Manu laid down six forms of stridhana consisting of gifts by relatives on various occasions : (i) gifts before the nuptial fire (*adhyagni*); (ii) gifts during bridal procession, while the bride is being led from her natal residence to her husband's house (*adhyavahanika*); (iii) gifts of love from father-in-law and mother-in-law (*pritidatta*) and gifts made at the time of obeisance at the feet of elders (*padavandanika*); (iv) gifts made by father; (v) gifts made by mother; and (vi) gifts made by brother. A dictate of Manu[13] which empowered a righteous king to punish as thieves, the relatives, who appropriated the property of a woman, is quoted in all the later smritis with approval.

Vishnu, a later smritikar, added four more categories to this enumeration—gifts by the husband to his wife on supersession, that is, on the occasion of his taking another wife (*adhivedanika*); (ii) gifts subsequent, that is, gifts made after marriage by husband's relatives or the wife's parents (*anwadheyaka*); (iii) *sulka* a marriage fee or a gratuity; and (iv) gifts from sons and relatives. The later sages, Yagnavalkya, Katyayana, Narada, Devala etc. widened the concept further. Yagnavalkya (around second century AD) expanded the scope of stridhana by adding the word *adhya* ('and the rest') to the enumerations of Manu and Vishnu.

The Katyayana Smriti lays great emphasis on stridhana and discusses the concept elaborately. Katyayana classified the stridhana property as *saudayika* and *asaudayika* and explained the concept as follows: What is obtained by a married woman or by a maiden, in the house of her husband or her father, from her brother, husband and parents is saudayika stridhana. The saudayika stridhana could include immovable property. He emphasized the exclusive ownership both in terms of sale and gift and laid down: Neither the husband, nor the son, nor the father, nor the brother have authority over stridhana to take it or to give it away. This injunction is almost in the nature of a warning to male members to lay their hands off the woman's property.[14] If the husband borrowed saudayika money, he was under a legal obligation to repay it with interest.

The wealth which was earned through mechanical arts or through gifts from strangers during the subsistence of marriage was categorized as asaudayika stridhana and only these were made subject to the husband's control. This is not to deny that these were also a woman's separate property or her stridhana which she could use according to her will. The stipulation was merely that a woman had to obtain her husband's consent before disposing off the property of this category during the subsistence of her marriage. There also seems to have been a usage that property upto the limit of two thousand *panas* should be given annually to a married woman by the father, mother, husband, brother or kindred (relatives) for her personal use.[15]

Sir Henry Maine in his '*Early History of Institutions*, while describing the institution of stridhana comments, 'It is certainly remarkable that the institution seems to have been developed among the Hindus at a period relatively much earlier than among the Romans.' But he seems to be under the erroneous impression that it gradually deteriorated to an insignificant position. There is no historical basis for this premise, if the later commentaries are the indicators.[16]

The *Mitakshara* (Vijnaneshwar, eleventh century AD), the most widely recognized source of the Anglo-Hindu law, expanded the scope of the term *adhya* mentioned by Yagnavalkya and laid that property obtained by a woman through inheritance, purchase, partition, seizure (adverse possession), and finding is her stridhana. Through this expansion, every category of property was brought under the scope of stridhana and the woman was granted exclusive ownership over it. While this was endorsed by many of the later commentators, *Vyavahara Mayuka* (of Nilakantha Bhatta, seventeenth century, Bombay school), further expanded the scope.[17]

The *Dayabhaga*, the accepted authority of the Bengal school, did not adopt the notion of joint male ownership or coparcenary. Upon the death of the head of the family, the property was partitioned equally between the legal heirs. Women as widows, daughters and mothers were conferred a share in the family property. Despite this, even the Dayabhaga school recognized the concept of a woman's specific property. But in the absence of a coparcenary spreading over four generations, the need to prescribe a wide interpretation to the term was absent here. So under the Dayabhaga system, stridhana was restricted to gifts and movables. Under all other schools, stridhana included movable, as well as immovable property. Property acquired by a woman by her own exertions was her stridhana according to the Bombay, Benares and Dravida schools.[18]

As can be observed, a system of property ownership by women seems to have been an integral and significant part of the ancient moral, ethical, and legal social norms. Due weightage was granted to this subject in Sanskrit scriptures. It does appear that patriarchal collusions constantly undermined the scriptural dictates of the dharma of stridhana. At each time the smritikars, with great effort, brought the emphasis back to women's ownership of property and in the process also expanded its scope. There seems to be a constant tussle between the smriti dictates and patriarchal subversions within the family. The task of the smritikars seems to have been challenging, as can be observed from the comments of Jimutavahana, the author of Dayabhaga, on completion of his chapter on stridhana. Thus has been explained the most difficult subject of succession to a childless woman's stridhana.[19]

The most distinguishing feature of stridhana property was its line of descent. Under *Mitakshara*, after the woman's death, it devolved firstly on the unmarried daughter, then on the married daughter who is not provided for, followed by the married daughter who is provided for. Next in line was the daughter's daughter followed by the daughter's son. The woman's own son could inherit it only in the absence of heirs in the female line.[20]

2.3 Women's Rights Under Customary Law

As already mentioned, custom was an important source of law. Two points need to be stressed regarding this source—(i) its validity under the smriti law; and (ii) its relevancy to castes and tribes who were not governed by the smriti law.

Local customs were held in high esteem and were acknowledged as an important source of law under the smritis. The widely used smriti terms, *achara, sadachara, shishtachara, loksangraha* etc. denote custom. Gautama, Manu and Brihaspati granted special recognition to custom.[21] Narada went further and proclaimed that custom overrides the sacred law. The local customs varied from region to region with the southern states granting women greater rights. Incidentally, it is believed that both Yagnavalkya and Vijnaneshwar, who had expanded the parameters of women's right to property, hail from the southern (*Dakshina*) region.[22]

The southern and predominantly Dravidian regions followed various pro-women practices of property inheritance even under smriti law. The liberal construction of stridhana under the Bombay and Madras schools is an indication. There were also several other lesser known local customs and practices prevalent in this region. For instance, there are many references to women and their use of property in inscriptions in Tamil Nadu which can be traced back to the thirteenth to fourteenth century AD during the reign of the Cholas, Pandyas and Pallavas. The inscriptions indicate that the ownership rights of women included the power of alienation through gifts and sales.[23]

Some recent studies indicate the prevalence of such a custom in various parts of southern India. A custom of handing over a piece of land to the daughter at the time of her marriage prevailed within the Madras Presidency. The income from this land was meant for the woman's exclusive use. This was her stridhana and devolved on the female heirs and passed from mother to daughter. Known as *manjal kani*, the land was perhaps meant to provide an independent income to the daughter which would be sufficient to provide for her personal expenses—manjal (turmeric) and kumkum (vermilion) while in her husband's house.[24] A similar custom of providing a piece of land for the daughter's personal expenses also prevailed in the Maratha region of Bombay Presidency by the name *bangdi choli* (which literally means bangles and blouse).[25] A woman's right to one-third of the property upon her husband's remarriage was also recognized within certain lower castes of Madras Presidency and was termed as *patnibhagam*.

Carol Upadhya[26] in her study of the coastal Andhra region has recorded a practice of giving land to the daughter at the time of her marriage which was known as *katnam*. As per her observation, this land owned by the woman was very distinct from the land owned by the husband's family and also distinct from the present day north Indian practice of dowry. Even after marriage, traditionally, women continued to exercise control over this land.

In another study of Virasaiva women from the Karnataka region, it was observed that twelve per cent women inherited property in the form of land from their mother and this property customarily passed on only to daughters, even when boys did not inherit from their fathers.[27] The Lingayat women of Dharwar region, who were categorized as sudras in various judicial pronouncements, also had rights of divorce, remarriage and property ownership. An illegitimate son was recognized as an heir, which is a marker of the status enjoyed by women in informal alliances. The Buddhist literature also indicates that women could own and gift property in their own right.[28]

The Brahminical-Aryan customs followed by the upper castes of north India exercised a strict control over women and their sexuality and the status of women among them was low, as compared to women from the lower castes and the Dravidian regions. Brahminical norms such as pre-puberty marriage, restraint on widow remarriage and divorce, the ceremony of *kanyadan* (the ritual of gifting away a bedecked bride to a scholarly groom), the theory of the *kshetra and beeja* (soil and seed symbolizing that the woman was a mere carrier of the children who actually belonged to the man), are an indication of the lower status of women among the north Indian higher castes.

The main aim of these rituals was to maintain the caste purity through a very strict control over women and their sexuality. Since the women of the lower castes were relatively free from these notions of purity and pollution, they were governed by a relatively lax code of sexual morality and women held a slightly higher social status. The lower castes or sudras were considered to be out of the varna system and hence they were not governed by the code of the smritis. The code was applicable only to dwijas or the twice born (upper castes) who had the sanction to study the sacred texts.[29]

The women from the lower castes worked and contributed to the household and hence were not totally dependent upon their men. Most lower castes practised the custom of bride price, (*kanya sulka*), where the father of the girl had to be compensated for the loss he suffered by the marriage of his daughter. Although the smritis shunned this practice, as it amounted to sale of a daughter, the fact that it is mentioned in most smritis and commentaries indicates its wide acceptance by the various castes including the Brahmins.[30] It continued to be followed by several castes in the southern region, northern Himalayan regions and various tribes right up to the pre-independent period.[31]

Marriages among the various lower castes were less sacramental and more contractual. The ritual of *saptapadi* (seven steps round the sacrificial fire, which is essentially a Brahminical ritual) or kanyadan did not prevail among these communities. Child marriages were not the norm. The contractual marriages were based on consent of adult women and the rituals and ceremonies reflected this element of consent and contract. The rituals of remarriage of widows and divorcees varied from those of virgin brides. Steele, while recording the customs of the Deccan region mentions an interesting phenomenon. Remarriages of women whose husbands had been absent for a long time was permitted. If the first husband eventually returned, the woman had a choice to live with either the first or the second husband, but the husband who was deserted had to be reimbursed his marriage expenses.[32]

A careful scrutiny of the contemporary customs of the various castes reveals the different customary forms of divorce and remarriage prevailing within these communities even to the present day. In the Deccan (Maratha) and Gujarat region, such practices are termed as *kadi mod* (literally, breaking of a twig symbolizing the termination of the relationship) or *chor chittee* (deed of divorcement drawn up by community or family elders after breaking the wife's neck ornaments). If the process is initiated by the woman, either she or her father would have to return the bride price and also a part of the marriage expenses.[33] Normally, the mother is given the custody of her younger children, while the father retains the custody over older children and is under an obligation to bear their marriage expenses. The practice of maintenance after divorce is not prevalent among these communities. This is perhaps because the women are gainfully employed and the husbands do not possess property, resources or a steady income upon which the women can lay their claim to maintenance. Also divorced women are accepted within the natal family and a subsequent remarriage or an informal alliance is not unusual.

The custom of divorce and remarriage was also prevalent among Lingayats of Karnataka, Kapus of Telengana, the Jats of Punjab and Ajmer, certain castes among the Maravars, Namo-sudras of Bengal and the Banias of Bihar. In northern parts of Bihar, Orissa, Chota Nagpur and Assam all castes and tribes except the Brahmins, Kayasthas, Banias and Rajputs permitted remarriage. It was also accepted as a universal custom in the Darjeeling and Manipur regions.[34] The prohibition to divorce and remarriages of widows and divorcees existed only among communities, who emulated the Brahmins in order to rise in social scale. As a community progressed economically, it took on Brahminical practices and exercised a stricter sexual control upon its women.

Among various castes and tribes, along the Malabar coast, there were female-headed joint family households and matrilineal inheritance patterns.[35] Of these the Marumakkathayam and Aliyasanthana received judicial recognition during the British period. The female-headed joint families were called Tarwad and Tavazi and the line of descendants was traced through the female line. These systems were in existence until recently and were brought to an end through specific state intervention in the form of legislations in the post-independence period.[36] Under these systems, the women contracted loose marriage alliances which were called *sambandham*, which could be easily terminated with the consent of both the parties.[37] Since property devolved along the female line, there was no premium on the sexual purity of these women.

From the above discussion it is evident that even a casual glance at the customs of the lower castes is sufficient to indicate an absence of a strict sexual code and correspondingly, a wider scope for negotiating women's rights of divorce, remarriage and property ownership among them.

2.4 'Hindu'—An Amorphous Society

If communities practised such diverse norms of marriage, divorce, remarriage, property ownership, notions of legitimacy and illegitimacy then, for the purpose of administering the Hindu law, who is a Hindu becomes a central issue. The question has baffled the judiciary for well over a century and has continued to be illusive to the present day. Is it a question of affiliation to a religious institution as the European Christians understood the term or a far more complex phenomenon?

While contextualizing the Hindu law and its diverse practices, it is necessary to highlight that the term 'Hindu' is not located within the smritis.[38] It is derived from 'Indoi', a term used by Greeks to denote the inhabitants of the Indus valley.[39] The first known use of the term to denote a community was in 1424, by Krishnadevaraya II in a plate Satyamangala, to distinguish themselves from the Muslim rulers.[40] The Portuguese referred to the 'natives' as Gentoos which is derived from the word gentiles indicating non-believers. The initial Regulations of the East India Company also used the same term to denote non-Muslim natives.

In the pre-colonial era, diverse local customs were administered by family or caste councils or village panchayats, which were termed as *kula* (family or tribe), *shreni* (artisan's guilds) and *puga* or *gana* (assembly or association).[41] These local panchayats which were non-state legal fora regulated civil life and family relationships. These local councils co-existed along with the royal courts *sabhas* and *samitis* where the king (or his appointees) administered justice according to the school or authority accepted in the area with the help of Brahmin Pundits. It was an accepted norm that territorial conquest did not lead to tempering of local customs. During the Moghul rule, although the Muslim rulers introduced the Islamic criminal courts, they did not interfere with the local customs and civil laws. Hence, during this period civil laws continued to be regulated by local customs and usages.

At various historical points, when the Brahminical hold over the scriptures became oppressive, several religious and social reform movements challenged the Vedic orthodoxy and Brahminical hegemony and formed various religions and sects i.e. Buddhism, Jainism and Sikhism, Virashaivism, the Bhakti movements, the social reform movements during the nationalist struggle etc. A common thread which runs through all these reformist religions is their revolt against the dominance of rituals, the supremacy of Brahmins and the Sanskrit language. In retaliation, the reformers preached in the language of the common people (the lower castes). Like the smritis, their preachings were also codes governing social relationships, i.e. denouncement of the caste hierarchies and concepts of purity and pollution laid down by smritis, simple forms of marriage, divorce and re-marriage, an elevated status for women and the lower castes as preachers, peaceful co-existence based on the principle of non-violence etc. Some sects like the Sikhs preached monotheism and some even atheism. But conversion did not necessarily entail a change in property regulations. The institution of property and religious affiliation were not co-ordinate. So although people converted to different religions, faiths and sects, they continued to follow the local customs and usages regarding property devolution.

As far as property was concerned, the law of the land was binding. Laws and customs applied to people locally, regionally and along family, tribe (or caste) and trade divisions. Hence, it is not surprising that there was greater similarity between customs and usages (as well as language and traditions) of people from a region irrespective of their religious faiths and affiliations, rather than between followers of a religion living in far flung regions. The Malabar region and the north-eastern tribal belts provide concrete examples of this. On the Malabar coast, not only the Nairs, but also the predominantly Muslim population of the Lakshadweep Islands of around 99 per cent, follow the matrilineal system of Marumakkathayam.[42] The Khasi, Jaintia and Garo tribes of north-east region who converted to Christianity continue to follow the matrilineal inheritance. The Khojas, Cutchi Memons, the Bohras and the Halai Memons, who were converts from the trading communities of Gujarat, followed the Hindu custom of joint family property, based on male coparcenary.[43]

The system of dividing the communities on the basis of their religion and applying to them their own 'divine law' disregarding their caste, tribe and race differences is of recent origin, introduced by the British. The British administrators tried to introduce a concept of institutionalized religion with clear affiliations along the lines of Christian church fellowships and subordinated the institution of property to it. The Indian sub-continental trend for well over 2000 years, right from Buddha and Mahavir around 500 BC had been to gravitate away from the structure of Brahminical superiority and Sanskrit orthodoxy. But the new colonial structure reversed the trend and subjected communities to the dominance of the smriti rules.

Since there were sharp differences in the customs and practices of Aryan and non-Aryan communities, the British system of deciding cases on the basis of a 'divine and ancient Hindu law' caused a lot of confusion and hardship. Whether Dravidians and other non-Aryan races should be brought into the pale of Hinduism through the application of the shastric law of Aryan origin was a highly contested issue. Whether the reformist sects, who had protested against Brahminical orthodoxy, ought to be governed by the same Vedic law which they had renounced was another disputed question. Several aboriginal tribes also challenged the application of shastric Hindu law to them. It is through this process of litigation over property disputes that the sharply defined community of Hindus governed by the present day Hindu code was constructed during the colonial regime.[44] The diversity of the communities to whom the Hindu law was made applicable led Derrett to comment as follows: 'The Hindus are as diverse in race, psychology, habitat, employment and way of life as any collection of human beings that might be gathered from the ends of earth.'[45]

The Brahminical smriti rules of marriage and property ownership were applied to people who could hardly be called Hindus and conversely, since the Hindu law was applied to them, these communities were termed as Hindus. Although, the ground for the construction of a Hindu community was laid during the colonial rule, this perceived homogeneous religious community of the Hindus was given the final seal of statutory recognition only in the recent past, when the 'Hindu Law' was codified in the post-independence period. By then the dilatory measures adopted by the courts had reached such a scale that it was easier to indicate a Hindu negatively, i.e. a person who is not a Muslim, Christian, Parsi or Jew.[46]

A precise meaning of the word 'Hindu' has defied all efforts at definition through statutes or judicial pronouncements. An attempt to define the term was made in 1966 by the Supreme Court in *Shastri Yagnapurushadasji v Muldas Vaishya*:[47]

> Acceptance of the Vedas with reverence, recognition of the fact that the means of ways to salvation are diverse and realisation of the truth that number of gods to be worshipped is large is the distinguishing features of Hindu religion.

Relying upon this definition, the court held that the Satsanghis are Hindus. The issue before the court was one of social justice, i.e. entry of Harijans to a temple belonging to the Satsanghis of Swaminarayan *sampradaya* (sect). The Satsanghis pleaded that they were not Hindus and hence were not governed by the pre-constitution temple entry legislation of the Bombay Presidency through which Harijans were granted the right to worship in a Hindu temple. By the time the judgement was pronounced, the courts were under the Constitutional mandate of equality, non-discrimination and social justice. And hence the question, whether the Satsanghis are Hindus had become irrelevant and was only of academic interest.

In the broad context in which the terms 'Hindu' and 'Hindu law' are used, the definition of the Supreme Court is highly inadequate. According to Paras Diwan, instead of a religious sect, had it been argued that *chamars* were not Hindus, the court would have faced an uphill task.[48] It would be problematic to define a community like the chamars, who apparently know little of Hindu religion and less of Hindu philosophy, as Hindus.

Under the present day statutes governing Hindus, any definition of Hindu in terms of religion will be inadequate. A person who practices or professes it, is a Hindu. But a person does not cease to be a Hindu, nor become less of a Hindu only because he/she does not have faith in Hindu religion/philosophy or does not practice or profess it. Even when a Hindu starts practicing, professing or having faith in a non-Hindu religion, he will not cease to be a Hindu unless it is conclusively established that he has formally converted to that faith. Even an atheist does not cease to be a Hindu.

So, the present day 'Hindu'. community governed by the 'Hindu laws' with their Brahminical tilt and an Anglo-Saxon base, is more a legal fiction than a religious entity or a social reality. In effect, it was an attempt to impose an alien and higher caste system of law upon a pluralistic society.[49]

Notes

1. Desai, S.T., (ed.), *Mulla's Principles of Hindu Law*, Bombay: N.M. Tripathi (1994) (16th edn.) p.3.
2. Sarkar Shastri, G.C., *A Treatise on Hindu Law*, Calcutta: B. Banerjee & Co. (1933) (7th edn.) p.12.
3. Bhattacharjee has argued that nibandhas had already replaced the smritis at the time of colonial intervention and hence smritis could no longer be considered as the 'source' of Hindu law. See Bhattacharjee, A.M., *Hindu Law and the Constitution*, Calcutta: Eastern Law House (1994) (2nd edn.) p.17 n.4.
4. Ibid. p.19.
5. Bhattacharjee has emphasized that smritis and commentaries were mere recordings of existing customs. Ibid. pp.12–39.
6. Raghavachariar provides a comprehensive list of various schools and the relevant authorities. See Raghavachariar, N.R., *Hindu Law: Principles and Precedents*, Madras: The Madras Law Journal Office (1980) (7th edn.), VOL. p.5.
7. Narada Smriti, XII 106–110.
8. See Alladi, K. (ed.), *Mayne's Treatise on Hindu Law & Usage*, New Delhi: Bharat Law House (1993) (13th edn.) p.146.
9. Desai, S.T. (ed.) *Principles of Hindu Law*, pp.157–63.
10. By the time the initial smritis were written roughly around 800–300 BC the pastoral and nomadic Aryans of the early Vedic period had settled into agriculture and feudal land relationships had been well established. The period of the early smritis coincides with the Mauryan period, the Magadha and Kosala kingdoms and early Buddhism. This is the period when agriculture was revolutionized by the use of the iron plough. See Chapters VI and VII of Sharma, R.S., *Material Culture & Social Formations in Ancient India*, Madras: Macmillan India Ltd. (1983), pp.89–134.
11. Under Dayabhaga school a woman had a right even to the undivided property of her deceased husband, while under Mitakshara the right was limited to the divided property.
12. The relevant passage is found in Gautama Dharmasutra, XXVIII, pp.24–6. The reference to this is made by Dr Jolly, J., 'Hindu Law' Tagore Law Lecture Series Publication (TLLS 1883) p.228. See Alladi, Mayne's *Treatise on Hindu Law and Usage*, p.874. Some scholars believe that the concept is rooted in the tradition of bride price.

13. *Manusmriti*, VIII : p.29.
14. Gill, K., *Hindu Women's Right to Property in India*, Delhi: Deep & Deep Publications (1986) p.301. Also see Mayne's *Treatise on Hindu Law & Usage*, p.877.
15. *Alladi*, p.875.
16. Ibid., p.875 fn.5.
17. According to him every category of property belonging to a woman was her stridhana.
18. Desai (ed.), *Principles of Hindu Low*, pp.163–9.
19. Banerjee, G., 'Hindu Law of Marriage and Stridhana' (TLLS-1878), Calcutta: S.K. Lahiri & Co. (1923) (5th edn.) p.290.
20. Desai (ed.), *Principles of Hindu Law*, pp.172–3.
21. The famous quote of Brihaspati, *'Deshe deshe ya acharah paramparayakramagateh; Sa shastrarthabalavanaiva langhaniyah kadhachava'*, which exhorts local, tribal and family usages. The principle was given judicial recognition by the landmark decision of the Privy Council in *Collector of Madura v Moottoo Ramalinga* (1868) 12 MIA 397, which laid down, 'clear proof of usage will outweigh the written text of law'. According to Mulla, the importance attached to the law-creating efficacy of custom in Hindu jurisprudence was so great that the exponents of law were unanimous in accepting custom as a constituent part of law. Desai (ed.), *Principles of Hindu Law*, p.2.
22. Mukund, K., 'Turmeric Land—Women's Property Rights in Tamil Society since Medieval Times', *Economic & Political Weekly*, XXVII/17 (1992), p.WS-2.
23. Ibid., p.WS-3.
24. Ibid., p.WS-5.
25. See the decision in *Yadeorao Jogeshwar v Vithal Shamaji* AIR 1952 Nag 55, where a reference to this custom is made.
26. Upadhya, C., 'Dowry and women's property in coastal Andhra Pradesh' (1990), in *Contributions to Indian Sociology*, New Delhi: Sage Publications(n.s.) 24, 1 (1990), p.29.
27. Mullati, L., *The Bhakti Movement and the Status of Women: A Case Study of Virasaivism*, New Delhi: Abhinav Publications (1986), p. 106.
28. Talim, M., *Women in Early Buddhist Literature*, Bombay: Popular Prakashan (1972).
29. Srinivas, M.N., *Caste in Modern India and Other Essays*, Bombay: Media Promoters & Publishers (1962) (Rpt. 1986) p. 55.
30. Ibid., p. 54.
31. Ibid., p. 44, 'A note on Sanskritisation and Westernisation.'
32. Ibid., p.44 Also K. Alladi *Mayne's Treatise on Hindu Law and Usage*, p.147.
33. The recording of customs of the Deccan and Gujarat region by Steele and Borradaile during the period 1820–1830 provides an ample proof of these practices. The fact that these customs still prevail among the lower castes was confirmed during various legal workshops in the Padra, Vagoria and Daboi districts of Baroda region organized by the Mahila Samakhya, Gujarat which were co-ordinated by the author

during the years 1996 and 1997. Women from various lower castes, Vankar, Baria, Vasava, Ratodia, Chamar and Rohit, participated in the workshops.

34. See Alladi, K., *Mayne's Treatise on Hindu Law and Usage*, p.147.
35. According to Mayne, The Marummakkathayam was practised by Warriers, Unnis, Padvals, Chakkiars, Thiyas, Nambiars (Brahmin) and Mopillas (Muslim). The Aliyasanthana was prevalent in south Kanara among the Billavas, Bunts, Maraveers etc. See Alladi, K., *Mayne's, Treatise on Hindu Law & Usage*, p.1209.
36. The Hindu Succession Act, 1956; The Kerala Joint Hindu Family System (Abolition) Act 1975.
37. Through the Malabar Marriage Act of 1896 the Sambandham marriages were granted legal recognition
38. The term used in the smritis is Arya.
39. Diwan, P., *Hindu Law*, Allahabad: Wadhwa & Company (1995), p.4.
40. Discussion with Prof. Sukumari Bhattacharji, author of *Women and Society in Ancient India*, Calcutta: Sasumati Corporation Ltd. (1994).
41. Desai (ed.), *Principles of Hindu Law*, pp.34–5.
42. Dube, L., 'Conflict and Compromise Devolution and Disposal of Property in Matrilineal Muslim Society', in *Economic & Political Weekly* (1994) XXIX/21, p. 1273.
43. Alladi, K., *Mayne's Treatise on Hindu Law and Usage*, p.63.
44. See Chapter 4 for a further discussion of this process.
45. Derrett, J.D.M., *Hindu Law Past and Present*, Calcutta: Mukherjee & Co. (1957), p.1.
46. S2 (c) of the Hindu Marriage Act, 1955. The same explanation is also found in the other Hindu Acts. The scheduled tribes are exempted from the application of these Acts.
47. AIR 1966 SC 1119
48. Diwan, *Hindu Law*.
49. It is relevant to note that the Brahmins constitute only around 5 per cent of the population. The upper castes who could have been governed by the smriti law could not, at any point, have been more than 20 per cent of the total Indian population. See *Table 1* for a caste-wise composition of the population.

3

Evolution of Islamic Law and Women's Spaces Within It

The Islamic law is of later origin than the smritis and also lays greater claim to divinity. Despite this claim, its evolution is not through a process of continuous revelations but through a rational method of interpretations.[1] A similarity can be traced between the smriti law and the Islamic law regarding the various schools and sects which flow from the original text which have led to plurality of practices. In this chapter, the origin and development of Islamic Law, its entry into the Indian subcontinent, women's rights under the Islamic jurisprudence as well as the later reforms are briefly sketched.

3.1 Origin and Development of Islamic Law

Islam means peace and submission.[2] The *Shariat* is the central core of Islam and is an infallible guide to ethics.[3] But this is not law in the modern sense. The jurisprudential law is called *Fiqh*. According to Fyzee, this is the name given to the whole science of jurisprudence. It is the knowledge and obligation derived from the four sources of Islamic law,[4] — the Koran, Sunna, Ijma and Qiyas.[5] The Koran which is the divine revelation (the word of God), is the highest source. Compiled from memory after the Prophet's death from the version of Osman, the third Caliph, it contains about six thousand verses but not more than two hundred verses deal with legal principles and only eighty verses deal with law of personal status. The Caliphs, as the Prophet's successors, took up the responsibility of adjudication of disputes among the people and while drawing upon the Koran, they continued the application of the ancient Arab system of arbitration and customary law.

The second source of Islamic law is *Sunna* or tradition. The word 'Sunna' means trodden path, Initially, the term was applied to the custom and practice of pre-Islamic tribes and the early

Muslims of seventh century AD. But later the word denoted the practice and precedents of the Prophet—Hadis. As a source of law, Hadis is as binding as the principles of the Koran. By the eighth century, Sunna became the ideal and established doctrine of the ancient schools, expounded by its representatives. Hence, in the present context, Sunna could either mean the living tradition of the schools or the traditions of the Prophet.

The third and equally binding source is Ijma, which is an agreement among legal scholars of any generation. This was supported by the Hanafi doctrine that the provisions of law must change with the changing times and of the Maliki doctrine that new facts require new decisions. In developing Islamic law by consensus, the doctrine of Ijtihad was developed. Ijtihad means one's own reasoning to deduce a rule of Shariat law. With the passage of time, liberty to reason was restricted and by ninth century Ijtihad was considered as the privilege of great scholars of the past.

The last source of Islamic Law is Qiyas which is reasoning by analogy. It does not involve laying down new principles but is merely a rule of interpretation. A principle laid down in the text can be applied to another situation, if it can be demonstrated that the rule laid down in the text governs the situation at hand by applying logic or reasoning, though the language of the text and the situation at hand are not strictly the same. It became a source of law as a sort of compromise by the Shafii and Maliki school. The Fatawas (legal opinions of scholars and judges), though not a source of law, have been instrumental in the development and enrichment of legal principles.[6]

There are two broad sects of Islam, the Sunnis and the Shias. The four recognized schools of Sunni Law are Hanafi, Maliki, Shafii and Hanbali. The Hanafi school founded by Abu Hanifa (699- 767 AD), has a wide following. The school is also known as Kufa school. Originating in Iraq, the doctrine spread to Syria, Afghanistan, Turkish Central Asia and the Indian subcontinent.

The founder of Shia school is Imam Jafar. The most important among the Shia schools of law are Ithna Ashari and Ismaili. The Ismaili sect of Shia school is the dominant majority in Persia. Elsewhere, they are generally in a minority. In India, the Bohras and Khojas (Agha Khani) are Shias belonging to the Ismaili sect.

The main difference between the Shia and Sunni sects is the

doctrine of *Imamat*.[7] According to the Sunnis, the leader of Muslims is Khalifa, the successor of the Prophet, who is a temporal and political ruler rather than a religious chief. For religious matters they must follow the Shariat. The institution of the Khalifat was abolished in 1924. According to the Shias, the Imam is the final interpreter of the law on earth. He is a leader not by the suffrage of the people but by divine right as descendant of the Prophet. Some Shia sects like the Dawoodi Bohras originated as an outcome of a rebellion against the oppressive Sunni theology in around eighth century BC and were considered to be reformative and emancipatory.

The laws of the two main sects and their sub-sects vary a great deal from each other. Among the various schools, the Maliki school is the most favourable to women and the Shafii school comes next. North Africa follows mainly the Maliki law and women enjoy greater rights. Under this doctrine, a wife has an option to dissolve her marriage on the following grounds: cruelty; non-payment of maintenance; absence of husband; insanity; leprosy; castration and sexual malformation.[8]

3.2 Introduction of Shariat Law in India

Islam came to India through the trade routes of the Arabs via the Arabian sea. Some of these traders settled down along the Malabar coast in eighth century and adopted the local customs and practices (Mopillas of Kerala). They did not follow the Shariat law.[9]

The Shariat was first introduced to the Sultanates of Afghan and Turkish rulers and entered India around the twelfth to the thirteenth century AD. The Muslim Sultans who invaded India were Hanafis. They relied upon the Ullamas to be the religious and legal arbitrators. The new Sultanates followed the basic law of Islam, the Shariat, as interpreted by the Ullama in the royal courts. The Moghul emperors were Hanafis and the Qazis appointed by them administered the Hanafi law. It is through this channel that the Shariat was established in India. The text books of Hanafi law are based on Fatawa Alamgiri, which is a collection of Fatawas compiled during Aurangzeb's regime and the Hedaya (the guide).[10]

The Muslim society as it evolved in India fell into three broad categories, the nobility, the peasantry and the artisans. The

Muslim population of the towns consisted of artisans and traders. Among the artisan classes, there was great assimilation between Hindu and Muslim rituals, ceremonies and customs.

There were many instances of the converted Muslims following their earlier non-Islamic norms and practices (for instance, the caste system or the joint family property system—coparcenary).[11] The Islamic law of pre-emption crept into Hindu customs and practices and came to be accepted as part of Hindu law. The population in the villages, both Hindus as well as Muslims, followed their own local laws and customs. The Bhakti and the Sufi movements of the fourteenth to sixteenth century, which were based on egalitarian principles of equality and love in opposition to the stronghold of religious orthodoxy and caste hierarchy, helped to bring further assimilation between the lower strata of Hindu and Muslim communities.[12] At the advent of colonial rule there were several amphibious communities which could not clearly be distinguished as either wholly Hindu or wholly Muslim due to the intermingling of their laws, customs and practices. The case of the Khojas, Cutchi Memons and other converted Muslim trading communities of Gujarat who followed the Hindu joint family system of property devolution and the matrilineal practices of the Mopilla community of the Malabar coast has already been mentioned in the preceding chapter. There were several other communities like the Meos of Rajasthan and the Satpanthis of Madhya Pradesh whose legal identity raised difficult questions of law. The Satpanthis and Pirpanthis of Gujarat, Cutch and Khandesh were by caste Matia Kunbis. They followed the *Atharva Veda* and worshipped the tombs of Muslim saints. They observed some Islamic practices like fasting during the holy month of Ramadan and repeated the Kalima. They buried their dead both with Hindu and Muslim prayers.[13]

In a rather recent case, the disputed issue was the right of females to inherit property. In an effort to deny females the right, it was pleaded that Meos follow Hindu family law and hence women have no right to inherit property. Over-riding this premise the court held that the Meo Mewati community is Muslim and is governed by Mohammedan law. Hence, daughters cannot be denied a right in the property in the absence of a conclusive proof of a custom to the contrary.[14] A curious trend in the litigation of the pre-independence period was for the females to plead the cover of the Mohammedan law while the opposing patriarchal subversive forces could be aided by a plea of customary Hindu practice of property devolution.[15]

According to R. H. Hutton, such an interesting illustration of the commixture of Hinduism and Islam was not restricted only to western India. He observed that at times great difficulty existed in deciding whether a particular body of people is Muslim or Hindu. Other such illustrations provided by him are those of the Naayitas of Malwa, the Kuvachandas of Sind, the Hussaini Brahmins and the Malkanas of Uttar Pradesh, the Bhagwanias or Satyadharmis of Bengal and the Chuhras of Punjab.[16]

3.3 Rights of Women Under Islam

It is important to contextualize the principles of Shariat law within tribal Arabia. The Arabs were traders and had mastered the law of contract.[17] The basic principle of contract was applied to other social relationships including marriage. Although the Shariat is premised upon a patriarchal familial structure, it is not based on a feudal economic structure. The matrimonial principles differ from the principles evolved within European feudalism reflected in the Canon law. The principal of indissolubility of marriage, which is intrinsically linked to inalienability of feudal land, did not govern Islamic law of marriage and divorce. The principles governing marriage transactions were similar to trade contracts—offer, acceptance and consideration—forming its base. The principles of a contractual marriage provided a better scope for defining women's rights than the status marriages under the Christian laws of feudal Europe during the corresponding period.

The Prophet converted the custom of bride price of tribal Arabia to mehr which would be a future security to a married woman.[18] In an era of unlimited polygamy, the Prophet restricted the number of wives to four with an injunction that each wife be treated with equal dignity and affection. Islam was also the first legal system to grant women the right of inheritance. Some positive provisions of the Islamic law of marriage and succession are listed below:

Marriage is a civil and dissoluble contract: This is in sharp contrast to the principles of Christianity and Hinduism where marriage was traditionally viewed as an indissoluble sacrament. Later at the advent of nineteenth century when Europe made a shift from feudalism to capitalism, the marriage was transformed from status to contract. This concept was later introduced into the Anglo-Saxon law and subsequently incorporated into the codified Hindu law in 1955.

The right to stipulated mehr: Stipulation of mehr at the time of marriage is an important aspect of a Muslim marriage. This is meant as a safeguard to the woman. Under the Shariat law, the woman has a charge over her husband's property for the payment of her mehr, even after his death. The high amount of mehr stipulated in the *nikahnama* (marriage agreement) was meant to act as a deterrent to unilateral divorce.[19]

The right to enter into a pre-marriage agreement (kabein nama): These agreements relate mainly to two aspects, (i) regulation of matrimonial life, and (ii) stipulations regarding dissolution of marriage. This can be an effective way of controlling polygamy. The woman can stipulate that in the event of the husband entering into a second marriage he should provide her with a separate residence. If the husband violates the agreement, the wife is entitled to divorce herself without the intervention of the Court.[20]

According to Ameer Ali, the renowned Islamic scholar, the following agreements can be enforced in a court of law.[21]

- the husband will not contract a second marriage during the subsistence of the first;
- the husband will not remove the wife from the conjugal domicile (matrimonial home) without her consent;
- the husband will not absent himself from the conjugal domicile beyond a certain period;
- the husband and wife will live in a specified place;
- certain amount of dower will be payable immediately after marriage or within a stated period;
- the husband will pay the wife a fixed sum of maintenance;
- the husband will maintain the children of the wife from her former husband; and
- the husband will not prevent her from receiving visits from her relations whenever she likes.[22]

The one third rule regarding testamentary succession:[23] As per this rule, a Muslim cannot will away more than one-third of his property. Wills also cannot be made in favour of legal heirs. The heirs have to inherit according to the rules of succession as laid down in the Shariat. Women are granted defined shares under the scheme of succession.[24]

The woman's share, under the Islamic law of inheritance, is not equal to that of her male counterpart. She is entitled to half the share of the male counterpart.[25] Although the stipulation falls short of the present concept of gender equality, it was a radical measure for its time and was based on a principle of equity. The man had to provide the mehr for the wife and bear the marriage expenses of unmarried daughters and sisters from his share of inheritance. The women were excluded from such encumbrances.

It is interesting to note that at the time of independence, women's rights under Muslim law were far superior to both the Hindu as well as the Christian laws. The subversion of women's rights by the constant pleadings of patriarchal interests for the application of Hindu personal laws on the basis of custom has already been discussed. Another interesting case decided by the Privy Council in 1898, *Skinner v Skinner*[26] reveals that the succession rights of a Muslim widow were even superior to those granted under the *Indian Succession Act*. The case concerned a couple who were Muslims but who had, at the time of their marriage converted to Christianity and performed the wedding ceremonies as per Christian rights. Subsequently thereafter, they reconverted to Islam and performed a nikah ceremony. An amount of Rs 50,000 was settled as mehr at the time of the nikah ceremony. Within a few years, the couple was estranged and the parties lived with other partners. The husband, prior to his death drew up a will and disinherited the wife of her rightful share in property and bestowed the property upon the children from the subsequent alliance.

After the death of her husband, the widow claimed her mehr and her share in the property and challenged the validity of the will under the Muslim law. The issue before the court was whether the couple was governed by the Indian Succession Act or the Islamic law. If the couple was governed by the Indian Succession Act, disinheritance through a will was valid. But the wife pleaded that she had never been divorced and both the parties were followers of Islam until the death of her husband and hence were governed by the Muslim law of succession. The trial court as well as the appellate courts, including the Privy Council, held that since a valid divorce could not be proved, and the parties had continued to follow Islam, the Islamic law would apply and the widow could not be disinherited of her rightful share in property through a will.

Although the Muslim law contains several positive provisions which would safeguard women's rights, these provisions have deteriorated due to socio-cultural reasons and patriarchal subversions of a later period. Practices like seclusion (*purdah*) and child marriage have rendered women vulnerable and dependent on their male relatives. Poverty and illiteracy have further contributed to the subordination of women. The amount of *mehr* which is fixed at the time of marriage has been reduced to a mere token and has ceased to be a safeguard against arbitrary divorce. The Brahminical custom of dowry has crept into most lower castes and Muslim communities. Recent studies indicate that among several Muslim communities the amount of dowry is substantially higher than the amount of mehr.[27]

A scrutiny of reported judgements would reveal that the amount of mehr was substantial during the pre-independence period and could function as an effective deterrent upon arbitrary and capricious divorce. But there is a marked decline on the reported cases on this issue in the post-independence period. Perhaps this is reflective of the lowered economic status of Muslims in post-partition India. So, for positive case law on this issue, one has to refer to Pakistani law journals.

The courts in Pakistan have consolidated the right of mehr through the following judgements:[28]:

(i) Various amounts paid by the husband to the wife during the marriage should not be presumed to be in lieu of dower;

(ii) Dower can be fixed or raised by the husband at any point during the continuance of the marriage. A declaration by him to this effect is sufficient;

(iii) Even after consummation has taken place, the wife may refuse to live with her husband unless he pays her prompt dower. Non-payment of mehr is a complete defense to a suit for restitution of conjugal rights and the wife is competent to refuse herself to her husband;

(iv) A woman can claim dower upon divorce if none had been fixed initially. This is applicable even in case of Muslim male and Christian female contracting a registered marriage abroad.

3.4 Reform Within Islam

Although the Islamic law is stated to be theocratic, several countries (Islamic as well as others) have modified the law to meet the demand of the changing social conditions and values. Furqan Ahmad maintains that the major portions of the statutory personal law enacted in most Muslim countries represent a mere codification of the traditional law and at best unification of divergent legal principles. But it cannot be denied that these changes have brought about significant reform in the classical Islamic law. The reforms have been either approved by the *Ullamas* or have been modified according to their suggestions.[29]

The process of change within the Muslim world has not been linear. The countries where Islam is the state or the predominant religion (particularly in the Arab world) have continued to preserve the uncodified Muslim law as locally followed. At the other end, countries like Turkey and Albania have opted for a complete abandonment of the traditional Islamic family law and replaced it with secular systems. Lebanon and Israel have incorporated the provisions of the Turkish family code and have made them applicable to the Muslim population.[30]

Many countries have adopted a moderate course—retaining the fundamental structure of the traditional family law of Islam but adapting its various locally prevalent versions to the contemporary social requirements. Around twenty countries have enacted either substantive or regulatory reforms to change the matrimonial law either partly or wholly, by relying upon the principle of Ijtihad within the broad framework of Islam itself.[31] Crossing the barriers of the officially adopted or dominant schools, laws have been codified on the basis of a selection of legal rules derived from the various schools of Islamic law.

For example, although the dominant school in India and Pakistan is Hanafi, the Dissolution of Muslim Marriages Act, 1939 incorporated the principles of Maliki law.[32] Similarly, on the basis of a doctrine of the Hanbali school of Islamic law, several countries have granted women the right to stipulate a restraint against bigamous marriages of their husbands.

Several countries have also regulated the husband's right to polygamy through statutory and regulatory provisions. Turkey and Tunisia have abolished polygamy altogether. In many countries, prior permission of the court is required for a bigamous marriage. Indonesia, Sri Lanka and Pakistan have imposed various restrictions on polygamy.[33] For instance during the regime of Ayub Khan, the *Muslim Family Laws Ordinance of 1961* was promulgated in Pakistan. Through this Ordinance, the husband's right to bigamy was regulated. It became mandatory for the husband to obtain prior permission of an Arbitration Council. These reforms are meant to mould the classical Islamic law according to the changing social needs.

Notes

1. Schacht, J., *An Introduction to Islamic Law*, New Delhi: Oxford University Press (1964) (Rpt 1975), p.1.
2. In its religious sense, it denotes submission to the Will of God and in its secular sense, the establishment of peace. In English, the word 'Muslim' is used both as a noun and as an adjective and denotes both the person professing the faith and something specific to Muslims such as law, culture, art etc. See Hidayatullah M. & A. Hidayatullah (ed.), *Mulla's Principles of Mohammedan Law*, Bombay: N.M. Tripathi (1981) (18th edn.), p. xix.
3. Fyzee, A.A.A., *Outlines of Muslim Law*, New Delhi: Oxford University Press (1974) (4th edn.), p.16.
4. Ibid., pp.17-18.
5. For the explanation of the four sources, I am relying upon *Mulla's Principles of Mohammedan Law*, pp. xix-xxiv.
6. Ibid., at p. xxiv.
7. Fyzee, A.A.A., *Outlines of Muslim Law*, pp.39-40.
8. Ibid., p.169.
9. See Chapter 2 ns.35 & 42.
10. The original texts were translated into English during the early phase of colonial rule and became the basis of Anglo-Mohammedan law in India. In Chapter 4, this issue is further discussed.
11. There were several cases concerning Bohras, Khojas, Cutchi Memons of Gujarat and Muslim Ghirasias of Bharuch, where during litigation the Hindu law of coparcenary was applied.
12. Thapar, R., *A History of India*, Delhi: Penguin (1992), Vol. I pp.298-312.
13. See Derrett, J.D.M., *Religion, Law and the State in India*, New York: The Free Press (1968), p.49, n.1; Also Fyzee *Outlines of Mohammadan Law*, p.65.
14. *Hooriya v Munna* AIR (1956) Madh Bh 556.
15. The *Khojas & Memons Case* decided by Lord Erskine Perry in 1847 (POC 1853 p.110), which is discussed in detail in the following chapter provides a concrete example of this trend.
16. See Fyzee, *Outlines of Muslim Law*, p.65.
17. According to Paras Diwan, Hindus perfected the concept of (gift) *dan* and applied it to marriage alliances, i.e. kanyadan. The Muslims perfected the concept of sale and found it convenient to express many transactions including marriage in the language of sale. Diwan, P.

Muslim Law in Modern India, Allahabad: Allahabad Law Agency (1993) (6th edn.), p.52-3.

18. The concept of mehr was latent in pre-Islamic Arabia. A gift is called Sadaq and the wife is called Sadaqi or woman friend. The Prophet released marriage from the bride purchase notion of Sadaq. Mehr became part of a marriage settlement to be paid to the wife. See Diwan, P., *Muslim Law in Modern India*, Allahabad: Allahabad Law Agency (1993).

19. No other legal system known to the Indian matrimonial jurisprudence subscribes to this concept. Both Hindu and English systems rely upon the concept of maintenance to safeguard women's economic right within marriage. Maintenance presumes a state of dependency. The concept of stipulating mehr is based on the more noble principle (a mark of respect for the woman) than maintenance and eternal dependency. Further, under all matrimonial laws, maintenance is linked to a woman's chastity and hence becomes a way of controlling the woman's sexuality. An unchaste woman is not entitled to maintenance either during the subsistence of marriage or after its dissolution.

20. Before the enactment of the Dissolution of Muslim Marriages Act, a Muslim reformist, Mrs Hamida Ali, on behalf of some of the leading women's organizations in India, had prepared a specimen form of such an agreement which was published in the *Bombay Law Journal* in the year 1936. See Fyzee A.A.A. The Muslim Wife's Right of Dissolving her Marriage in (1936) B.LR, p. 113.

21. Diwan, P., *Law of Marriage and Divorce*, Allahabad: Wadhwa & Company (1988), p.62.

22. The right to enter into a pre-marriage agreement is not available under any other matrimonial statute (except under the Goan law modelled on the French code). Since marriage under the Anglo-Saxon law was indissoluble, pre-marriage and post-marriage contracts stipulating conditions are held to be against public policy under the English law.

23. Hidayatullah & Hidayatullah (ed.), *Mulla's Principles of Mohammadan Law*, p.104.

24. Under the Indian Succession Act and the Hindu Succession Act there is no restraint regarding testamentary succession and a person can will away all the property and disinherit his legal heirs.

25. Although there are wide differences in the laws of various sects and sub-sects, the inheritance rights of women under the Islamic law can be broadly categorized as follows:
    ** the daughter inherits half the share inherited by the son, e.g. when there are no other heirs, the daughter inherits one third and the son inherits two thirds of the property.
    ** the mother inherits one sixth of the property while the father inherits one third.
    ** the wife (or if there is more than one wife then all of them jointly) inherits one eight of the husband's property [Hidayatullah & Hidayatullah (ed.), *Mulla's Principles of Mohammadan Law*, pp. 48-62].

26. *Skinner v Skinner* (1898) ILR 25 Cal 537 PC.

27. In a recent study of Muslim women conducted by Women's Research and Action Group, Bombay (WRAG) during 1994-6, most communities confirmed that they still follow the custom of mehr but it has been reduced to a mere token. The communities have now adopted the practice of dowry. They further confirmed that the amount of dowry is always higher than mehr. The final report of the study is yet to be published. I am relying upon the various newsletters brought out by WRAG during 1994 and 1995, where some of the preliminary reports of the research from Maharashtra, Gujarat, Kerala, Tamil Nadu, West Bengal and Assam have been published. See the following issues: I/2 (September, 1994); II/1 (February, 1995); II/2-3 (August, 1995) and II/4 (October, 1995).

28. See Balchin, C. (ed.), *A Handbook on Family Law in Pakistan*, Lahore: Shirkat Gah (1994) (2nd edn.), p.52.

29. Ahmad, F., *Triple Talaq: An Analytical Study*, New Delhi: Regency Publications (1994), p.113.

30. Mahmood, T., *Family Law Reform in the Muslim World*, Bombay: N.M. Tripathi (1972), p.3.

31. For a detailed discussion regarding reform in Muslim family law in various Islamic countries, see *Mahmood, T., Family Law Reform in the Muslim World*, pp.270-2.

32. According to Hanafi authorities, rules of other Sunni schools may be applied by command of the sovereign power. Through this principle, in 1931, the ruler of Bhopal enacted a code, *Dabita Tahaffuzi Huquqai Zawjain* (Law for the Protection of Rights of Spouses) incorporating Maliki rules. This principle was later incorporated into the *Dissolution of Muslim Marriages Act* of 1939, to grant Muslim women in British India the right of divorce. See Fyzee A.A.A., Outlines of Muslim Law.

33. Ahmad, F., *Triple Talaq: An Analytical Study*.

4

Colonial Rule and Subversion of Rights

Introduction

In order to study the judicial structure of modern India, a study of the process of colonization in the Presidencies of Calcutta, Bombay and Madras during the eighteenth and nineteenth century is essential. The Calcutta Presidency of the Bengal region, in particular, had felt the presence of the British through the establishment of the East India Company from the early eighteenth century. Here, what began as trading relations expanded into political domination. It is at this starting point that we will have to locate the routes of the present legal structure.[1]

With the advent of colonialism there was a substantial change in the legal structure of the newly established Presidencies. The non-state arbitration fora were transformed into state-regulated and state-controlled adjudicative systems. The transformation was at two levels: (i) through the introduction of a legal structure modelled on English courts, (i.e. Anglo-Saxon jurisprudence); and (ii) through principles of substantive law which were evolved and administered in these courts, (i.e. Anglo-Hindu and Anglo-Mohammedan laws). This set in motion a gradual process of homogenizing the local customs and practices which could be regulated through the state machinery.

During the initial period of the colonial rule, two different models of adjudication were adopted in the Presidencies of Calcutta and Bombay. While the Calcutta Presidency, under the administration of Hastings, adopted the Roman model of differentiating between the Canon and Civil law, the Bombay Presidency under the administration of Elphinstone, adopted the English model of King's law and Common law which provided greater scope for validating customary law. But gradually the

Bengal model was adopted for the centralized administration of British India. The adaptation of the canonical mould overriding the common law norm, curtailed women's customary rights which did not have a textual base. As the pluralistic communities became characterized as 'Hindu', the women's right to property ownership became curtailed. In addition, as already stated, the Bengal school followed the Dayabhaga principle of strict construction of stridhana. Gradually, this notion of a constrained and limited stridhana became the accepted principle of Hindu law for the whole of British India (with a few concessions granted to the Bombay Presidency). The transformation of the legal structure and its effects on women's rights is traced in this chapter.

4.1 Company Jurisdiction Over Natives

At the advent of the colonial rule, the Moghul power was on the decline and the law and order situation was at its lowest ebb. Although the Moghul courts arbitrated in family disputes, towards the end of the Moghul reign, the arbitration mechanisms had collapsed both in the Moghul Empire, as well as in the independent princely states. The Company officers, who were engaged in setting up trading establishments were often called upon to adjudicate over family and civil disputes in these areas.

The first seed of the Anglo-Saxon jurisprudence was sown at this juncture. Since the Company officers did not have a legal background, they relied either upon the local *qazis* and *pundits* or upon the principles of English law in an *ad hoc* manner. To provide legal validity to such arbitrations, after the Company established its rule, various charters of the British Parliament bestowed upon the Company, the jurisdiction over the natives and also deputed lawyers to adjudicate over these disputes.[2]

The initial charter, the Charter of Charles II in 1661, was the first in a series of charters, which authorized the East India Company judicial powers in India. The Charter of George I in 1726, authorized the establishment of Mayor's Courts (courts of the King of England) in Calcutta, Bombay and Madras. This Act was silent regarding jurisdiction over native inhabitants. The Warren Hastings' Plan of 1772, provided for the establishment of civil and criminal courts in each district (mofussil courts). This plan granted the Company jurisdiction over the natives. The plan explicitly protected the right of Hindus and Muslims to apply their own personal laws in civil matters concerning inheritance, marriage, caste etc.[3]

In 1774, the Mayor's Court of Calcutta was converted into a Supreme Court and in 1781, it was granted express jurisdiction over natives. It was laid down that in matters of inheritance, succession, land rent, goods and all matters of contract, the respective customary laws should be applied. In case the laws of the parties differed, the laws applicable to the defendant were to be applied. The practice of saving the personal laws of the natives which started at this juncture continued through all subsequent British Regulations. But the charters were not clear whether the native laws of Hindus and Muslims referred to their religious laws or to the customary usages or to both. Article XXIII of the Hastings' plan stated, *'the laws of Koran with respect to the Mohammedans and those of the shastras with respect to the 'Gentoos'*[4] S.17 of the Act of 1781 again stipulated that *laws of Gentoos and laws of Mohammedans* were to be applied.

The communities were categorized on the basis of their religion. The customs and laws, which the English administrators had decided to save, were in turn deemed to be religious. This created a legal fiction that the laws of Hindus and Muslims are rooted in their respective scriptures and further that Hindus and Muslims are homogeneous communities following uniform laws. There was also a presumption that the dividing line between the communities is their religion, over-riding other factors such as caste, sect, occupation, language or regionality. This legal fiction provided no space for validating the role of customary law which has no scriptural basis and is evolved at the local level transgressing boundaries of religious identities.

4.2 Anglicization of Scriptures

Since scriptures were unequivocally accepted as the source of both Hindu and Muslim family laws, the English administrations set the task of translating the ancient texts as an essential precondition to good governance. Translation of scriptures became the first priority for the political scheme of English administrators. The process of codifying the Hindu and Mohammedan laws was initiated by Hastings in eighteenth century and was facilitated by Jones, Halhed, Colebrooke and Macnaghten.

As discussed in the preceding chapters, till the advent of the colonial rule, civil law was enforced primarily by local and non-state legal fora applying the norms of customary law and adaptations of the smriti or quranic injunctions to suit local conditions. But when the Company officers stepped in to arbitrate in civil and criminal disputes, due to their limited understanding of local traditions and customs, they relied upon Hindu pundits and Muslim qazis to ascertain their respective laws. This set in motion the process of Brahminization and Islamization of laws.

The local systems of arbitration were a source of constant irritant to the colonial administrators due to various factors such as lack of regularity in procedures, delays, decisions based on maxims which were beyond the comprehension of the administrators etc. The plurality of customs often led to the pundits expressing contradictory opinions. The wide range of customs which had no shastric authority met with the disapproval of the administrators. They distrusted the pundits and felt that their opinions were biased and favoured the interest of their own caste. The administrators were of the opinion that if the original texts were made available, they could rule directly, without the help of partisan and corrupt pundits. So in their desire to be independent of the local clergy, they took upon themselves the task of translating the ancient texts. These translated texts became the basis of Anglo-Hindu and Anglo-Mohammedan law in India.

The activity of translation of the texts was based primarily in the Bengal region. In 1772, Hastings hired a group of eleven pundits for the purpose of creating a digest of Hindu law, which brought a heavy Anglo-Brahminical bias into the law. This was translated into Persian and then later into English and was published in 1776 under the title, *A Code of Gentoo Laws or Ordinations of Pundits*. The subsequent work of William Jones, has been compared with the Justanian *Corpus Juris*.[5] The code prepared by him had a strong bias in favour of the Bengal school. He then went on to translate *Manusmriti* which became one of the most favoured texts of the British. It influenced oriental studies far more profoundly than it had ever influenced the administration of law in pre-British India.[6] Colebrooke's translation of Dayabhaga and Mitakshara, became the two most frequently quoted sources of Hindu law in court judgements.

Jones also translated *Al Sirajiyyah*, the Mohammedan law of inheritance. In 1791, under directions from Hastings, Charles

Hamilton, translated the Arabic text, the *Hedaya* (the Guide) into English. But Muslim law proved to be too complex and the translation process had to be abandoned halfway.[7]

During this time, several Sanskrit scholars wrote treatises to meet with the British demand. But the work of European authors came to be trusted and used in preference even to the genuine shastric works.[8] The translated codes, backed by the authority of British courts, began to make alterations in custom. In their attempt to make the shastric injunctions precise and definite, to suit the structure of the Anglicized courts, the British forced it towards a straight-jacketed mould which led to a loss of complexities and localized contexts and also provided the scope for the biases of the English scholars to creep into the translated texts.

The administrators of Bengal, in their fervour to trace the correct and 'original' sources, totally disregarded local customs. But the Bombay Presidency Regulations of the same period, especially the 1799 Regulation (under John Duncan), did not follow the legal scheme devised by Hastings in Bengal. Here the English distinction between King's law and Common law was applied rather than the Roman categorization of Canon Law and Civil Law[9] and custom was granted due recognition as an important source of law.

From 1803 to 1827, through treaties with Gaikwad and the defeat of the Peshwa, the territories under the Bombay Presidency were expanded to Deccan. This resulted in a major reorganization of the legal and judicial administration. Mountstuart Elphinstone presided over this early organization of Company administration, first as Commissioner of the Deccan (1818–19) and then as Governor of Bombay Presidency (1819–27). The recorder's court of Bombay was replaced with a Supreme Court in 1823. Influenced by the English jurist Bentham, Elphinstone was of the opinion that the Bengal model of categorizing laws as 'Canon' and 'Civil' would not work in the Bombay Presidency. In his scheme, codification of Common Law was essential to guide the European judges in their administration of the native law to the natives. The Common Law had to be based on customary practices of the people rather than the archaic religious texts. This need for the compilation of common practices stemmed from two presumptions, a desire to preserve for the natives their way of ruling, which was combined with an unwillingness to allow the natives to manage their own affairs. To concretize this scheme, he set up a Regulation Committee and brought about the Regulation Code 1827 (also known as Elphinstone code). Two officers appointed by Elphinstone, Harry Borradaile and Arthur Steele, were assigned the task of recording the customs of the Deccan and Gujarat region.[10] Although the recordings were not systematic, the compilations provide some useful insights into the customs and practices of the various castes in the region.

4.3 Subversion of Women's Rights

The establishment of courts based on the model of English courts with English rules and procedures and a clear hierarchy of courts was meant to make the arbitration fora certain and definite. The English principles of justice, equity and good conscience were used as direct channels for introducing English laws and customs into areas reserved as personal laws.[11] These notions which crept into the Hindu and Muslim laws transformed the local traditions and usages in unforeseen directions.

Despite the initial policy of non–interference in 'personal' matters, as the British rule gained acceptance and stability, there was a gradual process of tampering with the established local customs through various means. The legal structure was seen by the administrators as an important forte of its civilizing mission.

At this stage, the process of evolving laws at the local level through commentaries, which incorporated within them the local customs, was arrested. The British interpretations of the ancient texts became binding and made the law certain, rigid and uniform. This clear marker of modernity was welcomed by the newly evolving English-educated middle class of Bengal and provided the British a moral justification for ruling India as harbingers of enlightenment.[12] Through their interventions the Hindu society could rid itself of its 'barbarism' and enter an era of 'civilization'. An image of the cruel and superstitious natives who needed Christian salvation was deliberately constructed by the Evangelists. The entry of Hindu social reformers into the campaign against Sati at the advent of nineteenth century strengthened the process of interventions not only by judicial decisions but also by legislative reforms.

The much-acclaimed *Sati Regulation Act of 1829* was followed by other legislations such as the *Widow Remarriage Act 1856*, the

Age of Consent Act of 1860, and the *Prohibition of Female Infanticide Act of 1872.* These legislations, focusing on the 'barbaric' customs of the natives, convey an impression that the exceptions to the rule of non-interference in the realm of 'personal' laws were for the benefit of women. There is a presumption that by incorporating the concepts of modernity into the native jurisprudence, the status of women in India was alleviated. But recent scholarship has questioned this premise.[13]

The British intervention did not stop at the level of welfare legislation for women but extended into two other spheres which have not yet received due attention. One set of legislations carved out a space for men's individual property rights into a system based on joint family property and rigid caste affiliations and laid the ground for the introduction of the capital mode of production in an urban setting.[14]

But the other area is even more disturbing for our purpose here. Simultaneously, through a series of judicial decisions the scope of women's rights was constrained beyond all recognition. As already discussed in Chapter 2, the Mitakshara had expanded the scope of stridhana to include property acquired by woman through every source, including inheritance and partition. But the judicial decisions changed this concept and laid down that inherited property is not stridhana. A new legal principle was gradually introduced through court decisions that whether the property is inherited by a woman through her male relatives (father, son, husband) or through her female relatives (mother, mother's mother, daughter), it is not her stridhana and that it would devolve on the heirs of her husband or father. The women lost the right to will or gift away their stridhana and it acquired the character of a limited estate. Any transaction by a widow in respect of the property inherited by her had to be justified on two grounds, legal necessity or religious or charitable purpose. Upon the widow's death, the property reverted back to the husband's male relatives. The introduction of this concept of 'reversioners' which is basically a legal principle under the English law, bestowed upon the male relatives the right to challenge all property dealings by Hindu widows.

To provide concrete examples of this trend, some decisions of the newly evolving legal machinery of British India are discussed below. These judgements have several commonalities. The litigations against the widows were initiated by the husband's heirs. In a significant number of cases, following local customs, the lower courts upheld the women's rights. The lower court decisions were reversed by the higher judiciary and then became binding principles of law. Significantly, in all the cases discussed below, the decisions were from property disputes within the Bengal Presidency but under the consolidated scheme of the hierarchy of courts, they became the binding principles of law for other Presidencies.

In 1868, in *Srinath Gangopadhya v Sarbamangala Debi*,[15] the Calcutta High Court held, that as per the Benares School, once a stridhana property devolves upon an heir, it loses its character as stridhana and devolves as per ordinary rules of Hindu law.

In another landmark case around this time, the Privy Council held that the property inherited by the widow from her husband was not her stridhana. The Privy Council reversed the judgment of the lower court and proclaimed:

> Under the law of the Benares School, notwithstanding the ambiguous passage in the *Mitakshara*, no part of her husband's estate whether movable or immovable to which a Hindu woman succeeds by inheritance, forms part of her Stridhana[16] (emphasis added).

The legal precedents set by the Privy Council became the binding rule of law and dealt a lethal blow to the property rights of Hindu widows, as the decisions of the various High Courts in the subsequent decade reveal.

This principle was followed by the Calcutta High Court in 1874 in *Gonda Kooer v Kooer Gody Singh*.[17] The widow had purchased property out of the accumulated income from her stridhana and pleaded that it should be considered as her stridhana. But following the rule laid down by the Privy Council, the Calcutta High Court held that the property was not stridhana and hence she does not have the right to dispose it off by will and upon her death it would devolve on her husband's heirs.

The courts also ruled that the property inherited by a daughter from her father is not stridhana.[18] This principle was then extended to the property inherited by an unmarried daughter from her mother[19] and later stretched to include the property inherited from all female relatives, thus sealing all avenues for the continuation of property devolution in the female line.

The substantial case law on this issue made it impossible to retreat from this position. In 1879, while holding that the property inherited from the father is not stridhana, the Privy Council expressly stated that since this rule has been established by a series of decisions in Bengal and Madras, a different interpretation of the old and obscure texts cannot be followed. The Privy Council further stated that the courts ought not to unsettle a rule of inheritance affirmed by a long course of decisions, unless it is manifestly opposed to law and reason. The Privy Council explained that the rule has been laid down by Sir William Macnaghten in his *Treatise on Hindu Law* , as follows: 'Under no circumstances can a daughter's son, daughter, husband or other descendants inherit the property which devolved on her at her father's death. Such property is not stridhana and will devolve on her father's heirs.' The court further held that this rule is not opposed to the spirit and principles of Mitakshara.[20] It is interesting to note that while during the early years of administration, contemporary practices were discarded in favour of ancient and 'obscure texts', during the later period, after the establishment of Anglicized courts, the court decisions and translated texts were granted greater validity than the written texts which now came to be discarded as 'old and obscure'.

The facts of two more cases on the issue of women's property are set out in detail. In the first case, *Mussammat Thakoor Deyhee v Rai Baluk Ram*[21], a childless widow Choteh Babee, gifted the property she inherited from her husband to her niece. It is reported in the judgment that Choteh Babee, despite being a *purdah nishin*, was an excellent business woman who managed her property well.

The husband's heirs challenged the deed, *inter alia*, on the ground that it was fraudulent and that she had no power of alienation over immovable property inherited from her husband. Sudder Ameen of Benares held that the widow was competent to gift the property. Sudder Dewaney Adawlut of Agra reversed the decision on the ground that the deed of gift was a forged document. At this point the right of the widow to gift her property was not a disputed issue before the court. The court only examined whether the gift deed was an authentic or a forged document. In appeal, the Privy Council ruled: 'The widow has no power to dispose immovable property inherited from her husband, whether ancestral or acquired.'

The second case decided by the Privy Council in 1903, *Sheo Shankar v Debi Sahai*,[22] provides yet another illustration of the judicial trend. The woman had inherited the property from her mother. After her death, her sons claimed the property as heirs of the mother and grandmother and deprived their sister. The subordinate judge of Gorakhpur, on 7 December 1897 held that the property inherited through the female line was the woman's stridhana and hence her sons had no right over it. On appeal, the Allahabad High Court reversed the decision. This resulted in an appeal to the Privy Council. In February, 1903, the Privy Council upheld the decision of the High Court and laid down that the property inherited by a woman from her mother is not her stridhana and hence it will not devolve on her daughter who is her stridhana heir, but will devolve upon her son.

Only the Bombay School which relied upon the local authority, Vyavahar Mayuka of Nilakantha Bhatta, which validated local customary practices of the region, provided a better scope for women's rights. The cases decided between the period 1862–5 and reported in the first issue of *Bombay High Court Reporter* are illustrative of this trend.[23]

In one of the cases, *Navalram Atmaram v Nand Kishore Shivnarayan*[24] the woman inherited property from her father. She died leaving a daughter and daughter's sons. Upon her death, her husband's brother took charge of the property. In a suit to reclaim the property, the trial court (Sudder Ameen) declared in favour of the daughter's son. On appeal, Assistant Judge reversed the decree. On second appeal, the Bombay High Court held that according to the usage of the caste and in accordance with Hindu law as interpreted by the authorities in the Bombay Presidency, the daughter was an absolute heir to the property which the woman had inherited from her father.

Ironically, while Hindu women were better protected by invoking the local customs in the Bombay region, the Muslim women's textual right to inherit property was defeated by upholding Hindu customs and usages. The Muslim trading communities of Gujarat, the Khojas and Cutchi Memons, followed the local custom of coparcenary or joint family property.[25] The male-headed coparcenaries denied women their right to a stipulated share in the property as per the Shariat. (As already discussed in the preceding chapter, under the rules of Shariat coparcenary is not recognized).

On 11 October 1847, by a common judgment, Justice Erskine Perry decided three cases filed by women claiming inheritance right to parental property.[26] In the first case, two daughters of a rich merchant Mir Ali, who did not leave behind a male heir, filed a suit to claim their father's property worth three lakhs. On their behalf, it was argued that the Hindu custom of disinheriting daughters, which has been adopted by Mohammedans, is most unreasonable. Hence public policy would dictate the adoption of the wiser rule laid down by the Koran by which daughters are awarded a fixed share. A contrast was drawn between the relative position which females held in Hindu and Muslim systems. On behalf of the woman, it was further argued that since the Muslim system was more beneficial to women, in larger interest of women's welfare, it was the duty of the court to give it effect when the two diverse practices are examined.

The comments of Lord Erskine Perry while disallowing the woman's claim make interesting reading:

> A custom for females to take no share in the inheritance is not unreasonable in the eyes of the English law for it accords in great part with the universal custom, as to real estates where there are any male issues and with some local customs mentioned by Blackstone through which in certain manors females are excluded in all cases.[27]

The judge commented further that since the attempt of the young women to disturb the course of succession, which has prevailed among their ancestors for many hundreds of years, has failed, they must now pay the price of this unsuccessful experiment by paying the cost to the defendants.[28]

While at one level the smriti law was distorted, at the other, this distorted law was applied to a wide range of communities following diverse customs. As the above case reveals, an interesting phenomenon during litigation seems to be for women to plead a non-Hindu status in order to protect their rights and for the men within the family to implore the protection of the distorted smriti law. If the courts could be convinced that the community was ruled by either the Muslim law, the *Indian Succession Act* or the customary law (by claiming a sudra status) the rights of women could be saved. If the courts bestowed a Hindu status upon the communities (or validated the application of the Hindu law as in the above case), women's right would be curtailed. Most of these were borderline cases where the pendulum would swing from one end to the other. But when the issue was finally decided by the Privy Council or the respective High Court as the case may be, the religious status of the community (and thereby the fate of its women and illegitimate children) would be sealed for all future litigations.

To provide some illustrations, in several litigations the widows from various Jain sects pleaded their right to adopt a son to their deceased husband under a separate law or a local custom. But the custom could not be proved to the level of legal validity and women lost their right of adoption as smriti law was applied to them. It is through these disputes that Jains became categorized as a Hindu sect. Another illustration is the *Asura* (or an un-approved) form of marriage. If a custom to this effect could be proved, the property could be saved from the 'reversioners'. Yet other examples are the disputes between widows and illegitimate sons within the Lingayat community. Since the existence could be proved of the custom of remarriages of divorcees and widows, the community was categorized as sudra and hence the illegitimate sons were declared as heirs to the father's property. The dispute could be confined between widows and illegitimate sons rather than its extension to reversioners.[29]

The period between 1850 and 1930 witnessed the elimination of a wide range of customs which diverged from the Anglo-Hindu law as the standard of proof required was very high. Unless it could be proved that the custom was ancient, certain, obligatory, reasonable and not against public policy, it had a very slim chance of survival. Derrett comments that in this manner, the Anglo-Hindu law with its Dharmashastra background was spread more widely than it had ever been before. The only customs which were saved from the crushing effects of the British courts were the customs of the agricultural classes in the Punjab and matrilineal practices of the Malabar region.[30] The tendency of both the British courts and of the urban Hindu middle class was to ignore the diversities and to impose a legal Hinduism upon these communities. Contrary to popular belief, many of the customs which were crushed were those in favour of women.

4.4 The Status of Women Under English Law During the Corresponding Period

During litigation, the courts often relied upon the principles of justice, equity and good conscience, while ascertaining women's rights. Since the Law Lords' notions of justice, equity and good conscience were the clinching factors, it would be relevant to glean over the decisions of English courts during the corresponding period, and assess the judicial notions of justice and equity regarding women.

The leading decisions indicate that the concept of modernity upon which the Anglo-Saxon jurisprudence rested did not encompass within its scope, the notion of women's rights. Since disinheriting women was not unreasonable or immoral as per the established legal precepts, the judges could, with ease, incorporate them into the Indian legal system.

Until the twentieth century, women in Britain could not vote. Married women did not have a right of disposal over their separate property. The husband could transact all property dealings on her behalf in respect of her separate property. Even worse, married women did not have a legal existence. As soon as a woman got married she lost her legal identity. Her identity merged with that of her husband. She could not even enter into a contract because she could not sue anyone nor be sued against. Since the husband was the woman's guardian he had a right to chastize her. Under the English common law, the husband had a right to whip the wife provided he used a switch not thicker than his thumb for correctional purposes under a legally accepted notion called thumb rule.[31]

At the social level, there are several judicial decisions which held that the women could not enter universities, that they could not hold elected posts, that they could not be enrolled to the bar and beyond this, that they are not even persons and further that the term 'he' does not include 'she'.[32] These 'persons cases,' as they came to be called, were launched by feminists in the hope of legally establishing the fact that an individual gender was irrelevant to his or her factual or legal capacity and that females were obviously to be included in the word 'person.' But what was self-evident truth to feminists, however, seemed an absurdity to the judges.[33] After a prolonged and sustained campaign by the suffragettes, finally in 1929, the courts granted women the right to be persons.[34] As a result of a sustained campaign, the women in Britain obtained the right to own property through a legislation in 1882[35] and the right to vote in 1918.[36]

But despite the near subordination of women in Britain, in order to rationalize the colonial rule, it was often projected in the colonies that the honour and respect in which women were held in Britain was one of the glories of British civilization and blessed fruits of Christianity.[37] The position of the English woman was extolled throughout the commonwealth as being without compare. This mystical sentiment served not only to obscure the true position of the great majority of women in Britain, but also to suggest a false status for English women when compared with that of women in the colonies.

While it was relatively easy to pose as 'rescuers' of Indian women from the clutches of 'barbaric' customs like Sati and infant marriages, it was indeed not easy to conciliate with the notions of civil right of property ownership which was a contentious issue in Britain at the time. The antagonism and hostility towards the women suffragettes demanding equality seems to have influenced the Law Lords of the Privy Council, while sitting in judgment over the appeal cases from the Commonwealth. The prolonged legal battles of English women for equality are an indication of the status-quoist attitude of the jurists who were modelled along Blackstonian notions of women's rights. These notions were adopted into the Indian system, even while posturing to liberate Indian women from the barbaric customs through legislative reforms.

An analysis of the legal cases of women's right to property reveals that with the benevolence of the English jurists, (who were aided by the subversion of women's rights in England) and the worst distortions of Brahminical smriti texts, the patriarchal modernity of India was ushered in.

Notes

1. Radha Kumar argues that this intimacy with the British later resulted in most social movements of the nineteenth century also being located in these two states. See Kumar, R., *The History of Doing —An Illustrated Account of Movements for Women's Rights and Feminism in India 1800 — 1990*, New Delhi: Kali for Women (1993), p.7.
2. Jain, M.P., *Outlines of Indian Legal History* , Bombay: N.M. Tripathi (1966), p.24.
3. Parashar, A., *Women and Family Law Reform in India* , New Delhi : Sage Publications (1992), pp. 61–9.
4. 'Gentoos' was the Portuguese term for Hindus. The term has its origin in the Biblical term 'Gentiles' meaning heathens or non-believers.
5. He set out to give his subjects their law in a similar fashion as Justanian guaranteed his Roman and Greek subjects their laws.
6. Derrett, D.J.M., *Religion, Law and the State in India*, New York: The Free Press (1968), p. 225.

7. Chhachhi, A., 'Identity Politics, Secularism and Women: A South Asian perspective,' in Zoya Hasan (ed.), *Forging Identities: Gender, Communities and the State*, New Delhi: Kali for Women (1994), p.82.

8. Kishwar, M., 'Codified Hindu Law: Myth and Reality,' *Economic and Political Weekly*, XXIX/33 (1994), p. 2145.

9: Amrita Shodhan has recorded how Macnaghten's *Principles and Precedents of Hindu Law*, written in 1827, relied only upon the works of Jones and Colebrooke and some Sanskrit texts. Cases brought before the courts were treated only as illustration of how the textual law was treated in the European court. He did not examine *Bebasthas* given by pundits and recorded only those cases adjudicated in British courts. See Shodhan, A., 'Legal Representations of Khojas and Pushtimarga Vaishnavas : The Aga Khan Case and the Maharaj Libel Case in Mid-nineteenth Century Bombay,' unpublished Doctorate dissertation, submitted to the Department of South Asian Languages and Civilizations, Chicago, Illinois (1995).

10. See Borradaile's *Report of Civil Cases 1820–1824*, and Arthur Steele, *Hindu Caste, Their Law, Religion and Customs*, Bombay: Courier Press (1827). Since most of the territory of the Bombay Presidency was newly acquired, perhaps it was felt necessary to record their customs.

11. This principle was laid down in a case of guardianship, *Waghela Rajsanji v Shekh Masluddin* (1887) 14 IA 89.

12. Kumar, R., *The History of Doing*, p. 9.

13. I am relying upon the work of Lata Mani and Uma Chakravarty on Sati and of Lucy Carrol on Widow Remarriage. Regarding the discourse on Sati for example, Lata Mani has commented that women were not the central concern of this debate. But rather, women were the site upon which the discourse on culture and identity was debated and women's rights did not figure in this debate. See Mani, L., 'Contentious Traditions: The Debate on Sati in Colonial India' (1989), in Sangari, K. and S. Vaid (ed.), *Recasting Women, Essays in Colonial History*, New Delhi: Kali for Women (1989), p. 88.

14. These legislations included:
    * The Caste Disabilities Removal Act 1850 set aside the provisions of Hindu Law which penalized the renunciation of religion by depriving a convert of his right in the joint family property.
    * The Hindu Inheritance (Removal of Disabilities) Act, 1928 prohibited the exclusion from inheritance of certain disqualified heirs.
    * The Hindu Gains of Learning Act 1930 stipulated that all gains of learning (income earned through professional qualifications) would be the exclusive and separate property of a Hindu male even if he had been supported to acquire professional qualifications from the funds of the joint family.

15. (1868) 10 WR 488.

16. *Bhugwandeen Doobey v Myna Baee* (1867) 11 MIA 487.

17. (1874) 14 BLR 159.

18. *Deo Parshad v Lujoo Roy* (1873) 20 WR 102.

19. *Dowlut Kooer v Burma Deo Sahoy* (1874) 22 WR 54.
20. *Chotay Lal v Chunno Lall* ILR (1879) 4 Cal 744.
21. (1886) 11 MIA 139.
22. (1903) 30 IA 202.
23. *Venayak Anandrav v Lakshmi Bai* (1861) 1 BHCR 117 and *Pranjivandas Tulsidas v Devkuvarbai* (1861) 1 BHCR 130.
24. (1861) 1 BHCR 209.
25. The Cutchis are originally from Sindh or Cutch and speak Cutchi language. They are believed to have been converted to Islam by Sadr Din. Although they practise Islam, their manners and customs continued to be Hindu. They believe in the ten incarnations of Lord Vishnu and during the period of litigation, as per the comments of the judge, not a single person knew Arabic or Persian.
26. The first two cases concerned Khoja women, *Hirbae v Sonbae* and *Gungbae v Sonabae*. The third case was by a Cutchi Memon, *Rahimatbae v Hadji Jussa & Ors.*
27. *Hirbae v Sonbae* POC (1853), p. 110 (also referred to as the Khoja's and Memon's case).
28. Ibid., p.121.
29. See Alladi, K. (ed.), *Mayne's Treatise on Hindu Law & Usage*, New Delhi: Bharat Law House (1993) (13th edn.), p.63-5, where some of these cases are cited.
30. Derrett, J.D.M., *Hindu Law Past and Present*, Calcutta: Mukherjee & Co. (1957), p.78.
31. See Martin, D., *Battered Wives*, New York: Pocket Books (1976), p.30-2. Also see Davis, E.G., *The First Sex*, New York: Putnam (1971), pp.254-5.
32. For the status of British women in nineteenth and early twentieth century, see the following cases:
1869—Manchester Voters case—*Chorlton v Lings* declared that common law disability prevents women from voting.
1873—Edinburgh Medical Students case—*Jex-Blake v Senatus*—Women's expulsion from University upheld.
1889—London County Council cases—Lady Sandhurst case exclusion of women elected to the county council upheld.
1903—Refusal by the Bar to enrol Bertha Cave upheld by the judges.
1908—Scottish University Voters case—*Nairn v Scottish Universities*—House of Lords, upheld trend to exclude women from public functions and voting.
1914—Women Solicitors case—*Beeb v Law Society*, refusal by Law Society to enrol a woman upheld by the courts.
1923—The Lady Rhondda case—House of Lords refused to seat Lady Rhondda.
1925—The Marriage Bar case—*Price v. Rhondda UDC*—judges upheld a requirement that only women (and not men) teachers resign on marriage as 'not unreasonable'.
The above list of cases is cited from Sachs, A. and J.H. Wilson, *Sexism and the Law*, Oxford: Law in Society Series, Martine Robertson (1967), p.227.

33. Ibid., p.6.
34. 1929—Canadian Senators case—*Edwards v. Attorney General*—the Privy Council finally acknowledged that women are included within the term 'Person'. Ibid., p.227.
35. *The Married Women's Property Rights Act of 1882.*
36. In 1918, the vote was granted to women aged thirty years and above. A decade later this right was extended to all adult women. In 1919, the *Sex Disqualification Removal Act* revoked all disabilities suffered by women in respect of holding public office and exercising public functions.
37. Alladi, K., (ed.), *Mayne's Treatise on Hindu Law & Usage*, p.139-140.

5

Politicization of Women's Rights

Introduction

The period of ninety years—1857–1947—which mark the nation's struggle for independence are also the years in which the edifice of personal laws was erected. Hence, the edifice is rife with the political undercurrents of the period. The struggle for women's rights within the realm of family laws is entrenched within these undercurrents and has become an integral and inseparable part of this discourse.

The process was initiated with the codification of laws after the administration of India was transferred from the Company to the British Crown. At this time a distinction was made between the laws of the 'personal' and 'public' spheres. The personal laws, to a large extent, were left uncodified to be governed by native jurisprudence. Despite this restraint, the legal structure of the personal laws, as we understand the term today, was shaped during the period 1860 to 1950. While women's welfare was the stated agenda, the political undercurrents played a crucial role in moulding this structure.

With the introduction of matrimonial statutes for Christians and Parsis and certain statutes of common application, English legal principles were introduced within the Indian jurisprudence. These principles gradually influenced even the uncodified 'personal laws' of Hindus and Muslims and remoulded them along the lines of English statutes to suit the requirements of an adversarial court system. The English principles of matrimonial jurisprudence could now be read into the native laws and customs. The anti-women bias and English norms of Victorian prudity could now be elevated into rigid legal principles of Indian family laws.

Towards the end of the nineteenth century, women's rights became a highly contested issue within the discourse of national identity and the plea of the reformers met with a great deal of hostility from the conservatives. The growing antagonism between Hindu and Muslim communities within the nationalist movement also rendered the project of evolving uniform family laws an impossibility.

Later, during the 1920s, in response to Gandhi's call, a large number of women entered the political arena. At their insistence, the question of women's rights was once again placed within the political sphere of the nationalist discourse. This resulted in the enactment of some statutes in the 1930s, which secured Hindu and Muslim women certain significant rights. In the years immediately preceding independence, during the debate in the Constitutional Assembly, the mandate on equality provided the necessary backdrop for formulating women's rights. But at this stage, the issue of women's rights was coloured by political concerns of an emerging nation. While laying the foundation of a modern democracy, the rights of citizens had to be defined. Here, the conflicting pulls between the rights of minorities to a cultural and religious identity and the concern for an integrated nation within clearly defined territorial boundaries, became the context within which the issue of women's rights had to be renegotiated. The legislative history of Hindu and Muslim family laws during the politically significant ninety years preceding independence is traced in this chapter.

5.1 Power from the Company to the Crown

After the political upheaval of 1857, when the administration of India shifted from the Company to the British Crown, a reassurance of non-interference in religious beliefs and practices became imperative. In her historic proclamation, Queen Victoria promised equal protection of the law for all religions and restrained the administrators from interference in the realm of personal beliefs and practices of the natives by declaring: 'We do strictly charge and enjoin all those who may be in authority under us that they abstain from all interference with the religious belief or worship of any subjects on pain of our highest displeasure.'[1] Since the British administrators had already concluded that practices governing family relationships are 'religious', this proclamation could be construed to protect the family laws from any interference from the administrators.

The *Government of India Act of 1858*, transformed every aspect of Indian administration. The legal structure went through a major change. The Supreme Courts in the Presidency towns of Calcutta, Bombay and Madras which operated with relative autonomy were replaced by integrated High Courts with the Privy Council as the final Court of Appeal. The Presidencies lost their autonomy and were joined into a unified imperial rule. The features of the administration as developed in Bengal were made the basis for new forms of unified administration for all the three Presidencies. The Bombay Presidency's treatment of self-governing groups and its acceptance of customary law gave way to the practice in Bengal Presidency of viewing all groups as possessing of a unified Hindu and Muslim legal entity.[2]

While the realm of the 'personal' was largely left untouched as per the proclamation, the new legal structure based on the model of the English courts necessitated the enactment of statute to regulate the 'public domain'. The extent of codification can be gauged by the fact that from 1861 to 1869, under Henry Maine, Member of Governor General's Legislative Council, 211 enactments were formulated, out of which 30 were major.[3]

The cornerstones of this new legal edifice were the Indian Penal Code and the Indian Contract Act, which facilitated smooth administration by laying down uniform laws regulating crime and punishment and commercial transactions. These two statutes formed the core of the criminal (penal) and civil (economic) legal principles in India. *The Indian Penal Code of (1860)* (along with the *Indian Evidence Act of 1872* and the *Criminal Procedure Act of 1898)* replaced the Islamic criminal system. *The Indian Contract Act of 1860* (along with the *Specific Relief Act of 1877*, the *Negotiable Instruments Act of 1881* and the *Transfer of Property Act of 1882)* laid down uniform laws to facilitate smooth economic transaction for the corporate world.[4]

As already discussed in Chapter 2, the Hindu notion of dharma differed a great deal from the British notion of law and justice. The term 'dharma' was broad and inclusive and could be applied to all aspects of life. Manu's categorization of 18 heads of law included both civil and criminal issues. The Islamic law also dealt with civil and criminal aspects. But the process of legislation adopted by the British was selective and affected only some aspects of civil and criminal law while a large area which was termed as 'religious' was left out of its purview, to be regulated by the natives as per their religious doctrines. But the categorization of matters to be dealt under personal laws was fluid, to be determined by the needs of the rising colonial empire. For instance, the initial charters had listed 'contract' as an issue left for the application of customary law. But since contract was essential to lay the foundation of a capitalist economy, it was taken out of the realm of 'religious' personal laws and was legislated upon. By treating only some aspects of these laws as religious, the British jurists were applying to them the Roman categorization of ecclesiastical and temporal (canon and civil) laws. Further, all issues concerning 'personal' matters were deemed 'religious' rather than customary. Over a period, the terms 'religious laws' and 'personal laws' were used as synonymous and interchangeable.[5] The First Law Commission's recommendation to codify personal laws was rejected on the ground that these laws are religious and since British legislature cannot regulate Mohammedan or Hindu religion, it also cannot (or shall not) legislate for Mohammedans or Hindus.[6]

But under the new system of adjudication, case law or judicial interpretation became an important new source of law entrusted with greater validity and binding force than the scriptures themselves. Through this source, inroads were made into the realm of personal laws. *The Indian Law Reports Act of 1875* strengthened the already established practice of relying upon the rulings of other courts. The subversion of women's rights through this process of case law has already been discussed in the preceding chapter. By the end of the nineteenth century the realm of uncodified 'personal law' was reduced primarily to case law reported in law journals.[7]

5.2 State Enacted Religious Laws

The restraint upon legislating in the realm of personal matters was applicable only to the Hindus and Muslims. The other religious communities, the Christians and the Parsis were not placed under this restraint. Hence statutes could be enacted to govern the matrimonial relationships of these communities.

The first few enactments in the realm of matrimonial laws were meant mainly for European Christians and Christian converts.[8] Significant among these is the *Indian Divorce Act* of 1869, which was modelled on the *Matrimonial Causes Act of 1857* of England. This statute was a milestone in the history of English matrimonial law as it transferred matrimonial jurisdiction from ecclesiastical courts to the civil courts in England and provided for the dissolution of Christian marriages.

Even prior to the enactment of the Indian Divorce Act in 1869, the British legal principles of morality, equity and good conscience could be effectively used as channels for incorporating the Anglo-Saxon jurisprudence into the Indian legal system. But in 1869, through a statutory process, the principles of English matrimonial law were firmly established within the Indian jurisprudence.

While some matrimonial remedies had already entered India through English lawyers practising in the Indian courts and by the application of the Civil Procedure Code,[9] the Indian Divorce Act gave a statutory recognition to the matrimonial reliefs like restitution of conjugal rights, judicial separation and annulment, which did not have any scriptural or customary basis in the Indian setting. It is significant to note that at this historical juncture, the laws and customs regulating most lower caste Hindus and the Muslim communities provided for the dissolution of marriages. These dissolutions could be effected through community-based arbitration fora by fulfilling certain minimum conditions and without engaging in lengthy legal battles nor incurring phenomenal costs. The relevant point to note is that these dissolutions were not effected through adversarial processes but through community arbitrations and with the consent of the parties or their families after returning the gifts received from the other spouse. In most cases, the party seeking dissolution had to pay back the marriage expenses and at times was called upon to pay a compensation to the other party. In communities practising the custom of bride price, if the wife was seeking dissolution, she herself, or on her behalf, her father or her future husband, would have to return the bride price. Among Muslim communities, if the wife was seeking dissolution, she would have to forego her mehr amount which was stipulated by the husband at the time of marriage.

But under the Christian view, marriage was deemed as an eternal and indissoluble sacrament. The *Matrimonial Causes Act of 1857* made some dent into the concept of indissoluble marital bondage by providing for the dissolution of marriage under certain stringent grounds. But divorce was a 'relief' available only to an innocent spouse, if a matrimonial fault could be proved against the guilty partner. The spouse could also obtain a lesser relief of judicial separation and keep intact the matrimonial tie and thus deny the guilty spouse the option of remarriage. The parties could also enforce conjugality through judicial proceedings and compel a deserted spouse to return to the matrimonial dwelling under threat of imprisonment or confiscation of his/ her property, a concept unheard of in the Indian setting. Overall, the Christian concept treated matrimony as a state of eternal bondage and the 1857 Act was meant to provide marginal respite from these archaic and anti-women notions. The aim of the *Indian Divorce Act of 1869* was to extend the progressive provisions for European Christians and British subjects residing in India. But gradually, these English notions of marriage and matrimonial 'reliefs', (e.g. restitution of conjugal rights, judicial separation and annulment of marriage) were incorporated into the personal laws of other communities either through judicial precedents or legislative enactments.

The Parsis who were governed by customary laws, demanded for a separate enactment to govern their marriage and succession. In response to this demand, a statute was enacted to govern Parsi marriages and the principles of English matrimonial law were incorporated into this statute.[10]

Although the statutes governing Christians and Parsis were state enactments, since they governed family relationships they came to be viewed as 'religious laws'. The implications of these statutes to Christian and Parsi women are addressed in Part Three of this book.

5.3 Remoulding of Indian Family Law Within a Western Model

The statutes governing Christian and Parsi communities set the trend of matrimonial adjudications for Hindus and Muslims. Within the new legal structure founded on adversarial principles of English civil law, family relationships of Hindus and Muslims came to be contested. The matrimonial rights and obligations were reinterpreted within the paradigm of the matrimonial remedies introduced by the new statutes.[11]

It is not intended to negate the fact that the customary

practices, as well as the doctrinal precepts of the pre-colonial Indian society contained several anti-women stipulations. But the scriptures were not statutes and contained several contradictions and ambiguities both internally within each authority, as well as between the different authorities within a region. Further, the language and the context of these texts was open to several interpretations leading to diverse customs within a pluralistic society. Hence, it would be logical to infer that the customs and interpretations were not uniformly anti-women and that there were spaces for negotiating women's rights.

The English translations of the original texts had already subverted the context and meaning of these precepts. The anti-women biases and the orientalist approaches of the translators would also have coloured the translations. Within the new litigation fora, the coloured opinions expressed in these translated texts became definite legal principles of universal application. Published in law journals and relied upon in subsequent litigations, the most negative aspects of Hindu and Muslim laws were highlighted and over a period of time became the settled infallible principles of Hindu and Muslim family law.

Many a times, the ancient texts were used mainly to co-opt the anti-women provisions of English matrimonial statutes. The application of the medieval European (Christian) remedy of restitution of conjugal rights (which was incorporated in the English matrimonial statutes in 1857), to both Muslims and Hindus in India by re-interpreting their ancient legal texts is one concrete example of this new trend.[12] Subversion of women's economic rights upon marriage, i.e. the Hindu woman's right to stridhana and the Muslim woman's right to mehr (both of which could include immovable properties) to the English concept of maintenance provides another example. The introduction of the English principle of widow's limited estate and the concept of 'reversioner' (to whom the property would revert back upon the death of the widow) is a third example of this trend.

Ironically, while the British used the issue of the status of Indian women to rationalize the political subjugation of India as a civilizing project, the Hindu revivalists tried to re-locate these principles into their ancient texts, armed by the orientalists approach of a shared distant Aryan past. The concern of reformers for changing the status of women became trapped within the binaries of a superior Hindu culture projected by the revivalists and the civilizing project of the British administrators. But the rigid Victorian morality was the parameter set by all factions for determining the status of women.[13]

During the last phase of nineteenth century, Hindu conjugality became the main battleground for the revivalist struggle for national identity and any reform within personal laws came to be viewed by this faction with extreme hostility. The issue was foregrounded in the controversy regarding the Age of Consent (and restraint upon child marriage) both in Bombay and Bengal.[14] The controversy was galvanized by the decision of the Bombay High Court in the case of Rukmabai, who was married in childhood and whose marriage had not been consummated.[15] The court had declined to pass a decree of restitution of conjugal rights in favour of the husband. The revivalists interpreted this judgement as an interference in the sacrosanct arena of Hindu conjugality by the British courts (and a breach of the assurance on non-interference). For the reformers, the intervention of the English courts was an armour in their campaign against the upper caste Hindu custom of child marriage.

The litigation, the judgement and the controversy which followed were all laden with ironies. The husband's case was trumpeted by the revivalists and it is with their support he had approached the English courts, rather than the caste panchayat, for the remedy of restoring his Hindu conjugality. As already stated, within the customary law, the relief of restoring conjugality was non-existent and the husband could not obtain any relief in this sphere. Conjugality has not been instituted and hence the question of 'restoring conjugality' an European Christian remedy did not apply to this case.[16] Also, the parties belonged to the lower caste among whom the custom of the caste recognized the right of the wife to dissolve her marriage. And most important, Justice Pinhey, who presided over the matter, had declined the relief on the ground that it was an outdated medieval Christian remedy under the English law and further that the Hindu law did not recognize such a barbaric custom.[17] But in the highly politicized climate, these subtle legal points were lost. The debate was confined within the binaries of the barbaric Hindu custom of child marriage by the reformers and the audacity of an English judge to intervene in the sacred realm of Hindu conjugality by the revivalists.

5.4 Option of Secular and Civil Statutes

During this period, certain uniform and secular statutes governing family relationships were also enacted. The *Indian Succession Act* of 1865 (re-enacted in 1925), the *Special Marriage Act* of 1872 (re-enacted in 1954) and the *Guardians and Wards Act* of 1890. Modelled on the principle of separation of the canon and the civil, which was gradually being accepted under the Anglo-Saxon law, these were purely civil enactments. There was no camouflage of religiosity here as in the enactments governing Christian and the Parsi communities.

The *Special Marriage Act* was a response to the demand raised by the Brahmo Samajis, as part of their campaign against Brahminical rituals and idol worship within the Bengal Presidency, for a law enabling registration of simple, non-ritualistic civil marriages. The Act was passed despite opposition from orthodox sections and provided the opportunity for Indians to contract a marriage, devoid of any religious trappings, in a civil registry. But it was mandatory for the parties contracting the marriage to declare that they had renounced their religion. The stipulation of renouncing religion narrowed the scope of the Act. In 1912, a demand was raised for the deletion of this provision, but was not conceded. But later, through an amendment in 1923, this clause was deleted. This facilitated the registration of civil marriages without the accompanying encumbrance of religious renouncement. After the marriage, for matters of property inheritance, the couple would be governed by the provisions of the *Indian Succession Act*.

The *Indian Succession Act* contained separate sections for Parsis and non-Parsis. The provisions governing Parsis granted daughters a share in the family property but followed the Islamic principle of granting them half the share of their male counterparts. The general section was more egalitarian. Daughters were granted equal right of inheritance along with their brothers. But the statute also simultaneously validated the English notion of testamentary succession. The individual acquired an absolute right in the property and there were no restraints upon alienation either by transfer or bequest. This concentration of rights upon an individual was contrary to the prevailing norms governing both Hindu and Muslim property inheritance.

Although applicable primarily to Christians, this statute could be deemed a residuary law since it was also applicable to persons contracting civil marriages. The *Guardians and Wards Act* of 1890 which authorized the courts to appoint guardians for minors was also applicable uniformly. Despite the limitation, the *Special Marriage Act*, the *Indian Succession Act and the Guardians and Wards Act*, provided secular and civil options to persons who did not want to be governed by religious enactments. These could have gradually developed into a comprehensive family code. But the growing resentment against the British rule and their policy of constituting Hindus and Muslims as separate, homogeneous and antagonistic communities restricted the scope for developing uniform family laws.

5.5 Sectarian Reforms Within Communalized Communities

The events at the turn of the century brought in a sharp cleavage between the two distinct political constituencies of Hindus and Muslims. The division of Bengal, the communal riots at the close of the century and the separate electorates introduced by the Morley-Minto reforms collapsed the space for any further enactments of uniform applicability in the realm of family law.[18]

But when women entered the political arena in response to the call given by Gandhi in the twenties, the issue of women's rights and family law reform gained limelight. Women leaders of the nationalist movement raised the demand for a comprehensive code regulating marriage, divorce and inheritance. Kamaladevi Chattopadhyay, Sarojinidevi Naidu, Muthulaxmi Reddy, Begam Shah Nawaz and other prominent members of the All India Women's Conference (AIWC) were the most vocal protagonists of this demand.

Lamenting over the plight of women, Captain Laxmi, a protagonist of women's rights, stated at the 1933 AIWC meet: 'The members of the Legislative Assembly who are men will not help us in bringing any drastic changes which will benefit women.' At the urging of Renuka Ray, another vocal member, 24th November 1934 was declared as a Legal Disabilities Day. The AIWC also initiated a comparative study of the family laws of different communities with a view to evolving uniform family laws.[19]

The pressure from women leaders led to the Indian National Congress ratifying the demand for a uniform code during its conventions. But when the Congress leaders acquired the power to legislate through the *Government of India Act* of 1935, the law reforms initiated by them were not only limited and short-sighted but also widened the gulf between the Hindu and Muslim family laws.

The Government of India Act of 1935, provided an opportunity for nationalist leaders to legislate and regulate family relations. Using this opportunity, both the Hindu and Muslim leaders pressed for law reform within their respective personal laws ostensibly to elevate the status of women. The issues addressed by the reforms, their impact on women's rights and the political motive beneath the reforms make interesting study.

The Hindu Women's Right to Property Act, 1937: The aim of the *Hindu Women's Right to Property Bill*, introduced by Dr G.V. Deshmukh, was to set right the problems created by the judicial decisions of the English courts which had constrained the scope of stridhana, during the later phase of the nineteenth century.[20]

While introducing the Bill in the Legislative Assembly on 4 February 1937, Deshmukh stated:

> The British concepts like 'reversioner' 'surrender' etc. had caused a great loss to women's right to property. The word 'reversioner' reflected an English notion peculiar to their own country. From that moment, the widow began to be infested by those pests called 'reversioners'. In fact, a majority of the litigation in connection with the property of widows was by and on account of the reversioners. The reversioner could harass the widow by challenging every act of hers in dealing with the property.[21]

Deshmukh added that due to the prevailing social conditions, the English judges had arrived at an erroneous conclusion that the temperament of the Hindu society was such that it did not want Hindu women to have an absolute right in the property.[21]

Through this Bill, Deshmukh hoped to achieve equality between Hindu men and women in respect of their property. Clause 3 of the Bill stipulated that no person should be excluded from inheritance and partition on the basis of sex. Regarding the devolution of the property of a Hindu dying intestate, Clause 4 of the bill specifically provided that it would devolve upon the wife, mother, daughter and wife of a predeceased son along with the sons and all would have equal share in the property. Clause 5 equated the status of women to that of men and made them absolute owners of the property.[22]

The Bill met with a great deal of hostility and Deshmukh was ridiculed for introducing this bill. After much debate, a watered down version of the original Bill was finally enacted. The provisions of the Bill granting women absolute right to property were mutilated and widows were granted only a limited right of inheritance through a concept called 'widow's estate'. The provision granting daughters a share in the parental property was excluded. The right of married women to separate property under the scriptural notion of stridhana, which the Bill originally set to restore was subverted. The women's right to property was confined within the limited sphere of inheritance rights of widows.

Reform within Islam (1937 and 1939): Using the same opportunity, the Muslim religio-political leaders enacted two important legislations which had far-reaching effect upon the Muslim communities. As mentioned earlier many communities which had converted to Islam continued their customary practices of property inheritance. The Muslim League with the support of the religious leaders, the Ullamas, initiated a legislation through which all Muslims would be mandatorily governed by the Shariat law.[23] The second statute[24] conferred on the Muslim women a statutory right of divorce under certain specific conditions.[25]

The arguments in favour of the Application of Shariat Act 1937 were that the customary laws of inheritance based on the concept of joint family property were discriminatory against women and that application of the Shariat would raise their status. M.H.M. Abdullah, who introduced the Bill in the central legislature spelt out the objectives of the Bill as follows:

> ...the bill aims at securing uniformity of law among Muslims in all their social and personal relations. By doing so it also recognises and does justice to the claims of women for inheriting family property who, under customary law, are debarred from succeeding to the same. If Shariat law is applied they will automatically be entitled to inherit the same.[26]

Another Muslim member Sir Mohammad Yamin Khan stressed that Muslim women had been lobbying for the passage of the bill and pointed out that

... being Muslim why (women) not get the benefit of Islamic law and why should they be deprived of their genuine right of inheritance on account of the customary law which gives to a man a much bigger share than what he is entitled to...(A Muslim woman) does not enjoy only the limited right of maintenance but she becomes the full owner of her property.... she is under no obligation to give the property to her husband .... not even have it managed by her husband ...human society must live on the right principles of equity....[27]

The Bill had the support of all Muslim legislators and women members. G.V. Deshmukh was another supporter of the Bill. The stated aim of the legislation was to declare that in matters relating to marriage, divorce and inheritance all Muslims would be mandatorily governed by the Shariat, (which is more progressive and pro-women) to the exclusion of other laws and customs, throughout British India. But beneath the stated objective, the Bill also had a deeper political agenda, of unifying Muslims and strengthening the political base, as well the religious hold over the community.[28] This was the period when the two nation theory was being formulated and within the nationalist movement there was a sharp divide between Hindu and Muslim leaders. A uniform law was viewed by the Muslim League as an important step towards unifying the community. Since unification of Muslims was the primary aim, customs of matrilineal inheritance were opposed as vehemently as those which denied women property rights. To achieve the crucial political motive beneath the Bill, an attempt had to be made to pacify the feudal land-owners who were opposed to the Bill. As a conciliatory move, M.A. Jinnah introduced an amendment to keep agrarian landholdings out of the purview of the Bill. Despite the tall claim of empowering women, women's rights were subverted to the political agenda.[29]

The second legislation during this period was the *Dissolution of Muslim Marriages Act*, 1939. As per the Shariat, on apostasy a Muslim marriage stood dissolved. Muslim women who felt trapped within oppressive marriages used the provision to dissolve their marital ties. The Act sought to arrest this trend by providing Muslim women a statutory right to divorce within their religious boundaries and thus retain them within the Islamic fold.

The Act was based on a book entitled, *Al-Hilat al-Nazjizalil Halilat al-Ajizah* (a lawful divorce) published in 1932 by the renowned Islamic jurist Maulana Ashraf Ali Thanavi. In defence of women's rights, he had enumerated the principles of the Maliki law by which a court could dissolve a Muslim woman's marriage under specified conditions.[30] Based on his recommendations, a Bill was introduced in the Central Legislature by Muhammed Ahmad Kazimi in 1936.[31]

The Islamic jurists, Asif Ali Fyzee and Maulana Thanavi actively campaigned for its enactment. The Bill was supported by several non-Muslim members. But some Hindu legislators cautioned that while they would support a bill granting divorce to Muslim women, they would oppose any move to confer a similar right on Hindu women.

The statement of objects and reasons mentioned that the aim of the Bill was to alleviate the unspeakable misery caused to Muslim women. The Act was applicable only to women. The Muslim men's right to unilateral divorce was not affected by the reform. Again, beneath the profound objective of women's welfare lay a deeper political motive of strengthening Islam. But despite the hidden agenda, it was a landmark reform in the history of Islamic (predominantly Hanafi) law in India.

5.6 Debate Within the Constitutional Assembly

The years immediately preceding independence were the years marked by the controversy around the Hindu Code Bill. Compared to their Muslim counterparts, the caste Hindu women lagged far behind. They had neither a right to divorce nor an absolute right of inheritance as widows and daughters. The consistent campaign by women leaders compelled the Congress to prioritize this issue. But although two separate committees were set up during the forties to explore the scope of reform within the customary Hindu law and these committees submitted detailed reports, the political developments necessitated the shelving of this issue until independence.[32]

It is interesting to observe that while laying the foundation of a new nation, the scheme of women's liberation had to be re-located within the master scheme of national integration and became subservient to it in all later developments, both legislative and judicial.

The issue of personal laws was debated primarily in the Constituent Assembly in the context of rights of minorities within the new nation. The trauma of partition had brought in its wake an insecure and defensive Muslim minority who had to be reassured of their right to religious and cultural freedom within the new democracy, which would be governed by majority concerns. The political impediments which necessitated this assurance bear resemblance to Queen Victoria's Proclamation after the Sepoy Mutiny almost a century earlier.

Within these political constraints, the debate around the Uniform Civil Code in the Constituent Assembly centered on the 'nation' and 'national integration'. The issue of gender and women's rights did not figure in this debate. It was deemed necessary that the integrated nation should be governed by a uniform set of family laws to facilitate national unity and smooth governance. The Indian leaders had inherited the British scheme of making laws certain, uniform and rigid for easy administration and carried a similar contemptuous approach towards plurality of laws and non-state legal systems which were deemed as pre-modern. But, the flip side of this objective of smooth governance was an assurance to minorities of their separate religious and cultural identity symbolized by the continuance of their personal laws.

The clause on the Uniform Civil Code became a highly contested issue and only after the rights were divided into two segments, i.e. Fundamental and Enforceable Rights (Part III of the Constitution), and Directive Principles of State Policy, which were non-enforceable (Part IV of the Constitution) that the Muslim members consented to placing this clause under Part IV of the Constitution. This move was opposed by liberals within the Constituent Assembly, M.R. Masani, Hansa Mehta, Rajkumari Amrit Kaur, K.M. Munshi, Alladi Krishnaswami Ayyar etc. in the context of evolving a new nationhood and ushering India into modernity and did not address the issue of women's rights. M.R. Masani, Hansa Mehta and Rajkumari Amrit Kaur voiced their notes of dissent on the ground:

> One of the factors that has kept India back from advancing to nationhood has been the existence of personal laws based on religion which keep the nation divided into watertight compartments in many aspects. [According to K.M. Munshi, the important point was whether] We are going to consolidate and unify our personal law in such a way that the way of life of the whole country may in course of time be unified and (become) secular. ...After all we are an advancing society. We are in a stage where we must unify and consolidate the nation by every means ... [Alladi Krishnaswami Ayyar added,] Are we helping those factors which help the welding together into a single nation, or is this country

to be kept up always as a series of competing communities?[33]

But withstanding this opposition, Dr Ambedkar pointed out that the Muslim members probably had read rather too much into this provision which merely proposes that the state shall endeavour to secure a civil code for the citizens of the country. It does not say that after the uniform code is framed, the state shall enforce it upon all citizens merely because they are citizens. It is perfectly possible that future parliaments may provide for an optional code.[34] Guided by these assurances, Article 44 of the Constitution is worded as follows: The State shall endeavour to secure for the citizens a *Uniform Civil Code* throughout the territory of India.

Notes

1. Desika Char, S.V., *Readings in the Constitutional History of India 1757–1947*, New Delhi: Oxford University Press (1983), p. 294.
2. I am grateful to Amrita Shodhan for sharing with me her unpublished doctoral thesis where she has dealt with this point elaborately. For reference, see Chapter 4, n.9.
3. Rankin, G.C., *Background to India Law*, Cambridge: Cambridge University Press (1946).
4. While enacting the *Indian Contract Act*, the fact that contract was initially treated as part of personal law was conveniently overlooked and it was transformed into territorial law uniformly applicable to all British subjects.
5. While a large part of the personal laws relates to family matters, the term also applies to issues like management of Hindu religious and charitable institutions and Muslim *wakfs*, as well as the Muslim law of pre-emption and the Hindu law of Damdupat.
6. Rankin, G.C., *Background to India Law*, p.67.
7. See Cohn, B.S., 'Anthropological Note on Disputes and Law in India' in Nader, L. (ed.), *The Ethnography of Law* (American Anthropological Association) (1965), pp.112-13.
8. The *Native Converts Marriage Dissolution Act*, 1866, the *Indian Divorce Act*, 1869 and *Indian Christian Marriage Act*, 1872 are illustrative of this trend.
9. See *Peerozeboye v Ardaseer Cursetjee* (1853) POC 57.
10. The *Parsi Marriage and Divorce Act* of 1865. The history of this legislation is discussed in detail in Chapter 9.
11. According to Bhattacharjee, with their bulk, alien appearance, exotic trappings and Westminsterish logomachy, the law of the country became alienated from the people. See Bhattacharjee, A.M., *Hindu Law and the Constitution*, Calcutta: Eastern Law House (1994) (2nd edn.), p.11.

12. See *Gatha Ram Mistree v Moohito Kochin Domoonee* (1875) 14 BLR 298 and *Moonshee Buzloor Ruheem v Shumsoonissa Begum* (1867) 2 MIA 551.
13. See Banerjee, S., 'Marginalization of Women's Popular Culture in Nineteenth Century Bengal' (1989), in Sangari, K. & S. Vaid (ed.), *Recasting Women, Essays in Colonial History,* New Delhi: Kali for Women (1989), p.127.
14. Sarkar, T., 'Rhetoric Against Age of Consent,' in *Economic and Political Weekly,* XXVIII/36, (1983) p.1870.
15. Chandra, S., 'Rukmabai: Debate over Woman's Right to Her Person,' in *Economic and Political Weekly,* XXXI/44 (1996), p.2927.
16. Among most lower castes which practised child marriage, the right of conjugality would commence not from the date of marriage but only after the performance of a second ceremony after attaining puberty.
17. *Dadaji Bhikaji v Rukmabai* (1885) ILR 9 Bom 529.
18. Sarkar, S., *Modern India 1885–1947,* Madras: Macmillan (1993).
19. Basu, A. and B. Rai, *A History of the AIWC 1927–1990,* Delhi: Manohar (1992), pp.46-7.
20. Gill, K., *Hindu Women's Right to Property,* New Delhi: Deep & Deep Publications (1986), p.485.
21. Ibid., p.104.
22. Ibid., pp.105-7.
23. The *Application of Shariat Act,* 1937.
24. The *Dissolution of Muslim Marriages Act,* 1939.
25. It is relevant to record that Hindu women were granted corresponding rights almost two decades later. The right to divorce was conferred on the Hindu women through the *Hindu Marriage Act,* 1955 and the absolute right of inheritance was conferred through the *Hindu Succession Act* 1956.
26. Lateef, S., 'Defining Women through Legislation,' in Hasan, Z. (ed.), *Forging Identities : Gender, Communities and the State,* New Delhi: Kali for Women (1994), p.43.
27. Ibid., p.45.
28. Parashar, A., *Women and Family Law Reform,* New Delhi: Sage Publications (1992), p.150.
29. Ibid., p.149.
30. Ibid., p.151.
31. Ahmad, F., 'Fatwa needed to make talaq revocable,' in *The Pioneer,* Delhi 17.V.94.
32. See the following chapter for a detailed account of the process of Hindu law reforms.
33. Dhagamwar, V., *Towards the Uniform Civil Code,* Bombay: N.M. Tripathi (1989), pp.2-3.
34. Ibid., p.4.

PART TWO:

POST-INDEPENDENCE DEVELOPMENTS

6

Hindu Law Reforms—Stilted Efforts at Gender Justice

Introduction

Constitution is rightly the most significant touchstone for determining the scope of women's rights in the post-independence period. The provisions of adult franchise, non-discrimination on the basis of sex and positive discrimination (or affirmative action) in favour of women and children placed Indian women far ahead of many of their western counterparts.[1] Equality and non-discrimination became fundamental and enforceable legal rights. The scope of Article 21, could be expanded to read into it issues of social and economic justice.[2] It is against this backdrop that we examine the major law reform of the post-independence period.

Although the reformed Hindu law is projected as the ideal piece of legislation which liberated Hindu women, the underlying motive of the reform was consolidating the powers of the state and building an integrated nation. This crucial objective could be achieved only by diluting women's rights to arrive at a level of minimum consensus so that the agenda of reform could be effected without much opposition. Several customary rights were sacrificed to arrive at uniformity. The statutes that were finally enacted were merely ornamental instead of being markers of genuine and concrete efforts at rectifying the gender discrimination written into the Hindu law. Some of the anomalies within the reformed laws, as well as the complex and labourious process of the reform is examined here.

In the years that followed, several discriminatory aspects of the personal laws came up for judicial scrutiny under the constitutional mandate of equality and non-discrimination. But the courts, in most cases, stopped short of declaring the discriminatory aspects as unconstitutional. Over the years, the courts have held that the discrimination under the personal laws of various communities is based on reasonable classification. This has thrown further stumbling blocks in the path of gender equality.

6.1 Concerns Governing the Reforms

The history of Hindu Law reform spans a period of fifteen years from 1941 to 1956. It was discussed in three Parliaments of historical significance i.e. the Federal Parliament, the Provisional Parliament and the first Parliament of the newly independent nation. At each stage, it went through a dilution of rights till finally, the political interests of the ruling party became the primary consideration. But the rhetoric continued to be 'liberation of women'.

The Hindu Law Committee, set up in 1941 to look into the anomalies of the 1937 Act, recommended a comprehensive code of marriage and succession, which led to the setting up of the second Hindu Law Committee in 1944. After soliciting opinions of jurists and the public, the Committee submitted its report to the Federal Parliament in April, 1947. The recommendations were debated in the Provincial Parliament between 1948 and 1951 and again from 1951 to 1954. Finally, a diluted version, in the form of four separate Acts could be passed only in 1955-6.

The three important factors which need to be examined in the context of the Hindu law reform are, (i) the opposition to it within the Congress leadership, (ii) the political impediments which necessitated the reform, and (iii) the veracity of its dual claim of being a code and of liberating women.

Opposition from Conservative Forces: Several provisions including the provisions of monogamy, divorce, abolition of coparcenary and inheritance to daughters were opposed. It was felt that the Hindu society will receive a moral setback if women were granted the right to divorce along with a right to inherit property. The reforms were opposed by the then President and Constitutional head, Dr Rajendra Prasad, senior Congressmen like Pattabhi Sitaramayya and the architect of the united Indian nation, Sardar Patel, the President of the ruling Congress, P.D. Tandon among others.[3]

The representatives of Hindu fundamentalist parties termed

it as 'anti-Hindu' and 'anti-Indian' and raised the demand for a uniform code as a delaying tactic. At this point, the women parliamentarians who had initially propagated a uniform code, reversed their position and supported the Hindu law reform. This is a significant political move, since an uncompromising demand for a uniform code would have meant an alliance with the most reactionary and anti-women lobby and would have caused a further setback to women's rights.[4]

Political impediments which necessitated the reform: The concerns which were instrumental in bringing about reform in Muslim Law, i.e. of homogenizing a community by uniting them under one law, were also the driving force for the Hindu law reform. The integration of Hindus from three different political regimes, i.e. British India, the princely states and the tribal regions into one nation could best be done by bringing them under one law. Hence, the primary concern was to define the term 'Hindu' in its widest sense and encompass all sects and castes and religious denominations within it. The Hindu Law Committee had defined 'Hindu' as anyone professing the Hindu religion. But later the word 'professes' was deleted to broaden its scope.[5]

Examining the motive for Hindu law reform, Archana Parashar[6] argues, that the hidden agenda was unification of the nation through uniformity in law. National integration was of paramount importance. Establishing the supremacy of the state over religious institutions was another important consideration. This could be best achieved by re-defining the rights given to women. Through the re-orientation of female roles the state could replace the claim of religion and religious institutions over people's lives. While bringing in reforms the state relied upon two conflicting claims of tradition and modernity. While professing that it was bound by the Constitution, the state projected the image of a continuity with the past (by preserving the provisions from the ancient sacred law) to bring in selective reforms.

For the state, the unifying potential of the common code became more important than its potential for ensuring legal equality for women. Hence, several customary rights of women, particularly from the lower castes and the southern regions, were sacrificed in the interest of uniformity. Local customs of matrilineal inheritance and other customary safeguards were not incorporated into the new code.

For instance, most lower castes had a right of divorce and remarriage under the customary law with consent of the parties. Through the *Marumakkattayam Act* of 1933, (applicable to the Malabar region) the right of divorce by executing a registered instrument of dissolution by the concerned parties was granted statutory recognition. Further, under the scriptural law as well as customary law, the right of females as stridhana heirs was superior to their male counterparts and that of parents was superior to in-laws. But under S.15 of the *Hindu Succession Act*, 1956, sons and daughters were granted equal rights. Further, under the provisions of the *Hindu Succession Act*, the property of a childless woman devolves upon the husband's heirs and only in their absence would it devolve upon the woman's own parents. A further and inexplicable distinction was made between the heirs of the father and those of the mother of a female and the mother's heirs were placed in an inferior category.[7] Despite the wide diversity under the Hindu law the reforms relied upon one school irrespective of its provisions favouring women.

The Congress party was dominated by lawyers trained in British law or those who studied law in England and consequently imbibed all the colonial biases regarding the functioning of Indian society, as well as the changes that were supposedly needed to modernize it. There was a fascination among social reformers with uniformity as a vehicle of national unity. The notion of the state as an instrument of social reform to be imposed upon the people without creating a social consensus derives essentially from the norms of functioning inherent in the colonialist state machinery and ideology. The English-educated elite had faithfully imbibed the colonial state's ideology, projecting itself as the most progressive instrument of social reform.[8]

The reforms did not introduce any principle which had not already existed somewhere in India. Despite this, the reforms were projected as a vehicle for ushering in western modernity. There were, however, several liberal customary practices which were discarded by the Hindu code for the sake of uniformity. In their stated determination to put an end to the growth of custom, the reformers were in fact putting an end to the essence of

Hindu law, and ironically, persisted in calling the codification 'Hindu'.[9]

Claims of liberating women: There is a general presumption that the Hindus are governed by a secular, egalitarian and gender-just code and that this code should now be extended to Muslims to liberate Muslim women. The judiciary has contributed to this myth by reiterating that Hindus have forsaken their personal laws and are governed by a common code.[10] This misconception forms the basis of the demand for the Uniform Civil Code. Hence, the veracity of this demand needs to be closely scrutinized.

Since the political impediment to reform Hindu law was grave, several balancing acts had to be performed by the state while reforming the Hindu law. Crucial provisions empowering women had to be constantly watered down to reach the level of minimum consensus. While projecting to be pro-women, male privileges had to be protected. While introducing modernity, archaic Brahminical rituals had to be retained.[11] While usurping the power exercised by religious heads, needs of emerging capitalism had to be safeguarded. Only through such balancing acts, the agenda of law reform could be achieved.

Unfortunately, the anomalies and anti-women bias within the Hindu code were not discussed widely in public forum. They remained hidden in statute books and legal manuals. There seemed to be almost a conspiracy of silence beneath which these inadequacies were crouched. This led to a fiction that the Hindu Code is sufficiently modernized and hence it is the perfect family code which ought to be extended to other religious denominations in order to liberate women.

The Acts were neither Hindu in character nor based on modern principles of equality but reflected the worst tendencies of both. Inheritance rights of daughters, the right of divorce for women and the imposition of monogamy upon Hindu males were the issues which were severely contended. Some aspects of these issues are examined here.

6.2 Illusory Inheritance Rights

The extent of opposition within the Congress to daughters inheriting property, was such that the then Law Minister C. C. Biswas, in 1954, on the floor of the house, publicly expressed his disagreement with this provision.[12] Due to severe opposition, coparcenary system had to be maintained, which resulted in the denial of rights to women in the ancestral home and property. When compared to the position of the brother, the sister's share was dismal.[13] Since the earlier safeguard provided by the ancient law givers to women by way of stridhana, a necessary concomitance to male coparacenary, had been corroded due to judicial decisions,[14] denial of equal rights to daughters only served to widen the gulf between the gender divide.

The daughters had equal rights only in the separate or self-acquired property of their father. But daughters could be denied a share even in this separate property by throwing the property back into the common stock using the doctrine of blending or by forming new coparcenaries. An incentive for such a move was provided by the state by conferring tax reliefs for coparcenaries under the *Income Tax Act*.[15]

While at one level coparcenary was retained, all the safeguards for protection of women's rights were abrogated. The main feature of the traditional Hindu joint family was its inalienability. But the new right granted to the male members to will away the property, further weakened the position of female members.[16] In this context, the daughters' right to be maintained from the family property or to claim marriage expenses out of this became illusory. The property inherited by the son from the father now became his separate property and the female members could not lay any claims to it.[17] While the English concept of alienation through testamentary succession was incorporated into the *Hindu Succession Act*, the protection granted to the family members under the English law did not find a mention here.[18] So individual men could will away both their share in the joint family property as well as the whole of their separate property with absolute abandonment. During Parliamentary debates, these loopholes were specifically pointed out to the members who were opposing the provision granting property rights to daughters to indicate how they could circumvent the provisions of the Act.[19]

While there were no safeguards to protect the right of daughters in their natal family, the capitalist, consumerist forces transformed the ancient custom of stridhana into a modern distortion called dowry.[20] Under its modern guise, the daughters lost control upon this property, which was presumably given on her behalf, to secure her happiness in her matrimonial home. In the subsequent years, the demand for dowry became an instrument of violence and subjugation of the newly married brides.

6.3 Implications of Formal Equality

The Hindu Marriage Act of 1955 was based on a formal concept of equality where the spouses were deemed equal and had equal rights and obligations towards each other. Both men and women were granted equal rights to matrimonial remedies and ancillary reliefs.

So, while a basic inequality between men and women persisted within the scheme of inheritance rights,[21] under the perverse logic of equality the Hindu woman was under a legal obligation to maintain her husband.[22] The concept did not exist under any prevalent notion of marriage in the Indian context—Hindu law, either scriptural or customary, or the Muslim law or even in the modern and secular *Special Marriage Act*, enacted in 1954. The concept was introduced for the first time under the *Hindu Marriage Act* and was based on the western notion of formal equality.[23]

It is pertinent to note that the enactment of 1955 did not grant Hindu women the right of divorce by mutual consent which had already been introduced under the *Special Marriage Act* in 1954 as it was considered too radical for the conservative Hindu Society.[24] And yet women from such conservative societies were deemed to be sufficiently progressive, liberated and economically advanced so as to provide maintenance to their husbands. While a boy of 18 years was not entitled to claim maintenance from his father on the ground that he had reached the age of majority and hence is capable of earning his own livelihood, an adult male was granted the privilege of exercising a choice of remaining unemployed and claiming maintenance from his employed wife. This, despite the social reality that a large number of women are engaged in unpaid domestic work and among those who are engaged in wage labour, a significant percentage are in low paying jobs or in the unorganized sector.[25]

Ironically, while women were burdened with the responsibility of maintaining the husband under a modern concept of equality, the courts continued to undermine a woman's right to retain her job against her husband's wishes under the ancient notion of the

Lord and Master and granted them the privilege of determining the choice of matrimonial home. If the woman was employed at a place away from the matrimonial home, the husband could claim restitution of conjugal rights against the wives.[26]

For decades after the enactment, in a series of decisions, the courts held that Hindu marriage is a sacrament and it is the sacred duty of the wife to follow her husband and reside with him wherever he chooses to reside. In all the cases, the women were working and supporting the family. The husbands had approached the courts for restoring conjugality just to spite the women. The courts upheld the husband's rights and granted them a decree of restitution. The decisions are summarized below:

- In 1958 in *Ram Prakash v Savitri Devi*[27] the court held: According to Hindu Law, marriage is a holy union for the performance of marital duties with her husband where he may choose to reside and to fulfil her duties in her husband's home.

- In *Tirath Kaur v Kirpal Singh*,[28] the wife pleaded that she was willing to carry on with the marriage but was not prepared to give up the job. But the court disallowed her plea and ruled in favour of the husband as follows: The wife's refusal to give up the job amounts to desertion. This would entitle the husband for a decree of restitution of conjugal rights.

- In 1966, the Madhya Pradesh High Court held: A wife's first duty to her husband is to submit herself obediently to his authority and to remain under his roof and protection.[29]

- In 1973, in *Surinder Kaur v Gardeep Singh* [30] it was held: The Hindu law imposes on the wife the duty of attendance, obedience to and veneration for the husband to live with him wherever he chooses to reside.

- In 1977, the issue came up before the Full Bench of the Punjab and Haryana High Court in the case of *Kailash Wati v Ayodhia Parkash*.[31] The wife was employed prior to the marriage. Seven years after the marriage, the husband asked the wife to resign her job and on her refusal to do so, filed for restitution of conjugal rights. The wife stated that she was prepared to honour her matrimonial obligations but was not prepared to resign her job. The Full Bench of Punjab and Haryana High Court held: According to Hindu Law marriage is a holy union for the performance of marital duties with her husband where he may choose to reside and to fulfil, her duties in her husband's home. The court reaffirmed that the wife's refusal to resign her job amounts to withdrawal from the husband's society, and granted the decree in favour of the husband.

So while under the modern concept of equality, the husbands had the right to be maintained by their wives, under the concept of a sacramental marriage, they could restrain them from gainful employment. The right was based on a plea that it was the sacred duty of a Hindu wife to reside under the care and protection of her husband, her lord and master. While the husbands' plea is not surprising, the judicial affirmation of this plea under a modern statute is disturbing.

It is only around 1975 that the courts began to recognize the woman's right to hold on to a job away from her husband's residence. Three important judgements of this time, secured for women their constitutional right of holding a job away from their husband's residence. The Gujarat High Court[32] while denying the husband the relief declared:

> In the modern outlook, the husband and wife are equally free to take up a job and retain it. Since there had been a mutual arrangement, it was not a case where it could be said that the wife had withdrawn from the society of the husband.

Similarly, the Madras High Court, in a case where the wife's income was used to sustain herself and her child, ruled: 'Under the modern law, the concept of the wife's obedience to her husband and her duty to live under his roof under all circumstances does not apply'.[33] In another significant development, the Delhi High court in 1978, in *Swaraj Garg v R.M. Garg*[34] dissented from the Full Bench decision in *Kailash Wati* and held that in the absence of a pre-marital agreement between the parties, it cannot be said that the wife who had a permanent job with a good income had to live at a place determined by the husband when the husband did not earn enough to maintain the family. Providing constitutional validity to the wife's right to hold on to the job, Justice Deshpande ruled that an exclusive right to the husband to decide the matrimonial home would be violative of the equality of sexes clause under Article 14 of the Constitution. In all the cases, the fact that the wives were earning more than their husbands and were substantially contributing towards household expenditure seems to have influenced the judges while denying husbands the decree of restitution of conjugal rights.

6.4 Consequences of Monogamy

The Hindu Marriage Act introduced the Christian concept of monogamy into the Hindu marriage and this provision seems to have caused a great deal of resentment among Hindus. The popular support for the demand for a Uniform Civil Code is rooted in the resentment that while the sexual tendencies of Hindu males are curbed by the introduction of monogamy, the Muslim males are left free to enjoy the privileges of bigamous marriages. The provision of monogamy was introduced ostensibly to elevate the status of Hindu women and it was a demand raised by women in the nationalist movement. Hence it would indeed be interesting to observe how the provision of monogamy under the Hindu Marriage Act has affected women.

Although it was claimed during Parliamentary debates that Hinduism is not a religion but a conglomeration of culture and the Act transformed the Hindu marriage from status to a dissoluble contract, the form of solemnizing the contract remained Brahminical and scriptural with saptapadi (seven steps round the sacred fire) and vivaha homa (the sacred fire) as its essential features. But within a pluralistic society, the Act also had to validate diverse customary practices.[35] But the notion of a valid custom remained ancient and that of time immemorial, as stipulated under the English law. This mingling of Brahminical rituals at one end, customary practices at the other, with English principles thrown in for good measure, has resulted in absurd and ridiculous rulings regarding the validity of Hindu marriages and women have been the worst sufferers of these legal absurdities.

In the process of urbanization, most customary forms have been modified and urban communities living in close proximity have adopted a synthesis of marriage rituals. The forms range from exchange of garlands to applying *sindoor* (vermilion) on the bride's forehead, declaring themselves married by signing on a stamp paper in a lawyers chamber or performing some rituals before a deity in a particular temple (for instance, marriages contracted at the Kalighat temple in Calcutta). The media and more particularly the Hindi films have contributed to the confusion by projecting these practices as valid forms of Hindu marriage.

This ambiguity regarding the valid form of marriage is not to be found under any law governing minority communities. Under the laws of minority communities, the formalities of solemnizing marriage are strictly prescribed and the officiating priest has to provide the necessary document by way of a marriage certificate or he is required to register the marriage with the Registrar of Births, Deaths and Marriages. Since Muslim, Christian and Parsi religions are more institutionalized, their rules and procedures for contracting marriage are definite and unambiguous and are strictly controlled by the religious hierarchies. But Hindu marriages (as well as the Hindu law) which were based more on community practices are relatively less institutionalized and hence their legality is more ambiguous. Due to the breakdown of traditional communities within which these marriages were performed, the situation has further deteriorated.

This ambiguity has provided a Hindu male ample scope to contract bigamous marriages. Since the law recognizes only monogamous marriages, the women in polygamous relationships are placed in a vulnerable situation. In the absence of any clear proof, the man has the choice of admitting either the first or his subsequent relationship as a valid marriage and escape from financial responsibility towards the other woman. When the man refuses to validate the marriage, the woman loses not only her right to maintenance but also faces humiliation and social stigma as a mistress. So much is at stake for the woman that it is not an uncommon sight for two women who are vying with each other for the status of a wife to come to blows during the court proceedings.

A random glance at law journals would reveal how widely prevalent is the ploy of refusing to validate the marriage in maintenance proceedings by Hindu husbands.[36]

The flip side of this predicament in maintenance proceedings is the dilemma faced by women in criminal proceedings in cases of bigamy. Here, years of litigation failed to end in conviction for the errant male due to the courts adopting a rigid view that Saptapadi, Vivaha homa and Kanyadan etc. are essential for solemnizing a Hindu marriage. If these ceremonies could not be proved by the first wife in respect of her husband's second marriage, the husband could wriggle out of conviction even though he had cohabited with the second wife, the community had accepted the man and the second wife as husband and wife or even if he had fathered children through the second wife.[37]

Later studies revealed that in spite of the provision of monogamy under the reformed Hindu law, the percentage of polygamy among Hindus is greater than polygamy among Muslims.[38] So the progressive sounding provision of monogamy not only turned out to be a mockery but in fact even more detrimental to women than the uncodified Hindu law which recognized rights of wives in polygamous marriages. For instance, in a case for maintenance where the husband pleaded that since the woman was his second wife he was not entitled to pay her maintenance, the court took recourse to the uncodified Hindu law and held that since the couple is governed by the ancient Hindu Law (which permits bigamy) and not by the reformed code, the second wife is entitled to maintenance.[39] This judgement speaks much for a law which was ushered in with great fanfare as an instrument of empowering Hindu women.

6.5 Constitutional Challenges

It is not surprising that the first challenge to the constitutional provision of equality, came from the Hindu male challenging the provision of monogamy. A petition was filed in the Bombay High Court challenging the monogamy imposed by the *Bombay Hindu Marriage Act*. In its eagerness to uphold the principle of monogamy among the Hindus, the Bombay High Court in *State of Bombay v Narasu Appa Mali* [40] held that the personal laws are not 'laws in force' and hence they are not void even when they come into conflict with the provision of equality under the Constitution.

In a subsequent case, *Srinivasa Aiyar v Saraswati Ammal*[41] it was argued that prohibiting polygamy denied Hindu men equality before the law and equal protection of law and further that it discriminated against Hindu men on the grounds of religion as it restricted the right to freely profess, practice and propagate religion. The Madras High Court did not address the issue whether the term 'laws in force' includes personal laws but held that even assuming that the term 'laws in force' includes personal laws, the Act does not offend Article 15 which stipulates non-discrimination on the basis of sex.

The judgments ruled that discriminatory personal laws do not violate the constitutional provision of equality. For obtaining the short-term gain of defending the provision of monogamy for

Hindu males, the judiciary erected an unsurmountable obstacle for gender equality within personal laws, by providing a legal basis for the continuation of discriminatory personal laws. However, in a recent judgment, *C. Masilamani Mudaliar v Idol of Sri Swaminathaswami Thirukoil*[42], the Supreme Court, while not referring specifically to the principle laid down in *Narasu Appa Mali*, has implicitly overruled the same. The Court held as follows:

> The personal laws conferring inferior status on women is anathema to equality. Personal laws are derived not from the Constitution but from the religious scriptures. The laws thus derived must be consistent with the Constitution lest they become void under Article 13 if they violate fundamental rights... .

The second issue which came up for judicial scrutiny was the provision of Restitution of Conjugal Rights under Section 9 of the *Hindu Marriage Act*. Justice Chowdhary of Andhra Pradesh in July 1983, struck down this provision as unconstitutional on the ground that it constitutes the grossest form of violation of an individual's right to privacy.[43] The court held that it denies the woman her free choice whether, when and how her body is to become the vehicle for the procreation of another human being and hence is violative of the right to privacy guaranteed by Article 21 of the Constitution.

Although s. 9 of the *Hindu Marriage Act* is based on formal equality and there is no distinction between the rights of husband and wife the court held that equality of treatment regardless of equality of the unequal situation is neither just nor equal. By treating husband and wife who are inherently unequal as equal, the judge held that this section offends the rule of equal protection under the laws ensured by Art.14 of the Constitution. He further added that in actual fact, the remedy works only for the benefit of husbands and is oppressive to women.

But later in the same year, the Delhi High Court took a totally different position and maintained that S. 9 of the *Hindu Marriage Act* is not violative of Art. 14 and 21 of the Constitution. The court held that the object of the restitution decree is to bring about cohabitation between the estranged parties so that they can live together in the matrimonial home in amity. According to the judge, it is a two-in-one provision. On the one hand, it enables the court to coax and cajole the parties to resume marital life and is designed to encourage reconciliation.

The court ruled further: 'Introduction of constitutional law in the home is most inappropriate. It is like pushing a bull into a china shop. It will prove to be a ruthless destroyer of the marriage institution and all that it stands for. In the privacy of the home and the married life, neither Art. 21 nor Art. 14 have any place'.[44]

Subsequently, the Supreme Court upheld this judgment in *Saroj Rani v Sudarshan Kumar Chaddha*[45] and stated the provisions of restitution of conjugal rights serves a social purpose and overruled the judgment of the Andhra Pradesh High Court. The main objective of this provision has always been to ensure conjugality through coercive measures. Whether the constitutionality of a legal provision can be tested by attributing to it a laudable social purpose for which it was never meant for, is a debatable question.[46]

So while the codification has brought some gains to Hindu women by granting a right to absolute ownership of property, monogamy and the right of divorce, these rights are more conceptual than actual. While attempting to resolve some issues, the codification has foregrounded others which have yet to find a satisfactory solution.

Notes

1. In contrast, the Canadian women were granted the right of equality in 1982, the Swiss women were granted the right to vote in 1972 and the United States has not yet endorsed the Equal Remuneration Act.
2. Art 21 of the Constitution ensures Protection of life and personal liberty. In recent years, the Supreme Court has read various socio-economic measures into this right to life. For instance in *People's Union of Democratic Rights v Union of India* (1982) 3 SCC 235, the Supreme Court read the right to minimum wages into Art 21. In *Olga Tellis v Bombay Municipal Corporation* (1985) 3 SCC 545 it was held that the right to life includes the right to livelihood. In *Mohini Jain & Ors v State of Karnataka* (1992) 3 SCC 666 and *Unnikrishnan J.P. & Ors v State of AP* (1993) 1 SCC 645, it was held that the right to education is a fundamental right.
3. Lateef S., 'Defining Women through Legislation,' in Hasan, Z. (ed.) *Forging Identities: Gender, Communities and the State*, New Delhi: Kali for Women (1994), p.51.
4. Karat, B., 'Step by Step Approach—Equal Rights, Equal laws,' in *Women's Equality* V/1, p. 20.
5. Parashar, A., *Women and Family Law Reform in India*, New Delhi: Sage Publications (1992), p.103.

6. Ibid., p.140.
7. S.15 (1)(d) and (e) of *Hindu Succession Act*, 1956.
8. Kishwar, M., 'Codified Hindu Law : Myth and Reality,' *Economic and Political Weekly*, XXIX/33 (1994), p.2145.
9. Ibid.
10. See the comments made by the Supreme Court in a recent judgment, *Sarla Mudgal v Union of India & Ors.* (1995) 3 SCC 635.
11. S.7 (2) of the *Hindu Marriage Act*, specifically mentions saptapadi which is a Brahminical ritual. Most lower castes were not permitted the ritual of saptapadi. Among some castes five steps were permitted and among others only four. Further, the ritual for the marriage of virgin brides differed from that of the second marriage of widows and divorcees.
12. Kishwar, M., 'Codified Hindu Law: Myth and Reality', p.2154.
13. For instance, as per the provisions of S.6 of the *Hindu Succession Act*, 1956, in a family where there are two sons and one daughter, upon the death of the father each of the sons would inherit one-third of the property as coparcenars. The remaining one third, is the father's separate property which would be divided in four parts, one for the wife, one for the daughter and one each for the sons. So while the sons would be entitled to one-third plus one-twelfth, the daughter's share would only be one-twelfth of the property. This dismal share is projected as gender equality.
14. See Chapter 4.
15. Under S.10.2 of the *Income Tax Act* an exemption is granted to income from the Hindu Undivided Family (HUF). Under SS.20 & 20A of the *Wealth Tax Act*, certain tax concessions are granted to members of HUF at the time of partition.
16. Under S.29(2) of the *Hindu Succession Act*, a power was granted to individuals to will away their property and in subsequent years this provision was used mainly to deprive the daughters their share in their parental property.
17. See the decisions in *Commissioner of Wealth Tax v Chandra Sen* ILR 1986 370 and *Yudhishter v Ashok Kumar* AIR 1987 SC 558, where the court held that the property inherited by the son is his separate property.
18. The English statute, *Inheritance (Family Provision) Act* of 1938 provided for a legal remedy, if the husband failed to make reasonable provisions for his wife and children. The right of a former wife who is entitled to receive maintenance was protected through the *Matrimonial Causes (Property and Maintenance) Act* of 1958 (subsequently re-enacted in the *Matrimonial Causes Act* 1965). Since this enactment placed a divorced wife in a superior position relative to the surviving spouse, a further statute was enacted entitled, *Inheritance (Provision for Family and Dependents) Act* 1975 through which the surviving spouse could claim not only maintenance but also a share in the capital.
19. Kishwar, M., 'Codified Hindu Law: Myth and Reality', p.2155.
20. M.N. Srinivas has argued that modern dowry is entirely the product of the forces let loose by British rule such as monetization, education

and the introduction of the 'organised sector'. To equate it with
dakshina is only an attempt to legitimize a modern monstrosity by
linking it up with an ancient and respected custom. See Srinivas, M.N.
Some Reflections on Dowry, New Delhi: Oxford University Press (1984),
p.11-13.

21. *Hindu Succession Act*, note 13.
22. SS. 24 and 25 of the *Hindu Marriage Act*, 1955. Also see S. Khanna,
'Padmasini's Quest for Justice,' in *The Lawyers* VII/2 (1992), p.25.
23. This concept has subsequently been incorporated into the Parsi
Marriage & Divorce Act, 1936 by the 1988 amendments (SS.39 and 40
of the Act).
24. The remedy of divorce by mutual consent was introduced into the
Hindu Marriage Act in 1976 through S.13 B of the Act. Cruelty and
desertion as grounds of divorce were also introduced in 1976.
25. As per the *Report of the Committee on the Status of Women, Towards
Equality* in the year 1971 only 11.86% of women were employed and
they constituted only 17.35% of the total labour force (p.153) and
women constituted only 10.9% of the labour force in the organized
sector (p.184).
26. S.9 of the *Hindu Marriage Act*.
27. AIR 1958 Punj 87.
28. AIR 1964 Punj 28.
29. *Gaya Prasad v Bhagwat* AIR 1966 MP 212.
30. AIR 1973 P&H 134.
31. ILR (1977) 1 P&H 642 FB.
32. *Praveenben v Sureshbhai* AIR 1975 Guj 69.
33. *N.R. Radhakrishna v Dhanalakshmi* AIR 1975 Mad 331.
34. AIR 1978 Del 296.
35. S. 7 (1) & (2) of *Hindu Marriage Act*, 1955.
36. In *Divorce and Matrimonial Cases* (1994), Volume I reported cases where
validity of marriages was an issue while claiming maintenance, were
as follows:
Reported cases relating to maintenance: 40–100%
Cases where validity of marriage was an issue: 9–36%
Cases where the Husband's plea was upheld: 4–16%
Admittedly Polygamous Marriages: 6–24%
37. For a detailed discussion on this issue, see Agnes, F., 'Hindu Men,
Monogamy and the Uniform Civil Code,' in *Economic and Political
Weekly*, XXX/50 (1995), p.3238.
38. Report of the Committee on Status of Women *Towards Equality*,
pp.66-7.
39. *Anupama Pradhan v Sultan Pradhan* 1991 Cri.LJ 3216 Ori.
40. AIR 1952 Bom 84.
41. AIR 1952 Mad 193.
42. (1996) 8 SCC 525, decided by Justices K. Ramaswamy, S. Saghir Ahmad
and G.B. Pattanaik.
43. *T. Sareetha v T. Venkatasubbiah* AIR 1983 AP 356.

44. *Harvinder Kaur v Harminder Singh* AIR 1084 Del 66.
45. AIR 1984 SC 1562.
46. See Bhattacharjee, A.M., *Matrimonial Laws and the Constitution*, Calcutta: Eastern Law House (1996), p.19.

7

Erosion of Secular Principles

Introduction

Under Art. 44, the state is bound by a constitutional mandate to secularize and homogenize the family laws. The enactment of a uniform code was a goal to be achieved through a gradual process.[1] This was a directive principle of governance. In this chapter, the extent to which the state adhered to this principle is examined.

The first departure from the declared objective was the codification of the Hindu family laws. Within the first decade after the adaptation of the new and revolutionary Constitution, the state enacted special laws for its 'Hindu' citizens. By validating diverse customary practices and rituals as 'Hindu', by grouping various castes and sects under the banner of a 'legal Hinduism' and by naming the attempts at modernizing family laws as 'Hindu' reforms, the state departed from its declared goal of secularizing the family law. Through these enactments, Hindus were not subject to the application of some statutes, which had hitherto been uniformly applicable to all citizens. For instance, the scope of the *Caste Disabilities Removal Act* of 1850, which prohibited loss of rights upon conversion was constrained, as apostasy constituted a matrimonial offence.[2] The non-Hindu spouse was not entitled to maintenance from the Hindu spouse either while living together or separately.[3]

The converted parent lost the right to be the natural guardian of a minor child.[4] Children born to a Hindu after conversion were disqualified from inheriting the property of a Hindu relative.[5] The scope of another secular provision, the *Guardians and Wards Act*, 1890, was restricted by the *Hindu Adoption and Maintenance Act*, 1956. Hindus were taken out of this secular and uniform provision and were placed under the new statute, which validated adoptions through the Brahminical Hindu ritual of giving and taking in adoption,[6] while the customs and practices of lower castes, which were more fluid and secular were disallowed.[7] By stipulating a special provision under S.18 (a) of the *Hindu Marriage Act*, Hindus were taken out of the general provisions of the *Child Marriage Restraint Act* of 1929 and were liable for lesser punishment for the same offence. In addition, while such marriages performed under other matrimonial statutes (for instance the *Parsi Marriage and Divorce Act*, 1936 and the Special Marriage Act of 1954), were held to be void, marriages performed in violation of the stipulations regarding child marriage were deemed valid under the *Hindu Marriage Act*.[8] Certain tax benefits were conferred upon Hindu coparcenaries within taxation laws.[9] These enactments violated the constitutional mandate under Art. 14 (equality) and Art. 15 (non-discrimination on the basis of religion) as the 'Hindu religion' was the sole criteria for the classifications.[10]

During the decades that followed, the state moved further away from its declared objective of a uniform and secular family law. In several instances, the vested, patriarchal and community interests of the influential sections superseded the rights of women and children.

The issue was further problematized by the erosion of secular principles within the polity. A steady decline of secular values can be traced through the debates on the enactment of the *Special Marriage Act* in the fifties, the fate of the Adoption Bill in the seventies and the controversy around the Muslim Women's Bill in the eighties. The policy on secularism had changed from the Nehruvian concept of maintaining equidistance from all religions to the increasingly instrumental use of religion for political gains during the Rajiv Gandhi rule in the eighties. Rather than maintaining a distance from all religious groups, the state became increasingly entangled with the communal factions. If the state granted one concession to one communal group, to set the balance right, it was compelled to grant another concession to another group. *The Muslim Women's Act*[11] was a direct outcome of this political jugglery. The economic interests of Muslim women were sacrificed by the state in this balancing act. The gradual erosion of secular principles is traced in this chapter.

7.1 Constraining the Scope of Civil Marriage Law

The enactment of the *Special Marriage Act* in 1954 is the only significant move in the post-independence period to secularize family laws.[12] In 1952, while introducing the Bill, the Law Minister C.C. Biswas had described it as the first step towards the attainment of the objective of a Uniform Civil Code contemplated in Art. 44 of the Constitution.[13] The Act provided for a civil marriage of two Indians, without the necessity of renouncing their respective religions.

The Act contained several redeeming features. It introduced the concept of 'breakdown theory'[14] or a divorce by mutual consent. The Act also provided for the re-registration of marriages solemnized in accordance with the customs or rituals of the spouses.[15] This provision of subsequent registration enabled parties to avail of secular and uniform remedies despite the solemnization of the marriage through the performance of religious ceremonies.[16]

Since a marriage under this Act is a secular and civil contract, conversion or apostasy of the spouse is not a ground for divorce. The marriage is contracted at the civil registry in the presence of a marriage officer appointed by the state and a certificate is issued to the parties which constitutes a clear proof of a valid marriage having been performed for all future litigation purposes. This serves as a restraint against husbands contracting subsequent bigamous marriages.[17] Once the parties opt for a secular form of marriage, in matters of succession they are governed by the *Indian Succession Act*, 1925 (which is more egalitarian and gender-just), and not by the provisions of their respective personal laws.[18] This was a concrete step towards gradual unification of family laws.

Conservative Hindu, Muslim and Christian opinion was strongly opposed to the Act. Although the concept of contractual marriage was closest to the Islamic concept of marriage, during parliamentary debates a demand was raised by a section of Muslims that the Muslim community should be exempted from its purview, as the persons marrying under it would not be governed by the Shariat. But this demand was not conceded. Prime Minister, Jawaharlal Nehru pointed out that the constitutional provision which guarantees the freedom to practise religion also includes the freedom not to practise a religion. He emphasized that since it is a facilitating legislation, no one was compulsorily bound by it and the state would not come in the way of any one opting for its provisions.[19]

The Act had the potentiality of being developed further into a comprehensive code of marriage and divorce which could incorporate adequate safeguards for women, without invoking the controversy of freedom of religion. The premise that the Act is merely a facilitating measure which would apply only to consenting couples had already been accepted both politically as well as legally. Hence equitable principles of gender justice could easily have been incorporated into this Act. But unfortunately, the Act has not been well publicized and there seems to be a manipulation to subvert its provisions.[20]

Despite its secular credentials, the Act leaned towards the dominant Hindu upper caste practices, which prohibit marriages between first cousins and close family relatives. Such prohibitions are not found in the customary practices of several lower castes, as well as among the practices of Muslims, Christians, Parsis and Jews. Among several south Indian communities marriages between uncles and nieces and first cousins are a norm. Similarly, marriages among first cousins are a norm among the Muslims.

In order to rectify this lacuna and widen the scope of the Act, in 1963, an amendment was introduced, which subordinated the Act to customary practices.[21] During the debate, the amendment was criticized as a retrograde measure by several members of the Parliament.[22] Prior to this Act, the *Special Marriage Act* subordinated the personal laws to its provisions. The amendment on the other hand introduced the pernicious principle of reversing this principle and subordinating the Act to the personal laws. The stated reasons for the amendment were the practices of south Indian communities which permit marriages between uncle and neice and first cousins.[23] The objective was to co-ordinate the Act with the provisions of the *Hindu Marriage Act* which validated customary practices. Its relevance to minority communities was not in context during the debate. This placed the Act further away from its objective of a secular code.

In 1976, major amendments were introduced within the *Hindu Marriage Act* by incorporating additional grounds of divorce and by introducing divorce by mutual consent. So superficially, it appeared that the *Hindu Marriage Act* and the *Special Marriage Act* are synonymous and provide similar reliefs. But the anomalies of the *Hindu Marriage Act* regarding proof of valid ceremonies were not addressed during these reforms and Hindu marriage continued to be an illusory legal incident.

At the other level, amendments introduced to the *Special Marriage Act* in 1976[24] conferred concessions to Hindus marrying under the Act, which led to an undermining of the secular provisions of the statute. If a Hindu couple married under the Act, they were taken out of the purview of the *Indian Succession Act* of 1925 and were permitted to be governed by the *Hindu Succession Act*. This move was to ensure that coparcenaries (and male privileges within it) are not dissolved by the contracting of a civil marriage by means of the Act. The interests of a Hindu male who contracted a civil marriage were protected so long as he married a woman within the broad Hindu fold (which would include inter-caste and inter-regional marriages, as well as marriages with women from Boudha, Jaina and Sikh religions and also Brahmos, Prarthana Samajis and Arya Samajis or even atheists).

At one level, it gave a further lease to coparcenaries, which, in any case, are anti-women. But the move was deemed progressive because it protected the interests of a Hindu male contracting a civil marriage. Even if one concedes to this reasoning, why a similar benefit was not conferred upon a Hindu male contracting an inter-religious civil marriage remains unexplained. In effect, the amendment was a deterrent to a Hindu male wishing to marry a woman from any minority religious communities, i.e., Parsi, Muslim and Christian. Such an event would result in the dissolution of coparcenary. The reasoning that the broad Hindu fold is only a legal fiction and that the idea of a sudra or a neo-Buddhist woman entering the household would be as abhorrent to an orthodox Hindu as of a Muslim or a Christian woman entering the household, seems to have escaped the law makers. The provision was clearly unconstitutional as the basis of discrimination was religion. Further, progressive Hindus who married under a secular Act were not given a choice to be governed by a uniform and secular law of succession.

This clear violation of the mandate towards uniformity and secularization of family laws did not warrant a public debate. The benefits conferred on a Hindu male contracting a civil marriage, were deemed a progressive step for the Hindu community. Hence the deterrent it would pose to marriages of

Hindu males with minority women and to the secular principle of the nation, did not figure in the public debate. The criticism against this amendment remained within the confines of legal academia[25] and did not result in a media furore.

7.2 Efforts at Introducing an Adoption Bill

The next attempt at uniformity was the Adoption Bill, which was introduced in the Rajya Sabha in 1972[26] and was referred to the Joint Committee of the Parliament.[27] The Joint Select Committee held public hearings. At these hearings, the representatives of Muslims and Scheduled Tribes expressed their desire to be excluded from its application.[28] The demand made by the Scheduled Tribes was conceded by the Committee and it recommended that the Bill should be uniformly applicable to all Indians except the Scheduled Tribes. The three Muslim members of the Committee, in their note of dissent, pressed for the exclusion of the Muslim community from its application.[29] The Joint Select Committee submitted its report to the Parliament in August, 1976. But in order to avoid any politically costly controversy over this issue, the Bill was not presented till the Parliament was dissolved in March 1977 and consequently, the Bill lapsed. The Janata government which was voted to power after the election, introduced a new bill but withdrew it following opposition from a section of the Muslims.[30]

In 1980 when the Congress party regained power, the government re-introduced the Bill in a modified version and paid heed to the Muslim demand for exclusion. This time the Bill was referred to the Minorities Commission. At this juncture, the Parsi community demanded exemption from it application.[31] Thereafter, the Bill was abandoned.

Although the opposition to the Bill was based on various factors, the economic motive was the most dominant. The adoption would affect the inheritance rights of other heirs or make inroads within the common property of the community. These were the two major concerns expressed by the voices of dissent.

The tribal communities opposed adoption of children from outside the tribe, as this could lead to the inheritance of the tribal property by non-tribal children who may be adopted. They also opposed the provision of registering the adoptions as it would pose technical difficulties. The change of name after adoption was also against the tribal custom.

The Parsis did not want their charitable trust funds and their fire temples to be thrown open to non-Parsi children. They had no objection to inter-religious adoption if the rights of the non-Parsi child were restricted to inheritance of private property and would not extend to community resources.

The Muslim religious leadership argued that the Bill would be against the tenets of Islam. Adoption would create prohibited degrees of relationships in matrimonial alliances (with the adopted parents) which would violate Islamic principles. But most important, the adopted child would become an heir to the property of the adopting parents and the shares of the natural heirs would be altered. This would amount to an interference with the scheme of succession under the Shariat.

Although the conservative segment of the Muslim religious leadership opposed the bill, it received the support of several prominent Muslim scholars and jurists.[32] Some scholars suggested modification to the bill which would make it more acceptable to the Muslim community. Justice Hameedullah Beg suggested that instead of excluding Muslims, the Bill should contain a provision to declare that adoption is not contrary to their religious beliefs and added that the Constitution gives every individual his or her religious freedom.[33]

A certain shift in the government's stand can be discerned in this debate. In 1954, while enacting the *Special Marriage Act*, the government had not accepted the claim that it would encourage Muslims to leave the fold of Islam. But two decades later, while debating the Adoption Bill the government accepted the religio-political leaders as the spokespersons for the entire community and conceded to their posture that no Muslim would have the opportunity of rejecting Islamic law through a State enactment.

7.3 The Shah Bano Controversy and the Muslim Women's Bill

The political events which followed the Supreme Court judgement in the Shah Bano case[34] eventually resulted in the enactment of the *Muslim Women (Protection of rights on Divorce) Act* in 1986. (Hereinafter, the *Muslim Women's Act*) But the issue of maintenance to divorced Muslim women which marked the controversy had a long and turbulent history, which is reflective of a collusion between two different legal systems.

As already discussed, the Muslim law evolved within the context of trading communities of Arabia and regulated their marriages in the language of their trade contracts. A sum of mehr was stipulated at the time of marriage as a future security. Since marriage was a dissoluble contract, and women had a right of remarriage, the legal system did not provide for any recurring liability after the termination of the contract. After the dissolution of the matrimonial bond, the wife was not entitled to any further reliefs such as maintenance.[35] But despite these restraints, the Holy Quran contained a provision, 'For divorced women, maintenance should be provided on a reasonable scale'. (*Surah* III *Aiyat* 241).

Under the English and Indian legal systems, marriage constituted an indissoluble bond and the husband was entrusted with a legal obligation of maintaining the wife for life. Later, the Islamic concept of marriage as a dissoluble contract was accepted by the English law in the nineteenth century and by the Hindu law in the twentieth century,[36] but under these legal systems, the husband's obligation to maintain his wife continued even after the dissolution of marriage. Only the wife's remarriage or unchastity would redeem the husband of his obligation.

During the debate on the *Dissolution of Muslim Marriages Act* in 1939, the primary concern of the reformers was the absence of women's right to divorce in contrast to the husband's right of arbitrary divorce. And perhaps due to the fact, that as the economic rights conferred upon women by the Islamic law were superior to the rights granted to women under other legal systems, the reformers did not address the issue of economic rights of divorced women. The Act did not contain any provision of ancillary reliefs found in other matrimonial statutes based on English law.

Within the cultural ethos, where the pro-women stipulations of a minority community can easily be subverted by aping the majority practices (and at the same time, anti-women practices can be strictly adhered to on the premise of preserving the cultural identity) stipulations of mehr have been reduced to a token amount and the custom of dowry has been adapted among most Muslim communities. Within this social reality, a divorced Muslim woman was left with no economic options to escape from destitution upon divorce. As a corrective measure, in 1973, S.125 of Cr.PC, which granted the deserted or destitute wife the right to claim a maximum amount of Rs 500 as maintenance from her husband, was extended to a divorced wife by expanding the scope of the term wife to include ex-wife (or divorced wife).[37]

The amendment came after an acrimonious debate on the Muslim woman's customary right of mehr. Conceding the demand raised by Muslim leaders, the government included a clause that if a woman had received the customary settlement, the amount of maintenance due to her would be set off against the amount she had already received.[38]

Although this had constrained the scope of the Muslim woman's right to maintenance, two significant decisions of the Supreme Court delivered by Justice Krishna Iyer in 1979 and 1980 respectively had placed the divorced Muslim woman's right to maintenance on a secure footing without arousing a political controversy around this issue.[39] These decisions examined the right of Muslim women from a humanitarian context of social justice.

But the controversial Shah Bano judgement delivered by Chief Justice Y.V. Chandrachud (for the Full Bench comprising of five judges) in 1985, apart from affirming the right of a divorced Muslim woman, also commented upon Islam and interpreted the Muslim Personal Law while deciding a right under a secular and uniform statute. The call for a UCC and the comments on the Quran evoked a communal backlash.

Relenting to the pressure exerted by the Muslim orthodoxy, the government introduced a Bill in Parliament titled, *The Muslim Women (Protection of Rights on Divorce) Bill* to exclude divorced Muslim women from the purview of S.125 Cr.PC. This move met with severe opposition from women's organizations and progressive sections.

As the debate progressed, the media projected two insular and mutually exclusive positions, i.e. those who opposed the Bill and supported the demand for a UCC as modern, secular and rational, while those in support of the Bill and opposing the demand for a UCC as fundamentalist, orthodox, male chauvinist, communal and obscurantist. To be progressive, modern and secular was also to be a nationalist. By the same logic, the opposing camp was projected as against national integration and hence anti-national. There was hardly any public space left for arguments which pleaded for conciliation or compromise.[40]

As the controversy over the judgement escalated, the 'Muslim' was defined as the 'Other', both of the nation and of the Hindus. Muslims all over India, in turn could be mobilized to view this as yet another threat to their tenuous security. The communal turn to the event finally, led to Shah Bano herself withdrawing her claim to maintenance. This strengthened the popular misconception that to maintain the religiosity in Islam, women's economic rights have to be subordinated and further the Islamic religion is opposed to granting women economic rights.

The rigid approach of the Muslim leadership provided further fuel to the Hindu right wing forces in their anti-Muslim propaganda. This placed the secular groups in a precarious position. In order to distinguish their position from that advocated by Hindu right-wing forces, opposition to the Bill had to be withdrawn.

For the first time, the women's movement was constrained to address the complexities of the demand for a UCC.[41] The issue could no longer be addressed within the binaries of a gender divide. The political sub-text beneath the apparent gender concerns warranted a more complex framework.

Analysing the political developments around this period, Zoya Hasan argues that the compromise of surrendering women's rights has to be viewed from the perspective of a communalized polity.[42] It was an outcome of a rightward shift in politics and the economy in the 1980s, resulting in a close interaction of politics and religion marked by a decline in the commitment to secularism, equal opportunities, and social welfare benefits for the under-privileged and the disadvantaged.

The Congress faced defeat in several state assembly elections in 1985–6 as the Muslim vote, angered by the Shah Bano verdict, tipped the balance in favour of opposition parties. The Congress responded to the crisis by a shift in strategy, highlighted by the appropriation of pro-Hindutva themes which were gaining popularity in north India. This won the support of some Hindu factions but further alienated Muslims, the traditional supporters of Congress, who were dissatisfied with the party's failure to alleviate their long-standing grievances. Their disenchantment was further aggravated by the Ram Janmabhumi movement for the liberation of the Ram temple in Ayodhya started by Vishwa Hindu Parishad in 1984.

Against this background of declining political support, the Congress government decided to open the locks of the disputed Babri Masjid in February 1986 and simultaneously, enact the Muslim Women's Bill. Together, these two decisions, i.e. the introduction of the Muslim Women's Bill and the reopening of the disputed shrine in Ayodhya were part of a 'grand' Congress strategy of using religious issues and sentiments to regain its hold over Hindu and Muslim votes.

The Muslim Women's Act was thus an effort to pacify Muslim sentiments which were ruffled over the reopening of the disputed site. The Congress government exaggerated the strength of the conservative opposition, manipulated by a politically ambitious Muslim leadership. The Congress viewed the All India Muslim Personal Law Board (AIMPLB) as the sole arbiter of Muslim interests. Opposition from liberal and progressive groups was ignored, allowing the Ullama to appropriate the task of defining the overarching concerns and interests of Muslims.

7.4 The Unpredictable Turn of Events

Only after the dust raised by the controversial Act had settled down, could the various contradictory implications of the enactment to Muslim women, Muslim Personal Law and the Muslim community be examined. Thus:

(i) Despite the claim of divine origin and the consequential claim that a secular Indian State does not have the right to legislate upon Muslim law, through this legislation, the Muslim religious leaders conceded to the state the right to modify the Shariat. The Act imposed obligations on Waqf board and family members which were not imposed by the Shariat and to this extent modified the rules of the Shariat and overruled the theory of its immutability.

(ii) Despite the mobilization of a large number of Muslim women against the judgement and in support of the Bill, a significant number of divorced Muslim women continued to approach the courts for claiming their right to maintenance, as the cases filed by Muslim women indicate. Hence the claim of religious leaders that Muslim women are opposed to accepting maintenance from their ex-husbands after divorce has not been substantiated. The divorced Muslim women were able to separate their religiosity from their temporal needs of economic survival.

(iii) The judicial decisions in the period immediately following the enactment of the Bill proved contrary to the fears expressed by women's organizations that the Act would snuff out the economic rights of divorced Muslim women. In a few cases, judges used the provision of the new Act to award substantial amounts as lump sum divorce settlements.[43] The Act seemed to provide a better remedy than the meagre amount which a Muslim woman could claim under S.125 Cr.PC prior to this Act.

These judgments interpreted the scope of S.3 (1) (a) of the Act to mean that the husband must pay a reasonable and fair provision for the future during the *iddat* period. For throwing light on the ambiguities contained in S.3 of the Act, the courts relied upon the preamble which proclaimed that the aim of the Act is to protect the rights of Muslim women.[44]

(iv) Although there were instances where Muslim women could be granted maintenance by a progressive interpretation of the provisions of the Act, Muslim men are constantly being advised by their advocates that they no longer need to pay maintenance to their wives and it is their religion that says so. Studies revealed that even when the lower courts granted maintenance to wives, the husbands, upon advice by their lawyers, filed appeals against orders of settlements, by relying upon the provisions of the Act, thus making the litigation processes far more cumbersome and ambiguous for Muslim women.[45] In response to the generous interpretations of the Act, Syed Shahabuddin (Janata Dal) moved a Private Member's Bill (Bill No. 155 of 1992) in Parliament in August 1992. The aim was to amend the Act and restrict its scope in clear terms to maintenance only for and during the iddat period.

(v) The Act has been used by court officials to express a general anti-Muslim bias. The general attitude within court rooms is that Muslim marriages are unstable, Muslim women remarry and Muslim men are polygamous. In a study of maintenance cases filed in the magistrate's courts at Calcutta, Maitrayee Mukho-padhyay recorded the following comments:

When a Muslim comes to our court we are already biased; their 3–4 marriages are repugnant to us. ...For them (Muslims) marriage is nothing. They get married, have a few children and then they leave their wives. ...Muslim marriages are unstable because of easy divorces and Muslim women are no better than prostitutes because they remarry; ...Muslim women are worse off than the household dog. ...We are Hindus, we do not like this law and it is repugnant ...but we have to give judgments according to this new law.[46]

As per the study, the magistrates declined from awarding maintenance even for the duration of the marriage or for the period before the act came into force.

Did the new Act protect Muslim women better than the earlier provisions under S. 125 Cr.PC, which entitles women to a paltry maintenance dole of Rs 500 per month? Could the controversy have been used to consolidate the traditional right of mehr (which has been corroded in recent years and has given way to the Hindu practice of dowry) and negotiate lump sum divorce settlements? These questions have now become redundant in the political climate which followed the enactment. The *Muslim Women's Act* has been projected as the most glaring instance of the defeat of the principle of gender justice for the Indian women, as well as the defeat of secular principles within the Indian polity. The Act has led to the further strengthening of the Muslim appeasement theory in judicial discourse and in popular media.[47]

For the women's movement, the Shah Bano judgement and the *Muslim Women's Act* was a watershed. From this point onwards, the gender discourse became far more complex. Identity politics and gender equality could no longer be placed as two mutually exclusive and hostile terrains. While gender equality continued to be the desired goal, the demand had to be reformulated within the context of cultural diversity and rights of marginalized sections.

Notes

1. See the assurance given by Dr Ambedkar to Muslim members of the Constituent Assembly (VII CAD, 23 November 1948 pp.550–1).
2. S.13 (1) (ii) of the *Hindu Marriage Act* 1955.
3. As per Hindu law, conversion results in the legal death of a Hindu. Hence, the Hindu husband is not under obligation to maintain his converted wife. In *Sundarambal v Subbaiah Pillai* AIR 1961 Mad 323, the courts went even further and held that an order for maintenance obtained prior to the conversion cannot even be enforced after the conversion.
4. A change of religion by the mother will disentitle her to the custody of her child as under Hindu law, since the father is the natural guardian, it is presumed that the child will automatically be following his religion.

5. Although the bar on conversion or change of caste was removed by the *Caste Disabilities Removal Act*, 1850 and the convert cannot be denied rights in the ancestral property, under the modern statute, the children of a converted parent cannot inherit property of a Hindu relative unless at the time when the succession opens, the child is a Hindu (S.26 of the *Hindu Succession Act*).

6. See S.11 (vi) of the Hindu Adoption and Maintenance Act, 1956.

7. Kishwar, M., 'Codified Hindu Law: Myth and Reality,' in *Economic and Political Weekly*, XXIX/33 (1994), p. 2145.

8. See Bhattacharjee, A.M., *Matrimonial Laws and the Constitution*, Calcutta: Eastern Law House (1996), pp.11-14.

9. See Note 15 of Chapter 6.

10. For a more detailed discussion on the constitutionality of the *Hindu Marriage Act*, see Bhattacharjee, A.M., *Matrimonial Laws and the Constitution*, pp.10-27.

11. The *Muslim Women (Protection of Rights on Divorce) Act*, 1986, which was enacted after the Shah Bano controversy.

12. This was a re-enactment of the 1872 Act, discussed in Chapter 5.

13. Law Minister's statement on the Bill made in the Rajya Sabha on 28.7.1952.

14. This is a later and more progressive doctrine of English law, than the earlier 'fault theory' where one spouse is required to prove a matrimonial fault against the other.

15. S.16 of *Special Marriage Act*, 1954. Prior to this, the remedy was available only under the Muslim law.

16. Since the provision of divorce by mutual consent was not available under the *Hindu Marriage Act*, until 1976, parties wishing to avail of the provision could re-register their marriage under the *Special Marriage Act* and then subsequently obtain the divorce. Since the *Indian Divorce Act*, 1869 governing Christian marriages does not provide for divorce by consent even today, a Christian couple can use this provision to re-register their marriage under this Act, prior to initiating court proceedings. But unfortunately, this provision has not been much publicized and the progressive option offered by the Act has remained mainly on paper. See Table 2A in this context.

17. In contrast, the Hindu marriage is an illusory legal entity. The ambiguity and laxity provided by the Act in respect of customary practices is manipulated by legal practioners to 'perform' hasty, fraudulent and at times invalid 'court marriages'. The lawyers resort to this practice to overcome the more stringent provisions such as the mandatory one month notice period. A public-interest petition, demanding rectification of the legal lacunae, filed by a centre providing legal advocacy to women, *Majlis Manch v State of Maharashtra* WP 1842 of 1996, has addressed this issue before the Bombay High Court.

18. S. 21 of the *Special Marriage Act*, 1954. The provision was meant to further secularize inheritance laws. *The Indian Succession Act* grants better rights of inheritance to daughters than the *Hindu Succession Act* of 1956 which continued to recognize male coparcenary.

19. Parashar, A., *Women and Family Law Reform in India*, New Delhi: Sage Publications (1992) p.161.
20. The gross under-utilization of this provision is indicated in Table 2B.
21. The *Special Marriage (Amendment) Act* of 1963 (Act 32 of 1963) added the following proviso to S.4 clause (d): Provided that where a custom governing at least one of the parties permits of a marriage between them, such marriage may be solemnized notwithstanding that they are within the prohibited degrees of relationship.
22. See the comments of U.M. Trivedi, L.M. Singhvi etc. Lok Sabha Debates XX No.12, Col. 3234 and 3250. 1962
23. Speech by Deputy Minister Bibhudhendra Mishra, *LSD*, XX No.12, Col.3228. 1962
24. The Law Commission of India, *Fifty Ninth Report* (1974), p.98.
25. See B.Sivaramayya, 'The Special Marriage Act, 1954 Goes Awry', in V. Bagga (ed.), *Studies in the Hindu Marriage and the Special Marriage Acts*, Bombay: N.M. Tripathi (1978), p.310.
26. *Gazette of India*, Part II, 1972, pp.601–10.
27. *LSD*, 26.viii.1972.
28. Joint Select Committee, *Evidence on Adoption Bill* Vol. II 1972 p. 111.
29. Ibid. Minutes of Dissent, IX-XI.
30. Baig, T. A., 'Urgency of Adoption Law,' in *Mainstream*, 15 November, 1980, pp.9-10.
31. *Fourth Annual Report*, the Minorities Commission (1983).
32. Justices Chagla, Hidayatullah and Beg and jurists Asaf Ali Fyzee, Daniel Latifi to name a few. Parashar, A., *Women and Family Law Reform in India*, p.171.
33. Ibid.
34. *Mohd. Ahmed Khan v Shah Bano Begam* AIR 1985 SC 945.
35. The various legal workshops conducted with rural women's groups reveals that a similar legal provision prevailed among communities which permitted divorce and re-marriage of women in Maharashtra and Gujarat region. The only difference was that the custom of bride price was prevalent and if a divorce was obtained at the initiation of the woman, she (or her father) was required to return the bride price.
36. The English women were granted the right of divorce through the *Matrimonial Causes Act* of 1857 and the upper caste Hindu women acquired this right under the *Hindu Marriage Act* of 1955.
37. Explanation (b) to S.125 of Cr.PC stipulates that wife includes ex-wife.
38. S.127 (3) (b) of Cr.PC provides as follows:

    (if) the woman has been divorced by her husband and (if) she has received, whether before or after the date of the said order, the whole of the sum which, under any customary or personal law applicable to the parties, was payable on such divorce (the magistrate) may cancel such order.

    The wordings do not specifically mention the right of mehr under Islamic law but the amendment was effected at the instance of Muslim legislators in the context of the Muslim women's right to mehr. *Supra* n.19, pp.164-8.

39. *Bai Tahira v Ali Hussain Fideali Chotthea* AIR 1979 SC 362 and *Fuzlunbi v K.Khadil Vali* AIR 1980 SC 1730.

40. Fazalbuoy, N., 'The Debate on Muslim Personal Law,' Paper presented at the Third National Conference on Women's Studies, Chandigarh, 1986. Also see Mukhopadhyay, M., 'Between Community and State: The question of women's right and personal laws,' in Z. Hasan (ed.), *Forging Identities: Gender, Communities and the State*, New Delhi: Kali for Women (1994), p.109.

41. Pathak Z. and R. S. Rajan, 'Shah Bano' *Signs* XIV/3 (1989); Kishwar, M. 'Pro-Women or Anti Minority? The Shah Bano Controversy,' in *Manushi* VI/2 (1986), p.4.

42. Hasan, Z. (ed.), : *Forging Identities: Gender, Communities and the State*, New Delhi: Kali for Women (1994), pp.67-8.

43. One of the judgments which received publicity was passed on 6 January 1988 by a woman judicial magistrate at Lucknow's Diwani Kacheri. A divorced woman, Fahima Sardar was awarded Rs 85,000 as mehr maintenance and fair and reasonable provision. See Gandhi, N. & N. Shah, *Issues at Stake*, New Delhi: Kali for Women (1991), p.242. In 1992, in a judgement of the Kerala High Court (*P.K. Saro v P.A. Halim*, Cri.MC 1331 of 1991), against which a challenge is pending in the Supreme Court, the High Court endorsed the session court's order which awarded Rs 3,00,000 towards reasonable and fair provision and Rs 7,500 per month as maintenance for the period of iddat. Case cited from Singh, K., 'The Constitution and the Muslim Personal Law,' in Hasan, Z. (ed.), *Forging Identities: Gender, Communities and the State*, New Delhi: Kali for Women (1994), p.96.

44. S.1 (a) of the Act which was meant to restrict maintenance to the iddat period states as follows:
'Notwithstanding anything contained in any other law for the time being in force, a divorced woman shall be entitled to (a) a reasonable and fair provision and maintenance to be made and paid to her within the iddat period by her former husband.' For clarifying the ambiguity of the words 'reasonable and fair provision and maintenance' the courts relied upon the preamble of the Act, which states that the aim of the Act is to protect Muslim women. See the decisions in *A.A. Abdulla v A. B. Mohmuna Sayedbhai*, AIR 1988 Guj 141; *Ali v Sufaira* 1988 (3) Crimes 147; *Mohd. Tajuddin v Quomarunnisa Begam & Ors.* 2 (1989) DMC 204 AP; and *Ahmed v Aysha* 2 (1990) DMC 110 Ker.

45. Maitrayee Mukhopadhyay has argued that the issue is not whether S.125 Cr.PC is more advantageous than S.3 of MWA since neither really protects women's claims to a share in their husband's property, here the claim that Muslim men need not maintain their wives once they have divorced them is being legitimized. The provisions are being interpreted to mean that Muslim men, by resorting to this section, have greater ability to deny their wives' claims for maintenance. The legal sanction to do so derives authority from the evocation of tradition, a term which is interchangeable with religion and culture. Mukhopadhyay, M., 'Between Community and State: The question of

women's right and personal laws', in Hasan Z. (ed.), *Forging Identities: Gender, Communities and the State*, New Delhi: Kali for Women (1994), p.109.

46. Ibid., p. 126.
47. Sathe, S.P., 'Uniform Civil Code. Why? What? and How?' (1995), in *Towards Secular India*, I/4 Bombay: Centre for Study of Society and Secularism (1995), p.31.

8

Communal Undertones Within Recent Judicial Decisions

Introduction

The fifth decade of independence witnessed a further erosion of secular principles. The events escalated to an extent that led inevitably to the demolition of the Babri Masjid at Ayodhya on 6 December 1992. The demolitions and the riots that followed are indicators of an aggressive majoritarianism. The gulf between the Hindu and Muslim communities widened. Along with the demolition of the ancient monument, the hopes that had been expressed by the Constituent Assembly, that after the independent nation settled down into political stability, the time would be ripe for the enactment of a Uniform Civil Code, came crumbling down. Ironically, the demand which was meant to be a symbol of India's claim to modernity, became a weapon in the hands of regressive and communal forces to beat down the minorities.

Along with these political developments, the judicial trends set by the Shah Bano judgement, echoing communal undertones, consolidated during this period. The wide media coverage which followed these judgements resulted in a further collapse of the parameters of the gender discourse.

Ironically, the judicial fervour of the nineties to reform Muslim personal law was not supported by individual Muslim women during the litigation process. But the judiciary seemed undaunted in its modernizing mission. One cannot help but strike parallels between the contemporary judicial zeal to modernize and civilize the Muslim community by abolishing polygamy and triple talaq, with the colonial zeal to reform the Hindu society through regulations on sati and child marriage in the last century.

The judgements were portrayed by the media as serving the cause of women's empowerment. But if they are stripped of this veneer of gender justice, they stand exposed in the garb of their communal hue. Beneath the rhetoric, they do not even further the cause of women's rights in actual terms. The implications of the judgements for gender discourse as well as identity politics are examined in this chapter.

8.1 Judgement of Justice Tilhari Invalidating Triple Talaq

The judgement invalidating triple talaq was delivered by Justice Hari Nath Tilhari of Allahabad High Court (Lucknow Bench) on 15 April 1994.[1] 'Since the practice of triple talaq denigrates women it is violative of the Constitution' the judgement proclaimed.

Apparently, the cause of Muslim women was served and the judgement was hailed as bold and progressive.[2] The response of Muslim religious leadership was predictable.[3] The comments by the *amicus curie* during the proceedings that knowledge of Arabic is essential for commenting upon the provisions of the Quran and the Hadis (which constitute the Shariat), provided further fuel to the communal myth that Muslims do not owe allegiance to the sovereign Indian state and that they are not governed by the state enacted legal system.[4]

The judgement caused concern to progressive scholars who, while criticizing the inertia of the All India Muslim Personal Law Board (AIMPLB) to declare the practice as invalid, apprehended that the judgement might hamper the process of reform from within the community.[5] Legal scholars also questioned whether a retrospective judgement of a single judge, in a land ceiling dispute, was the proper forum to examine the validity of triple talaq.[6] Several Muslim scholars and leaders who had supported the Supreme Court judgement in the *Shah Bano*[7] case and had opposed the Muslim Women's Bill in 1986, were critical of the Tilhari judgement and expressed their resentment about the sensationalization of the issue by the media.[8]

The media reportage led to a misconception that the High court had upheld a Muslim woman's petition challenging triple talaq and had protected her rights and consequently, the rights of all Muslim women. The implications of the judgement upon the woman concerned received least media attention.[9]

The press reports drew a comparison between the Shah Bano controversy and the triple talaq judgement.[10] However, the comparison was based on a warped understanding of the issue.

The only common denominator between the two judgements was the judicial interpretation of the Shariat. While Shah Bano herself had approached the court and had gained personally from the judgement, the judgement of Justice Tilhari had in fact deprived the woman concerned of her right to property.

Briefly stated, the facts of the case are as follows: When a notice was issued to Rahmatullah in 1974 under the U.P. Land Ceiling Act,[11] he pleaded that he had divorced his wife Khatoon Nisa in 1969 and that the land belonging to her was erroneously added to his assets. The judicial process which was initiated in 1974 had a long history and went through several stages and was examined by several state authorities. Finally, the issue before the court in two separate Writ Petitions filed by Khatoon Nisa and Rahmatullah was whether the plea of divorce was genuine or was resorted to only to defraud the state.

Initially, Khatoon Nisa was not a party to the case. But in 1980 she deposed before the concerned authority that she had been divorced eleven years ago. Under the Land Ceiling Act, a woman who is married relinquishes her right to hold separate property. However, the Act recognizes the right of a divorced or judicially separated woman to separate property. In such a situation, the property of the spouses is not clubbed together.[12] Hence the second issue before the court was whether a woman who is divorced as per the rules of her personal law is entitled to similar benefits as a woman who is separated or divorced through a court decree.[13]

The woman concerned did not dispute the fact of the divorce nor challenged the constitutional validity of oral and unilateral divorce (triple talaq). The opposing party was not her husband but the state authorities. Initially, the wife was not even a party to the case. It is pertinent to note that not just the advocates representing the parties and the *amicus curie* assisting the court, but even the advocate general appearing for the state (the opposing party) had pointed out to the judge that validity of triple talaq was not an issue before the court. But overriding these objections Justice Tilhari hastily pronounced the judgement after he received his transfer orders. When the advocate general questioned the constitutionality of such a move, rather curiously, the Avadh Bar Association passed a resolution to suspend him.[14]

The sum effect of the judgement for the concerned woman was that through a court decree her marriage which was dissolved twenty five years earlier was held to be valid and subsisting even against her own wishes and depositions and consequently, the land belonging to her was held to be surplus for the purpose of acquisition by the state under the Land Ceiling Act.

The judgement examined the serious issue of invalidating triple talaq in a flippant manner and relied upon a couplet written by an Urdu poet:

Talaq de rahe ho bare gharur ke saath;
Mere shabaab bhi lautaa do mere mehr ke saath

(you divorce me with such pride
give me back my youth along with my mehr).

The romantic poem cannot be treated as an authority to be relied upon in a judicial decision. While dealing with an issue of such magnitude, quoting a romantic couplet does not seem appropriate. The stanza had no relevance to a case where the wife herself affirmed her divorce.[15]

The rambling judgement of over a hundred and fifty pages lamented the position of Muslim women under their personal law and relied upon not just legal arguments but prose and poetry to prove the point. But the preoccupation with gender justice seems to be limited to the issue of Muslim women and triple talaq and does not extend to issues of gender discrimination under the Land Ceiling Act. The provision of clubbing the married woman's property with that of her husband is blatantly anti-women and smacks of European medievalism. It is based on the premise that the husband and wife are one unit (and that unit is the husband) and the unit is of a permanent nature. Under this concept, upon marriage, the woman lost her right over her individual assets and the husband acquired the power not only to manage it but even to alienate it. Incidentally, the Muslim law does not recognize the concept of the merging of the wife's assets with that of her husband.[16]

This blatantly discriminatory aspect of the Land Ceiling Act has been declared as constitutionally valid in an earlier judgement.[17] The Land Ceiling Act also provides for two additional hectares of land for each adult son but no such benefits are provided for adult daughters who form part of the domestic unit. The Act presumes that either women are not capable of owning and administering property or property is of no concern to adult females. So neither as unmarried daughters nor as married wives do they have an additional entitlement and their status is confined to that of dependents. The Tilhari judgement which claims to address the issues of gender equality, does not concern itself with this aspect.

One curious edge to the judgement is that while in this case the court went out of its way to declare the discriminatory aspect of personal laws as unconstitutional although the issue was not challenged before the court, in several instances when the discriminatory aspects of personal laws was an issue directly before the courts, the courts have upheld the constitutional validity of these discriminatory provisions.[18]

Even presuming that there was an intention to gain monetary advantage by defrauding the state through the misappropriation of the provision of oral and arbitrary talaq, such misappropriations and manipulations are not unique to this case. The right to form Hindu coparcenaries which grants tax benefits are routinely used for monetary gains. Several Hindu couples have also obtained collusive decrees for saving their land from the provisions of the Land Ceiling Acts.[19] Here the collusive factor had not led to invalidation of the decree of divorce.

In another instance, when the issue of collusive decrees was examined by the High Court of Bombay, the court specifically ruled that so long as the necessary conditions have been met, it is not up to the court to examine the motive for a divorce by consent. The question had arisen because the Family Court had refused to grant a divorce by consent on the ground that the Petition was based on an ulterior motive of defrauding creditors.[20]

Viewed within this broader context, there is reason to infer that the motive for the judgement lay elsewhere. Gautam Navalakha[21] has pointed out the communal tendencies underlying the judgements and has also pointed out other instances where a communal motive can be attributed. Immediately after the demolition of the Babri Masjid, when the issue of public worship of the idols of Ram in the newly erected temple was before the court, the judge permitted public worship on the site on the ground that Lord Ram is a constitutional identity. He based his logic on the fact that a picture of Ram appears on the copy of the constitution given to him by his father. In another judgement, while granting custody of a minor child born of a Christian mother and a Hindu father, the judge held that the father would be a better guardian as he is a Hindu.[22]

In his press interviews following the judgement on triple talaq, Justice Tilhari reaffirmed that he is a firm Hindu and that he believes that everyone born in Hindustan is a Hindu as this is his motherland. The language of motherland and cultural Hinduism of all Indians bears close resemblance to the propaganda by the communal Hindu factions in their anti-Muslim agenda.[23]

8.2 Supreme Court Directive to Implement a Uniform Civil Code

The second significant development in the debate on Muslim personal law and Uniform Civil Code is the decision of the Supreme Court in a case concerning polygamy of Hindu men after conversion to Islam.[24] While the issue before the court was bigamy of Hindu men and validity of their marriage contracted prior to conversion, the court primarily addressed the issue of Uniform Civil Code in the context of nation, national integration and minority identity.

In the much publicized judgement delivered by Justice Kuldip Singh (with a concurring judgement by Justice R.M. Sahai), the Court commented:

> Since Hindus along with Sikhs, Buddhists and Jains have forsaken their sentiments in the cause of the national unity and integration, some other communities would not, though the Constitution enjoins the establishment of a common civil code for the whole of India. ...Those who preferred to remain in India after the partition, fully knew that the Indian leaders did not believe in two-nation or three-nation theory and that in the Indian Republic there was to be only one Nation, the Indian Nation and no community could claim to remain a separate entity on the basis of religion. In this view of the matter no community can oppose the introduction of common civil code for all citizens in the territory of India.[25]

The obvious reference to Partition and to the choice to remain in India are targeted towards the Muslim minority as Parsis and Christians did not have any choice in the matter. The discourse of choosing to remain in India after Partition has long been a warning to Indian Muslims from the Hindu Right. The reference to 'civilized' and 'human' in relation to the Uniform Civil Code suggests that those who oppose the code (read Muslims) are barbaric and uncivilized. The comments seem to suggest that Hindu family laws are entirely secularized and gender just and further that Muslim community is the uncivilized enemy to national integrity.

Ratna Kapur and Brenda Cossman have argued that the language of the judgement in deflecting attention away from the continuing religious and discriminatory aspects of Hindu personal law and in attacking the Muslim community is disturbingly similar to the political rhetoric of the Hindu Right. In this view, all religious communities must be treated the same and it is the dominant Hindu community which is to be the norm against which equality is judged. [26]

But the norm of monogamy of the Hindu society, which was the issue under scrutiny before the apex court, escaped all public debate. The spotlight was turned on polygamy of Muslim men and the plight of Muslim women and solution offered to curb polygamy was the immediate enforcement of a Uniform Civil Code. There was a presumption that the uniform code would render Hindu marriages more stable by curbing the bigamous tendencies of Hindu men. A reading of the judgement seemed to indicate that the only breach of monogamy among Hindus was by conversion to Islam. To quote from the judgement, '...there is an open inducement to a Hindu husband, who wants to enter into a second marriage to become a Muslim...'.

The norm of Hindu monogamy presumed by the judgement needs further scrutiny. Monogamy was introduced among the Hindus through the *Hindu Marriage Act* in 1955. Prior to this, Hindu men were absolved of the criminal consequences of bigamy under s.494 of IPC. After 1955, a Hindu wife could divorce her husband on the ground of bigamy and also prosecute him under the penal law.

The right to dissolve the marriage on the ground of bigamy is also available, to a certain extent, to a Muslim wife under the *Dissolution of Muslim Marriages Act*.[27] The additional relief that the Hindu wife can avail of is criminal prosecution for bigamy. But since only the first wife can initiate prosecution, a popular notion prevails that a Hindu husband can remarry with the consent of his wife and at a practical level, this notion is not far from the truth. So although on paper the position of a Hindu wife appeared slightly better than a Muslim wife, in respect of her husband's bigamy, the statistics of bigamous marriages among Hindus and Muslims are comparable.[28] By declaring that the earlier marriage was valid, the only legal remedy (apart from a petition for divorce on the ground of bigamy) that the litigating women are entitled to is a prosecution for bigamy.

It is in this context that judicial attitude towards bigamy by Hindu men has to be posed as the central issue. The judgement seemed to indicate that the judiciary has dealt severely with all breaches of monogamy among the Hindus and the only loophole through which a husband can escape is conversion. But an examination of the decisions of the Supreme Court and the various High Courts reveal that bigamy of the Hindu male persists despite statutory restraints and the judicial attitude has been extremely lax towards Hindu bigamy.

Ten years after the provision of monogamy was introduced, the Supreme Court dealt with the case of Bhaurao Lokhande.[29] The errant husband was convicted by the lower courts. But the apex court acquitted the husband on the ground that essential ceremonies for a valid Hindu marriage, i.e *vivaha homa* and saptapadi (invocation before the sacred fire and seven steps round it) had not been performed in the second marriage. The court ruled that the bare fact of a man and a woman living as husband and wife does not give them the status of husband and wife unless valid ceremonies of a marriage have been performed and hence such cohabitation would not warrant conviction under s.494 of IPC.

This principle was followed by the Supreme Court in 1966, in Kanwal Ram's case and in 1971 in Priya Bala's case.[30] While acquitting the errant husbands, the Supreme Court reaffirmed that proof of essential ceremonies is a precondition for conviction. The court further ruled that this condition must be met even when the husband and the second wife admit the marriage or the fact of cohabitation.

In the intervening period of 30 years from Bhaurao in 1965 to Sarla Mudgal in 1995, the various High Courts not only followed the trend set by the Supreme Court, but in their zeal, advanced the logic to absurd ends, stamping out all hopes of justice and fairness in criminal prosecutions. Ceremonies performed in a temple, registration with the caste panchayats or temple authorities or even with a civil registrar fell short of the degree of clinching proof which the first wife was expected to produce. The paternity of the child of a second marriage if proved could only amount to its bastardization and not proof of bigamy by its father. The complainant wife could also lay herself open to the risk of invalidating her existing marriage.[31]

The decisions ignored the reality of a pluralistic Hindu society and thrust upon it an absurd notion of uniformity. The second marriages of lower castes were judged by the yardstick which can only be applied to marriages of upper caste virgin brides. The lower castes did not follow the Brahminical rituals and also permitted divorce and remarriage prior to the *Hindu Marriage Act* and followed distinct ceremonies to distinguish the first and the second marriage. Hence a remarriage of a lower caste person could never meet the high judicial standards set by the courts in co-ordination with the provisions of the *Hindu Marriage Act*.

A discernible pattern emerging from prosecution for bigamy is conviction by the lower judiciary and leniency by the apex court. The higher judiciary rescued the errant husbands by applying the standards of Brahminical rituals of homa, saptapadi and kanyadan. The complexities of bigamous Hindu marriages and the afflictions of both the first and the second wife were addressed neither by the courts nor by the media while the focus continued to remain on Muslim bigamy.

8.3 Implications for Identity Politics

The gains of the much publicized judgments for gender justice amounted to naught. The single judge decision invalidating triple talaq has been stayed by the Supreme Court. In the second judgement, the direction of the court to the legislature was criticized by legal scholars.[32] The then Prime Minister, P.V. Narasimha Rao, declared in a press statement that the government will not interfere with the personal laws of minorities. Within the stipulated period of one year the Parliamentary elections brought a change in government. The United Front which assumed power was a broad-based coalition of non-Congress, non-communal parties. Some of these parties had opposed the communal demand of UCC in its election campaigns.

At the expiry of the one year period, the government filed an affidavit in the Supreme Court expressing its inability to enact such a code.[33] A review petition filed against the judgement has been admitted. The Supreme Court has subsequently observed that its direction to the Union government to take necessary steps was only *obiter dicta* (not binding in law).[34]

The welcome change from the Shah Bano controversy to the triple talaq judgement was that in the post Babri Masjid political scenario, the triple talaq judgement could not polarize the issue within the binaries of progressive and secular Hindus and obscurantist and fundamentalist Muslims. The judgements met with criticism from several women's organizations and human rights activists for their communal undertones.[35]

The reactions of the AIMPLB were more subdued in comparison to the communal frenzy whipped up after the Shah Bano judgement. In a press release issued after the Tilhari judgement, the AIMPLB appealed to the community to restrain from taking the battle to the streets and assured them that the Board would approach the Supreme Court for redress.[36] In its meeting held at Lucknow on 1 May 1994, the Board assured the community that it would initiate the process of codifying sections of the Muslim law.

But the judgement provided a boost for the rhetoric of the Hindu Right. In Maharashtra, with the BJP-Shiv Sena in power since 1993, the judgement provided the impetus to fulfil its election manifesto of enforcing a Uniform Civil Code (which in effect, is confined to abolishing Muslim polygamy).[37] A hurriedly formulated Bill abolishing polygamy was rushed through both Houses without any public debate and was submitted for the President's assent. Since no effort is made to plug the loopholes within the *Hindu Marriage Act* or to protect women's rights, the only aim of the Bill seems to be to bring Muslim men under the penal provisions of S.494 IPC.[38] With a change in the government at the centre, the Bill seems to have lapsed.

So while the gains for the gender discourse have been nil, the judgements have dealt a severe blow to identity politics. The judgements have led even legal scholars, who had earlier advocated Uniform Civil Code, to re-examine their position. They have severely constrained the scope of gender discourse and have forced human rights activists and women's rights advocates to take a more restrained and cautious position in order to clearly distinguish their demand from that of the right wing communal forces.

Notes

1. *Rahmat Ullah v State of U.P.*, Writ Petition no.45 of 1993 and *Khatoon Nisa v State of U.P.*, Writ Petition no.57 of 1993 (unreported).
2. 'Triple Talaq Again', *The Times of India*, 19 April 1994; 'The practice is contrary to the spirit of Islam'. *Indian Express*, 25 April 1994; 'Muslim women welcome court verdict on talaq'. *The Statesman*, 22 April 1994, Anjana Basu, 'Behind the Four Walls The Veil.' *The Statesman*, 30 April 1994.
3. 'Muslims resent talaq verdict.' *The Times of India*, 18 April 1994; 'Divorced From Reality.' *The Pioneer* 25 April 1994.
4. Ahmad, F., *Triple Talaq—An Analytical Study*, New Delhi: Regency Publications (1994), p.104.
5. See comments by Tahir Mohammed quoted in, 'Beyond the law: The Strange case of Justice Tilhari,' *Frontline* 20 May 1994, p. 35.
6. Ibid. Also Advocate Daniel Latifi, who had represented Shah Bano in the controversial case criticized the Tilhari judgement in his article 'Verdict on talaq', in *Hindustan Times* 5 May 1994.
7. AIR 1985 SC 945.
8. Arif Mohammed Khan, the Congress Minister who had resigned in protest against the Muslim Women's Bill criticized the judgement in an interview with Neena Vyas, 'Much more at stake than triple talaq,' in *The Hindu*, 1 May 1994. In another article by Ajaz Ashraf titled 'A cap and a beard: Is that all to Muslims,' *The Pioneer*, 1 May 1994, several scholars expressed their resentment about the media coverage. Historian Harbans Mukhiya drew a parallel between the way the West covers India and the response of the media to Muslim issues. Mushirul Hasan opined that the media and the Muslim tend to stereotype each other.
9. Agnes, F. 'Triple Talaq Judgement Do Women Really Benefit,' *Economic and Political Weekly*, XXIX/20 (1994), p. 1169.
10. The report which appeared in *The Times of India*, 25 April 1994 was entitled, 'Another Shah Bano in the Making'. Several articles while commenting on the judgement carried a picture of Shah Bano. See for instance, 'Fear Behind the Purdah,' *Blitz*, 21 May 1994; 'One Nation, One Law', *Sunday*, 17 May 1994.
11. The U.P. Imposition of Ceiling on Land Holding (Amendment) Act 1972 (U.P. Act No.13 of 1972).
12. S.3 (7) and (17) provided for wives who were legally separated and divorced through a court decree to hold separate property.
13. Triple talaq under the Shariat law has statutory recognition under S. 2 of the *Application of Shariat Act*. 1937 Further talaq either in one sitting or in three consecutive months is the only remedy available for a Muslim man to divorce his wife. A Muslim man cannot approach a

court for a divorce either by consent or on fault ground. *The Dissolution of Muslim Marriages Act* of 1939 is applicable only to women.

The matrimonial relief of judicial separation is of western origin and is not recognized under the Muslim law. The fact that an orally divorced wife's right to hold separate property does not figure in the provisions of the Act while a legally separated wife's rights are recognized is an indicator of the state's blinkers towards the specificity of minority practices, while enacting legislations. In *Sita Devi v Additional Commissioner, Agra* AIR 1996 All 75, the court upheld the plea that the property of a judicially separated Hindu wife cannot be clubbed with that of her husband. If this is the legal position there, was no basis for holding that an orally divorced wife is not entitled to hold separate property.

14. 'Avadh Bar to Suspend Advocate General,' *Times of India*, 19 April 1994. The interest of the Bar Association of Avadh is another curious aspect of the case. Perhaps it is relevant to note that the advocates of the Avadh Bar led a demonstration to Ayodhya demanding public worship of Ram idols installed at the newly constructed temple after the demolition of Babri Masjid in December, 1992.

15. Ahmad, F., *Triple Talaq—An Analytical Study*, p.108.

16. The press note issued by the AIMPLB on 1 May 1994, from Lucknow, stressed that Muslim law is more progressive than the Land Ceiling Act in this respect. But ironically, the AIMPLB had not opposed this provision of clubbing together the properties of the spouses, by raising the plea of religious dictates, prior to this judgement.

17. *Ambika Prasad Mishra v State of U.P.* 1980 (3) SCC 719.

18. See *Dwarakabai v Prof. Mainam Mathews* AIR 1953 Mad 792 *Harvinder Kaur v Harminder Singh* AIR 1984 Delhi 66, *Krishna Singh v Mathura Ahir* AIR 1980 SC 707.

19. Mali, A., 'Uniformity among equals,' in *Hindustan Times*, 8 May 1994 and Kannabiran, K.G., 'Outlawing Oral Divorce,' in *Economic and Political Weekly*, XXIX/25 (1994), p. 1509.

20. *Leela Mahadeo Joshi v Mahadeo Sitaram Joshi* AIR 1991 Bom 105.

21. Navlakha, G., 'Triple talaq: Posturing at Women's Expense,' *Economic and Political Weekly*, XXIX/21 (1994), p.1264.

22. The judgement of Justice Tilhari in the case of *Indumati Koorichh v Yogendra Pal Koorichh* W.P. no. 325 of 1993 dated 29 July 1993. See Bindra, A., 'Child Custody for Hindus only,' in *The Lawyers* IX/2 (1994), p.11. Also see 'Beyond the law—The strange case of Justice Tilhari,' *Frontline*, 20 May 1994, p. 35.

23. Basu, T. et al., *Khaki Shorts Saffron Flags*, New Delhi: Orient Longman (1993).

24. *Sarla Mudgal v Union of India & Ors* (1995) 3 SCC 635.

25. Ibid., para 34 and 35.

26. Kapur R. and B. Cossman, *Subversive Sites*, New Delhi: Sage Publications (1995), p.260.

27. S.2 (viii) (f) of the *Dissolution of Muslim Marriages Act*, 1939. Under this section, if the husband does not treat both wives equitably, the woman

has a right of dissolution of marriage. A similar right also exists if the husband associates with women of ill repute.

28. As per the Census report 1961, incidences of polygamous marriages for the decade 1951–60 are as follows: Tribal—17.98per cent; Hindus—5.06 per cent Muslim—4.31 per cent. According to another study, the incidence of polygamy is as follows: among tribals—15.25 per cent, Buddhists—7.97 per cent, Jains—6.72 per cent, Hindus—5.8 per cent and Muslims 5.7 per cent. (*Towards Equality*, pp.66-7; 104) Since Buddhists and Jains are also governed by Hindu law, the statistics for Hindus collectively would be 6.83 per cent as compared to 5.7 per cent for Muslims. See Table 3.

29. *Bhaurao Shanker Lokhande v State of Maharashtra* AIR 1965 SC 1564.

30. *Kanwal Ram & Ors v The H.P. Administration* AIR 1966 SC 614; and *Priya Bala Ghosh v Suresh Chandra Ghosh* AIR 1971 SC 1153.

31. For a further discussion on this issue see Agnes, F., 'Hindu Men, Monogamy and the Uniform Civil Code,' in *Economic and Political Weekly*, XXX/50 (1995), p. 3238.

32. Seervai, H.M., 'Judiciary oversteps its Brief', *The Times of India*, 5 July 1995.

33. 'No change in Muslim personal law, says P.M.,' *The Times of India*, 28 July 1995.

34. 'Suggestion on civil code not binding says Court,' *Asian Age* , 12 August 1995.

35. Punwani, J., 'Women veto a common civil code,' *The Sunday Review*, 23 July 1995; Sathe, S.P., 'Uniform Civil Code Implications of the Supreme Court Judgement,' in *Economic and Political Weekly*, XXX/35 (1995), p. 2165; Also see Kannabiran, Ahmad, F., *Triple Talaq*.

36. See note 16.

37. Bill No. XXXII of 1995 introduced by Liladhar Dake, Minister for Law and Judiciary on 7 August 1995.

38. Gangoli, G., 'Anti-Bigamy Bill in Maharashtra,' *Economic and Political Weekly*, XXXI/29 (1996), p. 1919.

PART THREE:

DEVELOPMENTS IN
THE PERSONAL LAWS
OF NON-MUSLIM MINORITIES

9

Legal Significance of the Parsi Community

Introduction

The history of law reform of minority communities, Muslims, Parsis and Christians, can broadly be categorized into three phases: (i) the reforms during the initial phases when the administration was transferred from the Company to the Crown; (ii) the reforms initiated when the Indian legislators, under the *Government of India Act*, assumed the power to legislate; (iii) reform measures initiated during the eighties when the issue of gender was foregrounded by the women's movement and legislative reform became an important arena of women's rights discourse. It is significant to note that during the first decade after independence, during the process of nation building, when major rehauling of the Hindu legal system was undertaken, there were no attempts to reform laws governing minorities.

The legislative history of Muslim minorities has been discussed in the preceding chapters. In this and the following chapter, an attempt is made to trace the legislative history of Parsi and Christian communities. Although the recent debate on Uniform Civil Code has posed the problem within the narrow confines of Hindu majority and Muslim minority, the issue also has implications for other minorities, Parsis and Christians. Hence it would be relevant to trace the history of personal laws among these communities and examine the strategies adopted by them to bring in reform.

The initiatives by the Parsi and Christian communities, during the recent phase of reforms, have met with diagonally opposite ends. While the Parsi community has been reasonably successful in bringing about legislative reforms, the initiatives by the Christian community have met with hostility and procrastination. The fate of reform among the two communities indicates that, even when the process is initiated from within the community.

the official response is coloured with extraneous considerations and political undercurrents. To trace the linkages between political undercurrents and legal reform, it is necessary to locate the two communities within the context of the colonial and post-colonial political power structures.

9.1 The Ancient Civilization and the Transition to a New Land

The Parsis are a small and well-knit community. Numerically they are so insignificant that in the census report, under the classification, 'religious communities', they do not even merit a separate listing and are clubbed together under the head 'other communities'. The Parsi population in India is roughly around 1,00,000.[1] Since it was not a proselytizing religion, there was no significant increase in the population and the community continued to be homogenized. In 1851, the world population of the Parsis, including Persia, was around 1,50,000 out of which around 1,10,544 were in India.[2] As per a recent study, in 1986 the Parsi population of the world was around 2,50,800.[3]

The Parsis originate from Iran (abode of Aryans). The Greek writers called this land 'Persis' and the people Persians, hence the land acquired the name Persia. The country was divided into two parts, Media, the north-western region and Pars, the south-western region. The inhabitants of Pars were called Parsees (or Parsis).[4]

In AD 636, when the Arabs invaded Persia and Caliph Omar defeated the Parsi king Yezdezind, to escape persecution, they sailed off in boats in search of a new land, carrying with them their sacred fire. After a great ordeal at sea, the boat landed twenty-five miles south of Daman.[5] The head of the group implored the local king, Jadao Rane, to give them refuge with a promise that they would enrich his land. The history of India bears testimony to the fact that they kept this promise.

The king laid down five conditions: (i) the Parsis should adopt the local language; (ii) they should translate their holy texts into the local language; (iii) their women must change their dress and wear the local saree; (iv) their marriage ceremony should include the local rite of tying of the sacred knot; and (v) they should surrender their arms.[6] They consented to all the five terms and in return the king granted them permission to build their fire temples[7] and allotted to them a stretch of undeveloped country, near Diew (Diu). They renamed the place as Navsari[8], settled down to agriculture (some were also weavers and craftsmen) and lived amicably with the local Hindu community. Navsari became the centre of learning of the Parsi community. Due to the rigid caste system of the Hindus, assimilation was not possible and hence they were able to maintain their separate and distinct identity. But they adopted many local customs.[9]

Within this integrated community there are two sects Shensoys (or Shuhursaees) and Kudmis. The Kudmis are a breakaway sect formed in 1746 and consists of only around 10,000 Parsis. The difference between the two sects is not as major as among the Shias and the Sunnis in the Muslim community or the Catholics and the Protestants amongst the Christians.

The fortunes of this community seem to have transformed when they were touched by the magic wand of colonization. They were able to gain the maximum advantages of the economic and political transformation taking place during the colonial rule. Within the Bombay Presidency, they were the first to adapt to English education, new trading patterns, and later to commerce and industry. They fitted in well with the new colonial administrative structure and also played an important role in the nationalist politics. The contribution of the Parsi community to building the city of Bombay, after the English take-over, is particularly significant. It is through their close interaction with the British, that the community, though numerically insignificant in the post-colonial political map, evolved as an important economic and political force during the colonial regime and were able to negotiate for themselves a separate set of personal laws.

The records indicate that during the time of Portuguese rule, there was only one Parsi in Bombay, Dorabjee Nanabhoy.[10] After the island of Bombay was gifted over to the King of England by the Portuguese, the Parsis started trickling in and were able to obtain various commercial contracts from the British for building the new commerical centre of the British empire.[11] This helped the community to acquire a new economic and political status within the Bombay Presidency. The prosperity of Bombay attracted other Parsis who found life in famine-stricken Gujarat difficult. Over a period, 70 per cent of the Parsis in India began to live in Bombay. The more prosperous among them built hospitals, gardens, schools and housing schemes and were also significant contenders in the field of commerce, industry, science and art.[12]

9.2 Development of Parsi Laws of Marriage and Succession

The development of the Parsi legal system must be viewed within the context of the above mentioned role played by the Parsis within the colonial scheme. As already mentioned, after settling down, the Parsis adopted the local language and customs, while maintaining a distinct and separate identity. The adaptation of the institution of local panchayats for administration of their affairs is an important indicator of this adaptation.

During the initial phase of the Company rule, the various British charters explicitly saved the customs and usages of Hindus and Muslims in civil matters as they were deemed religious. But no such saving provision was granted to other communities like Parsis, Christians, Jews, Portuguese, Armenians and Europeans. The Presidency towns applied English law and in the Provinces, the law and custom of the parties (or the law of the defendant) was applied. In exercise of the discretion granted to the judges, English principles of justice, equity and good conscience were also applied as a residuary rule of law.[13] Under this legal scheme, English laws were applied to Parsis in all civil matters except marriage and bigamy.[14]

In 1778, after the Parsis petitioned William Hornby, the Bombay Parsi Panchayat was granted recognition and a lawfully constructed Panchayat came into effect from 1 January 1787.[15] This fitted in well with the legal scheme devised subsequently by Elphinstone of granting recognition to customary usages.

In 1835, a suit was filed by a son to appropriate the whole of the father's property through the application of the English principle of primogeniture (through which the eldest son inherits the whole property). Since this was not the custom followed by Parsis, the community was alarmed and pressed for a separate legislation. In their submission to the government, they pleaded that they were subjected to serious disadvantages in the absence of a fixed written code.

In response to this appeal, an Act was passed in June 1837,[16] which relieved the Parsis of Bombay from the operation of the English law of primogeniture. Through this statute, widows were granted a share in the property and the residue was divided equally amongst the children and their descendants. But English principles continued to be applied to them in all other respects.

In the case of the mofussil Provinces, it was almost impossible to ascertain with precision the Parsi customs because on many points the Parsis of Surat, Broach, Poona and Ahmedabad differed from each other and all of them differed from the Parsi in Bombay. So in November 1838, the Parsis forwarded to the Legislative Council a petition along with the answers which they had prepared to Borradaile's queries[17] and prayed that a regulation might be framed on the basis of those answers 'as embracing the rights of inheritance and succession that are acknowledged by the Parsi nation.'

The Parsis wanted to be protected from two primary principles of English law: (i) the English Statute of Distribution in case of intestacy; and (ii) from the English common law relating to husband and wife which denied married women independent control over their property during coverture.[18] But there was no further development on this issue. In a subsequent litigation, the Chief Justice of the Supreme Court of Bombay held that the ecclesiastical relief of restitution of conjugal rights applies to Parsi marriages.[19] At this juncture, the community renewed the demand for separate legislations to govern Parsi Marriage, Divorce and Succession. But the Third Law Commission rejected this demand as it felt that the demand was not substantiated. This left the community highly dissatisfied.

So on 20 August 1855, a meeting of the Parsis of Bombay was convened at central hall of the main fire temple to campaign for a separate law. The meeting was attended by 3,000 Parsis. A committee was appointed 'to prepare a draft Code of Laws adapted to the Parsi nation and to petition the Legislative Council of India for the enactment thereof.'

On 5 December 1859 the Managing Committee of the Parsee Law Association settled and adopted a body of rules titled a Draft Code of Inheritance, Succession and other matter. On 31 March 1860, this Draft Code was presented to the Legislative Council and was referred to a Select Committee. On 10 August 1861, the Select Committee of the Legislative Council presented their report and recommended that the Government of Bombay may appoint a Commission to make a preliminary inquiry into the usages recognized as laws by the Parsi community of India.

On 26 December 1861, the Government of Bombay appointed the commission, who recorded the evidence, both written and oral of the community representatives. As regards inheritance, succession and property between husband and wife, the mofussil Parsis objected to the rights of females to inherit the family property upon the death of a male Parsi dying intestate and to the right of married women during coverture to hold or dispose of their separate property. The mofussil Parsis, however, agreed with the Bombay Parsis that the English Law of Inheritance and Succession was unsuited to the requirement of the Parsi community. The commission submitted its report on 13 October 1862 and disallowed the contention that there should be two separate Inheritance Laws, one for the Parsis of Bombay and another for the Parsis of the mofussil towns.

As a next step, in 1864, the Parsi Law Commission was appointed and based on its report, in February 1865, two bills were introduced, Parsi Marriage and Divorce Bill and Succession and Inheritance (Parsis) Bill. They were referred to the Select Committee which presented its report on 31 March 1865.[20] Based on this report the two Bills were enacted, i.e. The Parsi Intestate Succession Act, 1865 and The Parsi Marriage and Divorce Act of 1865. Thus due to their perseverance, finally, the Parsis succeeded in securing a separate law for themselves.

The Parsi marriage and divorce law incorporated the provisions of the English matrimonial statute[21] which transformed the Christian marriage status to a dissoluble contract. Following the Christian model, the Parsi marriages were made monogamous and adultery was made into a ground of divorce.[22]

Through these statutes, the Parsis also secured legal recognition for their customary arbitration forum of the panchayat. Under the Act, a jury system consisting of seven representatives of the community was introduced. Through this process, the community obtained a hold over matters of marriage and divorce within the Anglo-Saxon court structure. In the process of emulating the English statutes, certain biases against women crept into the matrimonial laws. Despite the enactments, in matters not covered by the statute, either the English common law or principles of justice, equity and good conscience continued to be applied to Parsis.[23]

Like other communities the characteristics of the Parsi community also were 'fixed' in the process of litigation over property disputes. In an important case decided in 1908, the courts ruled that there is no conversion among the Parsis. The issue arose due to a dispute between the head of the Parsi Anjuman of Bombay, Sir Dinsha Petit and the Sir Jamsetji Jeejeebhoy, the industrialist. The issue before the court was the creation of private trusts and the relegation of huge properties to it by the industrialist. The Parsi Anjuman objected to the creation of such private trusts. But the issue which was foregrounded during litigation was that of conversion. The Parsi Anjuman pleaded that Juddins (converts) to whom the Navjot (initiation ceremony) is performed and are given the *sudra* and *kusti* become Parsis. In a lengthy judgement of around a hundred pages, a two member bench consisting of one Parsi (Justice Davar) and one English judge ruled in favour of Jamsetji and validated the creation of private trusts. In the process, they also invalidated conversions among Parsis. Adopting a rather curious logic, the court explained that while Zorastrianism is a religion, Parsis are a race and there cannot be conversion to a race. Just like a person cannot convert and 'become' an Englishman or a Frenchman, in a similar manner no one can convert and 'become' a Parsi the court explained.[24]

In order to prevent the Parsi trust property and fire temples from withering away from the Parsi fold, in another decision it was ruled that converts to Zorastrianism and children born to a Parsi woman, who is married to a non-Parsi are not Parsis.[25] The children of a Parsi father and a non-Parsi mother are deemed Parsis. Interestingly, the issue before the court did not concern the rights of children born to a Parsi woman through her non-Parsi husband. The case concerned a Goan Christian girl Bella, who was adopted and raised as a Parsi by a Parsi benefactor settled in Rangoon. Attracted to Zorastrianism, she expressed a desire to convert and was initiated into the faith through a ceremony of initiation by a Parsi priest. But when she started attending worship at the fire temple, the community elders raised an objection and filed a suit for an injunction restraining her entry into the fire temple in Rangoon. They pleaded that her presence in the fire temple caused distraction and prevented the Parsis from offering worship. Ironically, the land upon which the fire temple was built was a state endowment for religious worship, to the Parsis. The two lower courts held that since Bella had converted to Zorastrianism, her entry cannot be prevented and she was entitled to worship in the fire temple. But the Privy Council relying upon the Bombay High Court decision in *Dinsha Petit v Jamsetji Jeejeebhoy* held that the double requirements of religion and race are essential to worship in the fire temple, despite the fact that the legal deeds were drawn specifically in the context of religion. Through these two significant decisions, the avenues for conversion and adoption among the Parsis were sealed.

In 1925, when the *Indian Succession Act* was enacted, (which governs mainly Christian succession) the *Parsi Intestate Succession Act* was verbatim incorporated in Chapter III of this Act. Interestingly, during the years 1870 to 1925, considerable progress was made in the realm of married women's property rights under the English statutes and the concept of equality between men and women regarding inheritance had been accepted. Based on these developments, the *Indian Succession Act* did not discriminate between male and female heirs. But the Parsi inheritance laws, continued to maintain the discrimination and females continued to inherit half the share of their male counterparts.[26] This is a rather surprising development, given the context that the demand for a separate law for the Parsis originated with their resentment against the anti-women provisions of the English statutes being inadvertently applied to them.

9.3 A Wave of Reforms During the Thirties

When reforms were initiated in the family laws of Hindus and Muslims, the Parsis also initiated a process of reform. In 1933, the Council of the Parsi Central Association submitted a Draft Bill for the opinion of the Parsi public to amend the Parsi law of succession. The main objective was to improve the position of the widow and daughter under the statute and allotment of share to parents. The changes were incorporated into the *Indian Succession Act* in 1939.[27]

During the period 1865 to 1930, the status of women in England was radically transformed through various statutes and great strides were made in the English family laws. Against this backdrop, the *Parsi Marriage and Divorce Act* of 1865 had become outdated. So the Parsi Central Association took up the question of reforms in 1923 and a sub-committee was appointed to suggest suitable changes. The Parsee Laws Revision sub-committee submitted its report in 1927. The Parsi Central Association sent copies of this report to various trustees of the Parsi Panchayats, Parsi Associations, Parsi Anjumans, the delegates of the Parsi Chief Matrimonial court and to Parsi jurists all over India, as well as to Parsi Associations in China and Persia.[28] The report was also published in the press.

The Parsi Central Association made some modifications to the Bill after which it was circulated for public opinion. A conference was arranged under the auspices of the Parsi Panchayat. Twenty-five Parsi associations participated in this process and twenty-one associations approved the modifications.[29] Based on the various views expressed, a draft of the proposed Act was prepared and circulated which had the approval of leading members of the Parsi community including Sir Dinshaw E. Wacha and Right Hon'ble Dinshaw F. Mulla.

A Bill was introduced into the Council of State in 1935, by Sir Pheroze Sethna. It was circulated for opinion and a Joint Select Committee was appointed to consider the Bill. The Select Committee reported to the Council of State in the same year and the Bill was passed on 13 March 1936. The Federal Assembly considered the Bill in April 1936. Sir Cowasji Jehangir who moved the Bill, explained that an overwhelming majority of the Parsi community held progressive views and were anxious to modify the provisions of their archaic laws to suit the modern conditions.[30] The reforms expanded the scope of dissolving the marriage by introducing several new grounds— non–consummation of marriage, insanity, pre-marriage pregnancy, grievous hurt and desertion.

9.4 Reforms During the Eighties

The eighties witnessed the emergence of a new women's movement in India. Reform in personal laws was an important demand of this movement. There were significant reforms in various laws concerning women, rape, dowry prohibition, domestic violence etc. The controversy around the Shah Bano judgment and the Muslim Women's Bill also focused attention on discriminatory aspects of various personal laws. At this stage, the Parsi community again initiated reforms to modernize their laws.

The reforms were based on the recommendations of the Law

Commission's *110th report*. The process was initiated by the Board of trustees of the Bombay Parsi Panchayat. It submitted the recommendations to the government. The then Law Minister, Dhiraj Goswamy introduced two Bills for reforming the personal laws of the Parsis. While the amendment to marriage laws was passed in 1988, the amendment to succession laws had to be shelved and was enacted in 1991, during the Congress rule.

The *Parsi Marriage and Divorce (Amendment) Bill* was introduced in the Rajya Sabha on 24 November 1986. It was passed by both the houses in the following year, received President's assent on 25 March 1988 and came into force in April 1988.[31]

The provisions of marriage and divorce were modified along the lines of the *Hindu Marriage Act*. Grounds of divorce were further liberalized and divorce by mutual consent was introduced.[32] The disparity between the rights of legitimate and illegitimate children was abolished. In 1991, by amending the succession laws, the discrimination between female and male descendants was abolished.

The following aspects need to be highlighted in the context of Parsi law reforms:

i. At each juncture, the process of reforms was initiated from within the community and a broad consensus was reached before the Bills were introduced. So finally, when the Bills were presented to the legislature they were passed unanimously without much debate.

ii. Women from the community were conspicuously absent from the discourse. Although the community is liberal and holds a progressive stand on women's issues, women's names do not figure in any phase of the reform. The process seems to have been initiated at the instance of a few liberal male members. They interacted both with the community institutions at one level, and with the state institutions at the other.

iii. Although gender justice was the stated agenda, the motive of reform seems to be dual: (i) maintaining a separate community identity and once this is achieved (ii) ensuring that the laws do not lag far behind the dominant ideology, i.e. in the pre-independence period the British statutes and in the post-independence period, the *Hindu Marriage Act*. Since the *Hindu Marriage Act* grants the husband a right to maintenance, the same was also introduced in the Parsi laws. Under the *Special Marriage Act* of 1954, husbands do not have a similar right. It is significant to note that the reform followed the provisions of Hindu law rather than the *Special Marriage Act*, which is a secular legislation and more beneficial to women than the *Hindu Marriage Act.*

iv. The premise that gender equity was not the primary object is substantiated by the retention of certain outdated discriminatory notions inherited from the British statutes in 1865. The law provides for settling the property of an adulterous woman in favour of the children(S.50). The statute also treats women as legal minors and provides for a trust to be set up in respect of the maintenance allowance with the power to restrain women's access to the maintenance (S.41).

v. Even while modernizing the statutes, the community has maintained its hold over the matrimonial matters by retaining the jury system introduced in 1865. The jury system has been abolished under other Indian statutes. Constituting a special Parsi Matrimonial Court causes severe hardships and delays to the litigants. In the Bombay High Court, the Parsi Matrimonial Court is constituted twice a year and functions for about a week during each term. Even in the interest of uniformity or modernity, this system has not been abolished. This clause did not meet with any criticism during the legislative debate.

vi. The debate in the Parliament when the Bills were enacted has been cursory.[33] The members did not concern themselves with the implications of the Bill for Parsi women. The debate was confined to two spheres: (i) now that the Parsis have willingly modified their laws, it is time to enact a Uniform Civil Code; (ii) praises to the Parsi community that they are an enlightened and progressive community and thereby insinuating that other communities (more specifically the Muslims) are backward and reactionary. The fact that the Parsi community had also opposed the imposition of a Uniform Civil Code and the Adoption Bill, that they had retained the jury system in matrimonial adjudication and the relief of divorce by consent was introduced as late as in 1988, did not even figure in the debates. The Act also retained the sexist provision under S.50 of the Act, which empowers the court to settle a wife's property for the benefit of the children in case a ground of adultery is proved against her in a petition filed by her husband.

In conclusion, it is obvious that only through its political and economic significance during the colonial rule, the Parsi community could negotiate for a separate law, where *none* existed. The liberal leaders of the community, during each phase of reform, have ensured that the law does not lag far behind the dominant social norms, i.e. of the British, during the colonial rule and of the Hindu in the post-colonial rule. Although their initial demand for a separate law was premised on protecting the rights of women from the vagaries of the British legal principles, in the process of codification and reform, the community incorporated the biases inherent in the dominant system, both of the British and of the Hindu, which aided and reaffirmed the biases inherent within the customary practices. Hence their claim for a separate law to safeguard women's rights cannot be substantiated. But the existence of a separate law has substantially aided the numerically insignificant community to retain its own separate identity within the legal arena and granted statutory recognition to community interventions in judicial processes.

Notes

1. See Table 4.
2. Framjee, D., *The Parsees—Their History, Manners, Custom and Religion*, London: Smith Elder & Co. (1858), p. 52.
3. Cabinetmaker, P.H., 'Parsis and Marriage', Pune: International Institute of Population Studies (Mimeo) (1991), pp.2-3.
4. The Parsis are followers of Zarathushtra, the prophet of ancient Iran, born 1,500 years before Christ, who preached that life is a struggle between good and evil, with the ultimate triumph of good over evil. They worship the Supreme Being Hormuzd, the sun and five elements. Their ancient kingdom lays claims to many markers of civilization. In its hey day, the Persian kingdom extended from Egypt to Sind and from the Mediterranean to the Arabian Sea. Cyrus and Darius are the two illustrious Persian kings.
5. Framjee, D., *The Parsees*, p.10.
6. Cabinetmaker, P.H., 'Parsis and Marriage'.
7. The first fire kindled when they landed is preserved in the holiest of the holy shrines Imamshah at Udwada near Navsari.
8. New Sari, as it reminded them of a place they had left behind in Persia which was called Sari.
9. For instance, washing the toes of the bridegroom with milk during marriage rituals, offering *pan-sopari* on auspicious occasions, sprinkling of rose water etc. Framjee, D., *The Parsees*, p.84.
10. Framjee, D., *The Parsees*, p.26.
11. In 1735, when the British started building the Bombay dockyard, a

Parsi from Surat, Lowjeee Wadia was granted the contract of ship building (ship wright). Rustom Patel, another Parsi, helped the British to stall the Moppila attack. Rustomjee Cursetjee wrote the first book in English in 1780, called *Bombay Calendar*. On 1 July 1822, Mobed Fardoonje Marzben started the first newspaper in Gujarati, *the Bombay Samachar*. When the British started building the railways, the contract of laying the tracks was granted to Jamsetjee Dorabjee. In 1857, Rustomjee Byramjee, obtained a commission as a surgeon.

12. For a numerically insignificant community, the list of dignitaries in every field is endless. Sir Jamsetjee Jeejeebhoy, the first Baronet, Sir Nes Wadia, Dinshaw Jamsetjee Petit, the philanthropists, Sir Cowasjee Jehangir, the Patron of Art, Jamsetjee Tata, Homi Mody and Godrej, the industrialists, Behram Malabari, the social reformer, Homi Bhabha, the scientist, Sir Phirozshah Mehta, Sir Dadabhai Naoroji, Sir Dinshaw Wacha, Madam Bhicaji Cama, the nationalist leaders, Sir Dinshaw Mulla, the legal luminary and member of the judicial committee of the Privy Council and so on.

13. Jain, M.P., *Outlines of Indian Legal History*, Bombay: N.M. Tripathi (1966) (2nd edn.), p.59.

14. As shown by a case decided on 16 December 1817 by the Court of Appeal of Surat Adawlut, *Kaoosjee Roostumjee v. Mt. Awan Baee*, the matters concerning marriage and control over women's sexuality were regulated by Modees, Dustoors and members of the Parsi *unjoomun* and bigamous marriages were permitted under certain conditions. The case is discussed in *Mihirwanjee Nuoshirwanjee v Awan Baee*, Borradaile's Reports SDA Vol.I 1800–1824, pp.231–8.

15. Framjee, D., *The Parsees*, p.99.

16. Succession to *Parsees Immovable Property Act,* 1837, Act IX of 1837.

17. In 1828, a questionnaire was administered to the Parsis of Surat by Borradaile, who was assigned the task of recording the customs of various castes in the Gujarat region. The Surat Parsis did not respond to the questionnaire. So the Bombay Parsi Panchayat published it in 1832 and obtained the response of the Bombay Parsis to these queries. Framjee, D., *The Parsees*, p.120.

18. The history of Parsi law reform is based on the report in Roy Chowdhury, S.K. and H.D. Saharay Paruck's *The Indian Succession Act*, Bombay: N.M. Tripathi (1988) (7th edn.), p.73.

19. *Ardeseer Cursetjee v Peerozebai* 6 MIA 348.

20. Roy Chowdhury, S.K. and H.D. Saharay Paruck's *The Indian Succession Act*, p.74.

21. *Matrimonial Causes Act, 1857.*

22. With this, the penal provisions of bigamy under the Penal Code were made applicable to Parsis. But the Act did not have any retrospective effect and marriages contracted prior to the enactment could not be governed by the penal provisions. See Manchanda, S., *Parsi Law in India*, Allahabad: The Law Book Co. (1991) (5th edn.), p.14.

23. See the decisions in *Manchersha v Kamirunissa Begum* 5 BHCR 109 and *Mithibai v Limji N. Banaji* ILR 5 Bom 506.

24. *Dinsha Petit (Sir) v Jamsetji Jeejeebhoy (Sir)* (1909) ILR 33 Bom 509.
25. *Saklat v Bella* 1925 ILR 53 The court held that in a marriage between a Parsi woman and a non-Parsi man, there is a presumption that the wife will have to accept the religious faith of her husband. So it would follow that the children will be brought up according to the religion of the father.
26. This principle was borrowed from the then progressive Islamic law in 1865.
27. The Amending Act XVII of 1939.
28. Mentioned in the Statement of Objects and Reasons of the Act (Gazette of India, 1934, Part V p.221).
29. The non-concurrence of the rest of the associations was explained by Sir Phiroze Sethna as, 'This opposition chiefly comes from a small section who are ultra conservative in their views and do not, as a rule, approve of any changes in keeping with the changing times.'
30. *LAD* IV 1935, pp. 3246-7; *LAD* V, 1936, pp. 4149-53. Also see Parashar, A., *Women and Family Law Reform in India*, New Delhi: Sage Publications (1992), pp. 192-3.
31. The *Parsi Marriage and Divorce (Amendment) Act* 1988 (Act No.5 of 1988).
32. S. 32 (a), (b), (c), (e) and (g) of the Act.
33. For a discussion on the Inheritance laws, see *LSD* 10th Series, VI/10 4 December 1991, pp.662-7; 5 December 1991 pp.442-51.

10

Political Reformulation of Christian Personal Law

Introduction

The process of tracing the developments within the Christian personal law is far more complex than that of other religious communities, i.e. Hindus, Muslims and Parsis discussed in the preceding chapters. At one level the Christians are governed by the pioneering statutes which revolutionalized the scheme of personal laws in India and set the parameters of reform for all communities. At the other, these statutes have remained static for well over a century, while the other communities have made some attempts to keep abreast with the changing trends in matrimonial laws in the western world. Hence the statutes have now become archaic and redundant. This dichotomy is enmeshed within the political events which reduced Christianity from its hallowed position of being the religion of the colonial masters to the religion of an insignificant minority in the post-colonial phase.

Apart from this, two other factors of historical significance have also contributed to the complexity; (i) The laws governing Christians are shaped by two distinct colonial influences, the Anglo-Saxon jurisprudence introduced by the British and the continental system introduced by the French and the Portuguese within their respective territories (ii) The post-independence attempts of reform are marked by the conflict between the conservative Roman Catholic doctrine and the reformist Protestant theology which has its roots within European politics.

The concept of marriage as a permanent bond has gone through a full cycle, with the early churches of Orthodox traditions permitting customary forms of marriage and divorce; the medieval church of Latin rites evolving the doctrine of sacramental indissolubility, with the medieval European church moving in to regulate marriages through canon law and ecclesiastical courts[1] and the reformist Protestant traditions reformulating marriages as civil and dissoluble contracts to be regulated by state enactments.[2]

Keeping the above mentioned global trends in view, in this chapter an attempt is made to trace the complex legal history of the Indian Christian community, the attempts at reform in the post-independence period and recent judicial interventions.

10.1 Christianity in India and its Diverse Origins

While homogeneity is the characteristic of the Parsis, the Christian community is marked by its diversity. As per the 1991 census, Christians constitute 2.32 per cent of the total Indian population. Christians in India belong to three different traditions: (i) the Orthodox churches of west Asian traditions, i.e. Syro Malabar, Syro Malankara, the Mar Thoma Church etc.; (ii) the Roman Catholic Church of Latin rites and (iii) the various reformist churches of Protestant traditions now consolidated into the Church of South India (CSI) and the Church of North India (CNI).[3] There also exists a large population of Christians among various tribes, particularly in the north-east region. These tribes are granted protection under the constitution in respect of their culture, tradition, customs and laws[4] and hence are not governed by the Christian personal laws.

It is believed that Christianity was first brought into India by a disciple of Jesus Christ, Saint Thomas, soon after the crucifixion in the first century. As per the oral history, Saint Thomas landed on the Malabar coast. A church in Quilon is believed to have been built by the saint.[5] The Christianity of this period was affiliated to the orthodox traditions of west Asia, i.e. Syria, Armenia, Antiochia and also Constantinople.

The Indian Christian community of this early period, concentrated along the south-western coastland, was loosely structured and was assimilated with the local communities. The Christian priests were invited to participate in local rituals like *chattam* and *sradhas* and the non-Christians joined the Christians in their annual pilgrimage to the tomb of Saint Thomas.[6] The priests were not governed by a separate dress code or celibacy and Christian marriages were not indissoluble unions. Hence divorce and remarriage was accepted.

The second phase of conversion was carried out in the sixteenth century after the Portuguese established the trade routes and conquered a few Indian territories. As the popular saying goes, the white man landed on the Indian shores with a sword in one hand and a cross in the other. The conquests of this period were concentrated along the western (Konkan) coast. In 1550, the Pope (the Patriarch of the Church of Rome) entered into a pact with the Portuguese king to evangelize the newly acquired territories and in return granted the king a voice in the appointment of bishops in these territories.[7] The popular saint of this period, Saint Francis Xavier, landed in Goa in May 1542[8] and travelled along the western coast and instituted the Roman Catholic church in India.[9] The evangelists were engaged not only in proselytizing but in Latinizing the Thomas Christians of west Asian traditions.[10]

The third phase of Christianity is the Protestantism and the theology of enlightenment brought in by the missionaries of various European and American churches during the nineteenth and twentieth centuries.[11]

While being shaped by the European philosophies of the conservative and highly institutionalized Roman Catholic Church and the liberal and loosely structured Protestant theology, the indigenous Christian community also incorporated the local customs, traditions and languages resulting in wide regional diversities. The converted Christians also retained their pre-conversion caste hierarchies.[12]

10.2 Family Laws Governing Christian Communities

The laws governing the Christian communities have three distinct sources, i.e. the statutes enacted by the British in the nineteenth century; the Civil Code introduced by the Portuguese and the French within their colonies and the local customary laws. In addition, the Roman Catholics are governed by a dual system of civil law and canon law. Since the Roman Catholic church does not recognize divorce, to deal with the practical aspect of breakdown of marriages, it provides for liberal grounds of annulment under a legal fiction that marriages which are annulled were not valid marriages in the first place. This legal fiction enables the church to hold on to its dogma of indissolubility *vis-à-vis* the Protestant doctrine and at the same time provide for dissolution of broken marriages. Since Protestants are not saddled with the doctrine of sacramental indissolubility, a civil dissolution of the contract of marriage is recognized by the Protestants as valid.[13]

Until the nineteenth century, the converted Christians followed the local customary practices of pre-conversion traditions in respect of property inheritance and marriage rituals. The concept of a distinct Christian personal law evolved much later, i.e. only during the later half of the nineteenth century with statutory enactments introduced by the British and the Portuguese.

The two initial statutes enacted by the British were meant only to aid the process of proselytization. The *Caste Disabilities Removal Act* (or the Freedom of Religion Act) of 1850, was aimed at protecting the Christian converts from disinheritance from their respective families.[14] The *Native Converts Marriage Dissolution Act* of 1866 provided for the dissolution of the converts' marriages contracted prior to conversion.

Later, two more statutes were enacted to regulate Christian marriages. The *Indian Divorce Act* (IDA) of 1869 was modelled on the British matrimonial statute, the *Matrimonial Causes Act of 1857*[15] and provided for adultery as the sole matrimonial offence (which, as far as the wife was concerned, had to be coupled with either cruelty, desertion, incest or bestiality). The later enactment, the *Indian Christian Marriage Act* (ICMA) of 1872, provided for the solemnization and regulation of Christian marriages. The primary aim was to extend to the British and other Europeans the beneficial provisions of the English statute. The inclusions of indigenous Christians was only incidental, as a careful reading of the ICMA reveals.[16]

The subsequent British enactments liberalized divorce and by 1937, adultery, cruelty, desertion and insanity were made into independent grounds of divorce in England. Attempts were made to incorporate these liberal grounds into the laws governing Parsis, Muslims and Hindus in subsequent years through the enactment of *Parsi Marriage and Divorce Act* of 1936, the *Dissolution of Muslim Marriages Act* of 1939 and the *Hindu Marriage Act* of 1955. Ironically, during the period 1935–1955, when the three religious communities went through a process of remoulding their laws along the Anglo-Saxon matrimonial principles, there were no attempts to modernize the Christian family laws.

Two diverse factors, one political and the other legal, could have led to this stalemate. The political factor being that perhaps the nationalist leaders viewed the Christian religion (and laws) as the religion of the colonial masters, which would not warrant any reform through nationalist interventions. Absence of an Indian Christian political leader of repute within the nationalist movement, perhaps resulted in the invisibility of issues concerning indigenous Christians.

The legal factor being that the *Indian Divorce Act* of 1869 (modelled on the English statute of 1857) was so structured as to automatically incorporate the developments in the English matrimonial statutes within its scheme.[17] The comments of the Full Bench ruling of the Madras High Court in 1936 are revealing. While interpreting S.7 of IDA, the court held:

> The Indian courts have to keep pace with the practices in England and to note changes that are made in the principles and rules of the English divorce law from time to time since the English statute is the parent law.[18]

Hence, the necessity of statutory reform may not have arisen.

After independence, the changes in the political structure brought about a new status for indigenous Christians who were now reduced to the status of a politically insignificant minority. But the community continued to be governed by archaic and unreformed British statutes of the Victorian era.

Another significant development of the post-independence reformulation was that the dominant Protestant ideology with which the Christian community in British India was governed during the colonial rule, was replaced by the Roman Catholic Church, which became politically the most powerful among all the constituents of the Church in India. The Victorian ideology of indissolubility of marriage fitted in well with the Roman Catholic doctrine and the Catholic Church became an ardent supporter of a statute enacted by the British (Protestant) government and resisted any attempt of reform.

The Civil Code of Goa: Roughly around the time of British reforms, the Portuguese colonies of Goa, Daman and Diu also introduced a comprehensive civil code in 1867 in keeping with the European trend of separation of church and state.[19] Based on the French Civil Code (also known as the Napoleon Code), it contained among other civil matters, provisions regulating marriage and succession.

The French code was evolved in reaction to the Roman law of pre-industrial Europe which advocated the doctrine of dissolubility of marriage and also deprived married women of their right to own property. Hence, granting married women the right over property became a predominant feature of the French code. Under this code, the principles of common matrimonial property and pre-marriage agreements in respect of the separate property of the spouses were granted legal recognition. These were revolutionary principles which secured married women crucial economic rights.

The Portuguese code introduced in Goa is based on similar principles. Validation of ante-nuptial (pre-marriage) agreements in respect of the separate property of the spouses[20], protection of a woman's separate property by way of gifts and inheritance.[21] and joint ownership of matrimonial property[22] are significant features of the Goan Code which are not found in any matrimonial statutes founded on English common law traditions. Since the wife is deemed as the joint owner, the property cannot be disposed off without her consent.[23] The restraint upon testamentary disposition is another important provision. Within the scheme of joint ownership, the husband can dispose off only half of his property by a will.[24] The widow also has a right to retain possession of property until it is partitioned and a share is allotted to her.[25]

While these are positive, pro-women stipulations, the code also contains several discriminatory aspects. The power of managing all the properties of the conjugal society is vested on the husband and only in his absence is the wife empowered to manage it. But even in these circumstances, she cannot alienate any immovable property without the authorization of the family council.[26] The husband cannot be deprived of his right of administering the family properties including those which belong to the wife through an ante-nuptial agreement.[27] The initial code also contained a provision restraining the wife from publishing her writings without the consent of her husband.[28] But these provisions must be viewed within the context of the nineteenth century European traditions.

While the initial code provided only for legal separation, in

1911, the right of divorce both by contest and consent was granted statutory recognition.[29] Under Article 2 of the Law of Marriage enacted in 1911, marriages were rendered as civil contracts which had to be compulsorily registered.[30]

In the debate on UCC, the Goan Code is projected as the model of uniformity for the rest of India.[31] This projection is based on an erroneous understanding of the Goan code which, in fact, grants recognition to various customary practices including Hindu polygamy.[32] The situation in Goa is unique as compared to the rest of the country. Here Hindus are granted the customary right of polygamy, while Muslims are governed by the principle of monogamy. Neither a nikah nor a talaq is recognized and Muslim marriages and divorces are regulated by the code. The fact that this situation has not led to any political controversy can be attributed to the non-politicization of the issues concerning Muslim minorities, who in any case are numerically insignificant (as per 1971 census, 3.76 per cent).[33]

The code also grants certain concessions to Catholics who were the dominant segment. While marriages of other communities have to be performed in the office of the Registrar, a Catholic marriage is valid only when solemnized before a minister of church in accordance with canon law. Hence the sacramental aspect of only a Catholic marriage is granted statutory recognition.[34] An annulment granted by an ecclesiastical tribunal is also granted automatic recognition.[35] Hence, the Catholics in Goa do not have to go through a dual process of obtaining a civil divorce and a canonical annulment as the Catholics in the rest of India. After the liberation in 1961, Goa, Daman and Diu were incorporated into the Indian nation as union territories. But at this time, the Hindu Code Bill or the personal laws of other religious communities were not made applicable to these territories and the laws which were in force were allowed to be retained.[36]

While the Goan Code would provide useful guidelines regarding the concept of community of property, its claim to a model of uniformity cannot be substantiated. The positive and the negative aspects of the code cannot be isolated from the context of the Continental legal system, as well as the colonial policies of the Portuguese within which it is located. The legal system, which worked well for a small and homogenized territory under the rule of assimilation cannot be applied to a vast and pluralistic nation which was governed for about two hundred years by the British policy of divide and rule.[37]

Customary Laws of Succession: In matters of succession, the Christian subjects of British India were governed by the provisions of *Indian Succession Act* of 1865 (re-enacted in 1925). The *Indian Succession Act* of 1925 is a progressive piece of legislation which grants equal rights to daughters and sons in the parental property. The concept of ancestral property or coparcenary is also not recognized by this Act. Hence it granted better rights to women than the Hindu legal system (including the *Hindu Succession Act* of 1956), as well as the Muslim and Parsi (until it was amended in 1991) legal systems. But this legislation seemed to apply mainly to Europeans and other foreigners than to Indian Christians, as large sections of the Christian community governed by customary laws were excluded from the application of this Act.[38]

As already mentioned, even after conversion, communities continued to follow the pre-conversion laws regarding succession. Most Christian communities followed the rule of coparcenary or joint Hindu family property. The leading case on this issue is *Abraham v Abraham*[39] decided by the Privy Council in 1863. The case concerned the issue of succession to the property of a Roman Catholic who had subsequently converted to the Protestant religion. The dispute was between the widow and her husband's brother. The brother pleaded that although they had converted to Christianity they continued to follow the Hindu law of coparcenary. While holding that the property is joint, the Privy Council laid down the rule regarding conversion as follows:

> The profession of Christianity releases the convert from the trammels of the Hindoo law but it does not of necessity involve any change of the rights or relations of the convert in matters with which Christianity has no concern such as his rights and interests in and his powers over property.

But subsequently, the *Indian Succession Act* came into force and when the issue came up before the court again in 1886, the Madras High Court, in *Tellis v Saldanha*[40] held, that after the enactment of the *Indian Succession Act*, the Christian converts are governed by the provisions of the *Indian Succession Act*. The case concerned Roman Catholics of Mangalore who had converted several centuries ago. While the widow pleaded the application of the *Indian Succession Act*, the brother of the deceased pleaded that they are converts from a Brahmin sect and are governed by the Mitakshara law of coparcenary. But a subsequent decision of the Bombay High Court in the year 1907, dissented from the view expressed in *Tellis v Saldanha* and held that Christians are governed by the Hindu law of coparcenary.[41] The customs were also granted validity under S.5 of the *Punjab Laws Act* 1872.

Despite the enactment of the *Hindu Succession Act* of 1956 which improved the situation of Hindu women and granted daughters and wives a share in the parental property (but not in the ancestral property), Christians continued to be governed by the discriminatory provisions of the uncodified Hindu law, which denied daughters a share in the parental property.[42] In 1957, the Cochin and Travancore High Courts affirmed that Christians in the region are not governed by the *Indian Succession Act* and the discriminatory statutes enacted by the princely states apply to them.[43]

In 1974, a single judge of the Madras High Court adopted a progressive stand and ruled that the *Travancore Succession Act* stood repealed after independence and Christians in the region are not governed by this discriminatory statute but by the *Indian Succession Act*.[44] But this decision was overruled in 1978 by the Full Bench of the Madras High Court which reaffirmed that Christians in the state are governed neither by the progressive provisions of the *Indian Succession Act* nor by the *Hindu Succession Act* but by the uncodified Hindu customary law and under this law, the brother is the sole heir to the father's property to the exclusion of the daughter.[45] The controversy was finally resolved in a ruling given by the Supreme Court in Mary Roy's case.[46] The court struck down the discriminatory provisions on a technical ground that after independence the laws enacted by the erstwhile princely states, which were not expressly saved have been repealed. While the repeal was welcome and overdue, the court restrained itself from examining the provision under the constitutional mandate of equality and non-discrimination on the ground of sex under Articles 14 and 15 of the Constitution which could have set the precedent for examining gender discrimination under other personal laws.[47]

10.3 Law Commission Recommendations and Community Based Initiatives

Amongst the several discriminatory provisions of their personal laws, the narrow and constrained ground of divorce has caused the greatest hardships to Christian women. Cruelty and desertion do not constitute independent grounds of divorce. Under S.10 of the *Indian Divorce Act*, the husband's grounds of divorce are also constrained but he can obtain a divorce on the ground of adultery *simpliciter*, whereas the wife has to prove an additional ground either of cruelty or desertion. Since adultery is extremely difficult to prove, and not all husbands who treat their wives with cruelty or desert them also commit adultery, Christian women face great hardships and are discriminated against both *vis-à-vis* Christian men and *vis-à-vis* women governed by other matrimonial statutes. Though subsequently, cruelty to wives has become an offence under the penal code, such cruelty does not entail the Christian wife to a divorce.[48] The hindrance to reform has been caused by the Catholic dogma and the Protestant women have been the worst sufferers as their religion does not even subscribe to the theory of stringent divorce. Christian women (and more specifically, the Protestant women) set the task of reforming the archaic divorce laws as their first priority. These attempts have had a long and checkered history.

To initiate the process of reform, private member's bills were introduced in Parliament in 1958–1959 and in response, the matter was referred to the Law Commission (LC).[49] A draft bill titled, *The Christian Marriage and Matrimonial Causes Bill, 1960* was circulated by the LC to religious leaders and community organizations. The representatives of the Roman Catholic Church raised the plea that in adherence to the canonical doctrine, the Catholic community should be exempted from its application. The LC overruled these objections on the basis that the provision of divorce exists since 1869 and the Church had not raised any objection to this relief. The proposed bill was merely widening the scope of the existing provision and was not providing for any new reliefs.[50] After ascertaining the views of representatives of the community, a comprehensive report (*Fifteenth Report*) was prepared and submitted to the Ministry of Law by the LC on 19 August 1960. Due to the resentment expressed by the Catholic church hierarchy to the proposed Bill, the government returned the Bill with a request to further elicit public opinion.[51] Some of the clauses in the proposed Bill were re-examined and a Report (Twenty-Second Report) was submitted to the Law Ministry in December 1961. Following the recommendations of the LC, the government introduced the Christian Marriage and Matrimonial Causes Bill (Bill LXII B of 1962) in the Lok Sabha.[52] But the Bill was not debated and lapsed in 1971.

In 1983, in response to the letters received from Christian women, under the Chairmanship of Justice K.K. Mathew, the LC again took up the limited question of amending S. 10 of IDA.[53] After considering various options, the LC made a strong recommendation for amending the discriminatory provision as follows:

> If the Parliament does not remove the discrimination, the Courts in exercise of their jurisdiction to remedy violations of fundamental rights, are bound some day, to declare the section as void .... The Ninetieth Report of the LC was submitted to the Law Ministry in May 1983, but despite the recommendations, the government did not introduce the amendments in Parliament.[54]

This set in motion a chain reaction within the community which culminated in the Marriage Bill of 1994. Jyotsna Chatterjee, Director of Joint Women's Programme (JWP), a branch of the Christian (Protestant) institute for the Study of Religion and Society, mobilized community support and a memorandum signed by around ten thousand people, was sent to the Union Law Minister demanding changes in the personal laws.[55]

In February, 1986, members of various Women's Fellowships of the Churches in Delhi, representing the opinion of a wide cross-section of the Christian community, presented a memorandum to the Prime Minister of India.[56] It seemed that without the approval of the religious hierarchy, the government would not respond. So Jyotsna Chatterjee, with the backing of Church of North India (CNI) drafted a bill titled *'Christian Marriages and Matrimonial Causes Bill, 1988'* (CMMC), which was sent to the representatives of various churches.[57] At a Conference organized by CNI at Delhi, which was attended by representatives of various churches, as well as representatives of the Law Commission and Minorities Commission, a broad consensus among the various churches was arrived at. The Catholic church supported the recommendation to repeal the IDA, the provision of automatic recognition of church annulments by civil courts as in Goa but instead of a new Bill providing for divorce, suggested a *via media* that provisions of the *Special Marriage Act*, 1954 should apply to all marriages solemnized under ICMA.[58] This was a tactical and face-saving move which would save the church embarrassment that may be caused even by a tacit acquiescence to a Bill liberalizing divorce.[59] The rigid stand of the Catholic clergy was resented by the Catholic laity and several Catholic organizations extended their support to the proposed Bill.[60] Due to pressure from these organizations, finally, the Catholic church relented from its rigid and orthodox stand and withdrew its opposition to the proposed Bill. Following this, a broad forum titled, 'Ecumenical Committee for Changes in Christian Personal Laws' was formed, consisting of representatives of various churches, as well as secular organizations. The Committee finalized three draft Bills dealing with (i) marriage, divorce, custody, maintenance and right to matrimonial property; (ii) succession; and (iii) adoption. The Catholic Bishops Conference of India (CBCI), 27 Member Churches of the National Council of Churches in India (NCCI) and some other independent churches of west Asian traditions extended their support to the draft bills.[61]

Despite these sustained, systematic and marathon efforts, the government did not introduce the Bills. When a question regarding the status of these Bills was raised in Parliament, the government gave an evasive reply to the effect that the Joint Women's Programme, a women's organization had submitted certain draft legislations relating to marriage, divorce, adoption, maintenance and succession. Further, that since the policy of the government had been not to interfere with the personal laws of the minority communities, unless the necessary initiative came from the community concerned it would not be possible to bring in reform. The government also assured the house that the matter was being referred to the Minorities Commission.[62] These comments undermined the decade-long efforts initiated by community leaders and women's organizations to arrive at a consensus within the community to present a united front to the government. With this statement, the ball was thrown back to the religious hierarchy to reaffirm its commitment to Law Reform and women's concerns were once again made subject to the vagaries of the religious dogmas. This was a cause of concern for the community, as the response of the religious clergy to this new challenge could be highly unpredictable.

Through a stroke of luck, the bills endorsed by NCCI and CBCI were submitted to the government through the Minority Commission on 27 October 1997.[63] But while the community was awaiting eagerly for the presentation of the Bills to the Parliament, the government lost its majority and mid-term polls were declared. This political development has again delayed the process of reform. During the last round of deliberations, for reasons best known to the leaders, the consolidated Bill for marriage and divorce has been shelved and two separate Bills titled, *The Christian Marriage Bill* and *The Indian Divorce Bill* have been submitted along the lines of the current statutes. The provisions of matrimonial remedies have been brought on par with the *Hindu Marriage Act* and the *Special Marriage Act* with the additional provision of community of property or joint matrimonial property.

The thwarted efforts of Christian reforms, in comparison to the successive efforts of the Parsi reforms, reveal that in this political game, there is more to reform than a mere initiative from within the community as is publicly propagated. Perhaps there are extraneous considerations which have a bearing on the issue which can only be hinted at:

i. Except in pockets like Kerala, Goa and the north-east India, the community has neither the numerical weightage of the Muslims nor the economic clout of the Parsis. Hence, issues concerning women from this insignificant minority do not warrant serious political debate and can safely be rendered invisible.

ii. The Christian reforms were not initiated by the Church hierarchy of male leaders. Initiatives by women met with hostility from the conservative church leadership. Since the women's groups which supported the initiatives were mainly of an autonomous nature, they could not create the required political pressure to bring in legislative reforms. The government did not take a serious note of the initiatives by women as compared to the Parsi reforms initiated by the liberal male community leadership.

iii. The diverse viewpoints hindered the process of reforms. The community could not present a unified view to the government, as was the case with Parsi reforms. The government did not want to antagonize the conservative and politically powerful Catholic church.

iv. By the time the Catholic church withdrew its opposition and a unanimous front could be presented to the government in 1994, (in the post-Babri Masjid phase), the political climate had deteriorated as compared to the period when the reforms in Parsi law were enacted. The Hindu communal forces made the demand for a UCC an important political plank. Introduction of the Bill reforming Christian law would give an opportunity for the Hindu communal forces to rake the controversy and cause embarrassment to the ruling government. The minority Congress government led by the Rao ministry or the subsequent coalition government of the United Front could not afford this political impediment or to antagonize its Muslim supporters. What is the fate of this Bill in the hands of the new government is yet to be seen?

10.4 Constitutional Validity of Discriminatory Provisions

Confronted with this intricate political maze, the courts became the only avenue left for the community to bring in marginal respite. The constitutional validity of the discriminatory provisions of S.10 of IDA was first challenged before the Madras High Court in Dwarakabai's case. Adopting an extremely anti-women posture, the court ruled that the discrimination is based on a sensible and reasonable classification, after taking into consideration the ability of men and women and the results of their acts and hence it is not arbitrary. The court explained this logic further as follows:

> Adultery by a man is different from adultery by wife. A husband cannot bear a child and make it legitimate to be maintained by the wife. But if the wife bears a child the husband is bound to maintain it.[64]

Later judgments departed from this extremely sexist premise, but the courts refrained from striking down the offensive provisions as unconstitutional. In 1968, the Madras High Court held that the *Indian Divorce Act* is wholly out of date.[65] In 1989, a special bench of the Calcutta High Court in *Swapna Ghose v Sadananda Ghosh*[66] ruled that the offensive provision 'smacks of sex-discrimination.' The judgment also quoted with approval the recommendations of the *Ninetieth Report* of the Law Commission while it observed that if Parliament did not amend the offensive provision, the courts would be compelled to strike it down as unconstitutional. It however, stopped short of striking down the section as unconstitutional.

In 1990, in an interim application, in Mary Sonia Zachariah's case, the Kerala High court, set a time limit and directed the Government of India to give effect to the recommendations of the Law Commission within six months of the order.[67] But the government at the centre ignored these directions. So in February, 1995, in a landmark judgment, the Full Bench of the Kerala High Court stuck down the offensive provisions of S.10 of the IDA as arbitrary and violative of Articles 14 and 21 of Constitution.[68]

The court held:

> The legal effects of the provisions of S. 10 is to compel the wife who is deserted or cruelly treated to continue a life as the wife of a man she hates. Such a life will be a sub-human life without dignity and personal liberty. It will be humiliating and oppressive without the freedom to remarry and enjoy life in the normal course. Such a life can legitimately be treated only as a life imposed by a tyrannical or authoritarian law on a helpless deserted or cruelly treated Christian wife quite against her will and will be a life without dignity and liberty ensured by the constitution. Hence the provisions which require the Christian wives to prove adultery along with desertion and cruelty are violative of Article 21 of the Constitution of India.[69]

The community's eagerness to reform their laws can be judged by the number of interveners to the Petition. Protestant churches belonging to CSI, Bishops of the Eastern Orthodox Church, Christian institutions and women's organizations filed affidavits to be included as interveners in support of the petitioners.[70]

Since it was a High Court ruling, its effects were confined only to the State of Kerala. So in the years 1995–96, Christian women filed similar petitions in the Bombay High Court and by a judgment of the Full Bench delivered on 6 April 1997, the Bombay High Court also struck down the discriminatory provisions.[71] Whether Christians in other parts of the country will have to file similar proceedings, or whether the benefits can now be extended to the whole of India through a clarification by the Supreme Court is yet to be seen.

The Christians are also constrained by the denial of the remedy of divorce by mutual consent. The consenting couple has to take the circuitous route of first re-registering their marriage under the provisions of the *Special Marriage Act* and then filing a joint petition for divorce by mutual consent.

When this issue came up for scrutiny before the Supreme

Court, the Court commented that there was no point or purpose to be served by the continuance of a marriage which has so completely and signally broken down and recommended legislative intervention to remedy the situation.[72] But it held that even while adopting a policy of social engineering, the judiciary cannot introduce a new remedy into the matrimonial statutes.[73]

10.5 Judicial Responses to Challenges Posed to the Sovereignty of the Indian State

It is interesting to observe the manner in which the post-independence state established its sovereignty over its Christian subjects *vis-à-vis* two different sources of power, i.e. the statutes enacted by the British Parliament which was deemed as the parent law and the religious hierarchy of the Roman Catholic Ecclesiastical Tribunal.

As already mentioned, under S.7 of the IDA, the principles and rules of English Divorce Courts were to be automatically applied to matrimonial litigations by Christians in British India. The issue before the Madras High Court was whether after declaration of the country as a Republic, it was prudent for a free country, in the administration of justice, to adhere to the principle that the laws and regulations of its colonial masters should continue to be automatically adapted. In 1955, the Full Bench of the Madras High Court held that as per the provisions of the enactment of the *Laws Order Act* of 1950, English laws and procedures should be applied and it directed that the courts must follow the law and practice of the English matrimonial courts.[74]

In 1970, the special bench of the Madras High Court reversed this position and held that S. 7 cannot be read to incorporate the statute of a foreign country as part of the law of the land. But instead of striking down S.7, the court provided an explanation that practices and principles of the English matrimonial courts should be subjected to the scheme of IDA.[75]

In 1995, the Supreme Court in another significant judgment undermined the authority of Ecclesiastical Tribunal by holding that annulments granted by the Tribunal are not valid under the civil law and a couple who has gone through such annulment cannot contract a valid remarriage.[76]

Although Christian marriages are solemnized in church, they are simultaneously registered with a civil authority, i.e. the

Registrar of Births, Deaths and Marriages.[77] This transforms them into civil contracts and these contracts can only be dissolved through a court decree under the provisions of the IDA.[78] But most Christians are unaware of this dual procedure and believe that an annulment granted by the Tribunal qualifies them for remarriage. Since the church will not remarry the couple without a canonical annulment, generally a couple facing problems is encouraged to file a petition with the Tribunal and Christian couples are under the misconception that the annulment granted by the Tribunal constitutes a final dissolution of their marriage.

In the case before the Supreme Court, the woman had remarried after a church annulment. When marital discord arose, the husband approached the court for annulment on two grounds, i.e. i) the wife is insane, and ii) the annulment granted by the church in her earlier marriage is not valid under the civil law and hence her subsequent marriage to him is not valid.

In the proceedings before the trial court, the wife admitted her previous marriage and pleaded that it was annulled by Ecclesiastical Tribunal and this fact was known to the husband. Based on her admission of the earlier marriage, and disregarding her plea of the church annulment, the trial court granted a decree in husband's favour. The woman approached the High Court and not satisfied with its ruling, approached the Supreme Court. Dismissing her appeal, the Supreme Court declared:

> A marriage cannot be dissolved by a declaration granted by the Ecclesiastical Tribunal. Such annulments are not binding on the District Court or the High Court. The Ecclesiastical Tribunal cannot exercise a power parallel to the power which has been vested in the District Court or the High Court by the provisions of the Indian Divorce Act. The Church Authorities would continue to be under disability to perform or solemnize a second marriage for any of the parties until the marriage is dissolved or annulled in accordance with the statutory law in force.[79]

Through these decisions, the state has established its sovereignty over its Christian subjects subordinating the procedures laid down by the colonial state, as well as the religious hierarchy to its laws. This could be interpreted as a welcome move, but these decisions rendered the Christian marriages even more stringent and blocked all avenues of any progressive interventions.

In the case decided in 1955, the lower court had reduced the mandatory period between granting of a decree and its confirmation to six weeks from six months, following the developments under the English matrimonial statutes. But the 1970 judgment reversed this position and restored the period to six months, blocking the process of relaxing the stringent stipulations prescribed in 1869.[80]

In the second instance, the woman had taken recourse to the liberal grounds of annulments under the canon law, as is the common practice. As already mentioned, Christians to a large extent are unaware of the dual procedures. Due to its rigid stand on divorce, information about a civil decree of divorce is not easily forthcoming.[81] By subsequently holding such marriage as invalid, the stranglehold round Christian married women seems to have been tightened.

This judgement also raises other issues of legal ethics. In a situation of limited grounds of divorce, advocates are bound to exploit all possible legal loopholes to aid their clients. A common tactic adopted by advocates who specialize in Christian divorces is to advise their clients to file for a civil decree of annulment on the grounds either of relative impotency, insanity or fraud. It does seem that the legal strategy to question the validity of the marriage was formulated in the lawyer's chamber as can be seen from the two grounds pleaded by the husband: (i) insanity of the wife; and (ii) a technical ground of invalidity of marriage due to inadequate annulment.

As pleaded by the wife, the second husband had married the woman with the full knowledge of her previous marriage and its annulment by the church. So his act of entering into a marriage with her would amount to collusion and connivance. Matrimonial statutes specifically bar parties from taking advantage of their own wrongs while claiming reliefs. Since the remarriage was performed by the church with full knowledge of the previous annulment, it would seem that by the act of solemnizing her second marriage, the church led the woman into believing that the annulment, as well as the remarriage are legally valid and binding.[82] But finally, exploiting the procedural lapses, the husband was able to turn the situation in his favour, while rendering the woman a convenient scapegoat of a complicated legal maze. The Supreme Court seems to have aided this manipulation on the part of the husband and his advocate.

The judgement is a stark reminder that reforms cannot be confined to statutes but must extend to coherent and simple drafting style, easily comprehensible procedures and adequate dissemination of legal information regarding crucial issues like solemnization of marriages, their validity, women's rights within invalid marriages, their rights to custody and maintenance etc. Acknowledging the fact that literacy levels, in any given social strata, are lower for women and further, women would find it more difficult to access legal information under the prevailing socio-economic conditions, an additional responsibility is cast on the state by Art. 15 (3) of the Constitution to protect the rights of women and children. The state must ensure that the naive and the unassuming do not become victims of manipulative tactics adopted by legal practitioners. But it appears that the Supreme Court did not concern itself with this constitutional mandate while delivering this judgement invalidating an existing marriage. The only fault on the part of the woman seems to be her inadequate knowledge of the complicated and archaic law which governs her life.

In conclusion, it must be emphasized that to unravel the legal maze within which the Christian family laws are ensnared, a whole range of legal reforms are necessary and imperative. Unfortunately, even though the community is ready and willing, the political will to legislate for them is sadly lacking.

Notes

1. By the twelfth century the Western Church began to enact legislations for marriages of Christians. Pope Alexander III clarified the principle of indissolubility, declaring that once a Christian sacramental marriage was consummated no power on earth could dissolve it. Monterio, R., 'Belief, Law, and Justice for Women,' in *Economic and Political Weekly*, XXVII/43 & 44 (1992), pp., WS-74, 77.

2. In 1800, under the French Civil Code the power to regulate marriages shifted from the church to the state and thereafter the concept of contractual dissolubility was introduced. Gradually, the doctrine of separation of state and church and marriages as dissoluble contracts spread throughout Europe and later to the colonies.

3. Formation of these federations is a post-independence phenomenon. The Church of South India (CSI) was formed on 7 September 1947, within a month of India attaining independence. See note 11, p.73. The formation of Church of North India (CNI) is a more recent development of the seventies.

4. Article 371 A (Nagaland), 371 B (Assam) and 371 C (Manipur) of the Constitution of India.

5. It is believed that the trade routes between south India and west Asia were in existence from the tenth century BC during the time of King Solomon and Queen Sheba. See Mundadan, A.M., *History of Christianity in India Upto Sixteenth Century*, Bangalore: The Church History Association of India (1982), Vol.I p.20. Major religions of west Asia, i.e. Judaism, Christianity, Islam and Zorastrianism entered India through this trade route.

6. Thekkedath, J., *History of Christianity in India—1542–1700*, Bangalore : The Church History Association of India (1982), Vol.II, p.27.

7. Ibid., p.5.

8. Ibid., p.1.

9. Various religious orders, i.e. Franciscans, Jesuits, Augustinians and Dominicans set up their institutions in the coastal regions of Goa, Konkan and Bassein. Ibid., p.6.

10. Of particular significance is the Synod of Diamper which was held in 1599, through the initiatives by Archbishop Menezes. Ibid., p.28.

11. The Methodist Church, Anglican Church Mission, Church of Scotland Mission, Danish Missionary Society, Leipzig Evangelical Lutheran Mission, Free Church Mission, American Madurai Mission etc. See Grafe, H. *History of Christianity in India: Tamil Nadu in the Nineteenth and Twentieth Centuries*, Bangalore: The Church History Association of India (1982), Vol.IV (Part 2), p.24–34.

12. Ibid., p.98, Thekkedath, J., History of Christianity in India—1542–1700, p.23.

13. One of the fundamental differences between Roman Catholic and Protestant doctrines in the West is their diagonally opposite view on divorce. The Council of Trent rejected the opinion propounded by Luther and other reformers that marriage should be made into a civil contract and should be brought under the jurisdiction of civil courts. See Diwan, P., *Law of Marriage and Divorce*, Allahabad: Wadhwa & Company (1988), p.17.

14. Apart from Christians, the Act also protected persons converted to reformist sects like Brahmos and Arya Samajis who suffered loss of caste. The principle was first introduced through S.9 of the Regulation VII of 1832 of the Bengal Code. In 1850, the principle contained in the Bengal Code was made applicable throughout British India. It was a very brief Act consisting of only one section.

15. Under the provisions of this Act, the matrimonial jurisdiction was transferred from the ecclesiastical courts to the civil courts and the remedy of divorce was provided on a narrow and stringent ground of adultery (coupled with other offences). Prior to this a divorce could only be obtained through an Act of Parliament, a procedure which was extremely expensive. This statute rendered divorces within the reach of commoners.

16. For instance, Part IV of the ICMA lays down special procedure for registering the marriages of native Christians.

17. S.7 of IDA provides as follows: Court to act on principles of English Divorce Court.

18. *Sumathi Ammal v D. Paul* AIR 1936 Mad 324 FB.
19. The code became enforceable in the colonies w.e.f. 1 July 1870.
20. Art.1096. The ante-nuptial agreements could not be revoked after marriage (Art.1105), thus providing further security to women.
21. Arts. 1134–77.
22. Arts. 1130–33.
23. Art. 1119.
24. Art. 1766.
25. Art. 1122.
26. Arts. 1189 & 1190.
27. Art. 1104.
28. Art. 1187.
29. Ch. I, II & III of the *Decree of Divorce* promulgated on 3 November 1910. The enactment came into force w.e.f. 26 May 1911.
30. Art. 3 of the Family Law No. 1 promulgated on 25 December 1910.
31. Vargo N. and R. Goldfaden, 'The Goa Uniform Civil Code—Alive and Kicking,' *The Lawyers* X/7 (1995), p.21.
32. Art. 3 of *Usages & Custom of Gentile Hindus of Goa*. Identical statutes were enacted also for Daman and Diu.
33. The Portuguese did not resort to the divide and rule policy of the British which led to the constitution of Hindus and Muslims as distinct and mutually hostile communities. The Portuguese policy was one of assimilation and codification to facilitate smooth administration and hence various castes within their colonies were listed and their customs and usages were codified. But Muslims in Goa have lived on the periphery of social and political activity and there does not seem to be any categorization of their customs and usages under Portuguese rule.
34. Art. 1069. Also see Chadha, K., 'The Law that breaks the Constitution,' in *The Hindustan Times*, 8 August 1993.
35. Hence the Catholic community in Goa does not have to go through the rigours of a civil divorce, as is the situation in the rest of India under the IDA.
36. S.5 of the *Goa Daman and Diu (Administration) Act, 1962.*
37. In this context, also see the note of caution in the 'Foreword' by Chief Justice Sabyasachi Mukherji to Usgaocar's very useful translation of the Goan Family Code. Usgaocar, M.S., *Family Laws of Goa, Daman and Diu*, Panaji: Vela Associates (1988) Vol II.
38. S.29(2) of the *Indian Succession Act*, 1925.
39. *Abraham v Abraham* (1863) 9 MIA 195.
40. *Tellis v Saldanha* (1986) ILR 10 Mad 69.
41. *Francis Ghosal v Gabri Ghosal* (1907) 31 Bom 25.
42. In *Premchand & Anr v Lilavathi Shanti & Anr* AIR 1956 HP 17, while validating a custom which grants sons the right of inheritance to the exclusion of daughters, the court held that Christians are governed by S. 5 of the *Punjab Laws Act* of 1872 and not by *Indian Succession Act* which grants equal inheritance rights to daughters.
43. *Kurian Augusty v Devassy Alley* AIR 1957 Tra-Co 1.
44. *Solomon v Muthiah* (1974) 1 MLJ 53.

45. D. *Chelliah Nadar & Anr v Lalitha Bai* AIR 1978 Mad 66.
46. *Mary Roy v State of Kerala* AIR 1986 SC 1011. Under the *Travancore Christian Succession Act*, the right of daughter was limited to a quarter of the share of the son or Rs 5000 whichever is less. Under the Cochin *Christian Succession Act* 1922, the share of daughter was one third of the son or Rs 5000, whichever is less.
47. Part B *States (Laws) Act*, 1951.
48. S.498(A) of IPC which was introduced in 1983, makes cruelty to wives and dowry harassment a criminal offence.
49. Fifteenth Report of the Law Commission, p.1.
50. Ibid., p. 26.
51. *Twenty-Second Report of the Law Commission*, p.1.
52. *Gazette of India*, Extraordinary, Part II, S.2, 22 June 62.
53. *Ninetieth Report of the Law Commission*, p.1.
54. Ibid., p.17.
55. I am relying upon a comment made by Archana Parashar to this effect. See Parashar, A., *Women and Family Law Reform in India*, New Delhi: Sage Publications (1992), p.190.
56. Ibid.
57. Two more Bills were also drafted at this time, i.e. Indian Succession Bill 1988 and Indian Christian Adoption Bill 1988.
58. Circular from the Catholic Bishops' Conference of India (CBCI), 90/cir-17, Sub-Christian Marriage Law II, 6 June 90.
59. See note 1.
60. The organizations include: All India Council of Christian Women (AICCW), All India Catholic Union (AICU); Satyashodhak, Bombay; United Christian Women's Association (Prerana), Pune; Justice and Peace Commission, Bombay etc.
61. This fact was brought to the notice of the court by the pleader for the state in *Ammini E.J. v Union of India & Ors* AIR 1995 Ker. 252 FB, p.258.
62. Unstarred question No.752 raised by Shrimati Susheela Gopalan answered on 6 March 1996.
63. A letter from the Secretary, NCCI to the author dated 7 November 1998.
64. *Dwarakabai v Prof. Mainam Mathews* AIR 1953 Mad 792.
65. *Solomon Devasahayam v Chandirah Mary* 1968 MLJ 289.
66. AIR 1989 Cal 1 SB. Also see, *Ramish Francis Toppo v Violet Francis Toppo* 1 (1989) DMC 322 (Cal).
67. *Mary Sonia Zachariah v Union of India & Ors* 1990 (1) KLT 130.
68. *Ammini E.J. v Union of India & Ors* AIR 1995 Ker 252 FB (Also reported as *Mary Sonia Zachariah v Union of India & Ors* 2 (1995) DMC 27 FB.
69. Ibid., head note (B) also para 31.
70. Ibid. para 3.
71. *Pragati Verghese & Ors v Cyril George Verghese & Ors* 1 (1998) DMC 375 (FB).
72. *Jorden Deigdeh v S.S. Chopra* AIR 1985 SC 935.
73. Ibid. Also see the Supreme Court directives in *Reynold Rajamani & Anr v Union of India* AIR 1982 SC 1261.

74. *George Swamidoss Joseph v Harriett Sundari Edward* AIR 1955 Mad 341 FB.
75. *T. M. Bashiam v M. Victor* AIR 1970 Mad 12 SB.
76. *Molly Joseph & Anr v George Sebastian & Anr* 1996 AIR, SCW 4267.
77. Under the provisions of Ss.36, 55 and 62 of the *Indian Christian Marriage Act*, 1872, every person authroized to solemnize Christian marriages is bound to send a copy of all the marriage certificates of the marriages solemnized by him to the Registrar General of Births, Deaths and Marriages at monthly or periodical intervals. Any marriage which is not solemnized as per the provisions of the Act is void as per S.4 of the Act.
78. Here it is necessary to emphasize that although Christian marriages are solemnized in the church they are governed by purely civil statutes, the *Indian Christian Marriage Act*, 1872 and the *Indian Divorce Act*, 1869.
79. See note 72, paras 3 and 5.
80. Several judgements have commented that the statutory waiting period of six months under S.17 of the IDA constitutes procedural unreasonableness. See *Neena v John Pormer* AIR 1985 MP 85 SB; *Swapna Ghosh v Sadananda Ghosh* AIR 1989 Cal 1 SB and *Ramish Francis Toppo v Violet Francis Toppo* 1 (1989) DMC 322 Cal.
81. The Metropolitan Tribunal of the Archbishop of Bombay has clarified the legal position through a pamphlet, *'Questions People Ask About Annulments.'* But the functioning of smaller tribunals is rather haphazard and the legal position ambiguous. See note 1.
82. Under the Goan code, annulments granted by the church are granted recognition by the civil court and the parties do not have to initiate separate proceedings. The proposed reforms include the suggestion of civil ratification of church annulments.

PART FOUR:

CURRENT DEBATES

11

Model Drafts and Legal Doctrines

Introduction

The diverse sources of personal laws, the uneven developments within different communities, politicization of women's rights during colonial rule and the aggressive majoritarianism of recent times provide the backdrop against which an ideal family code will have to be assessed. Although the contemporary debate is more a political rhetoric, there have been some attempts at formulating model drafts during the decade following the Shah Bano judgement. These attempts can broadly be grouped into three categories, i.e. drafts by legal scholars, women's organizations and the official fora. The legal doctrines on which the various recommendations are premised are examined in this chapter in the context of their implications to women's rights and their claim to modernity. The positive and negative features of these drafts, as well as their contradictions and internal inconsistencies are also highlighted.

The drafts are tentative and their aim is to initiate a debate and arrive at a consensus. While some drafts are comprehensive and deal with the entire gamut of personal laws, others address primarily the issues of marriage and matrimonial reliefs. The discussion in this chapter is confined to marriage, divorce, rights upon marriage and its dissolution, with a focus on economic rights of women. While the drafts by legal scholars and the official fora are fully formulated bills, the recommendations from women's organizations are principles and strategies which have yet to be formulated as legal drafts.

The drafts attempt to modernize and bring uniformity into the diverse family laws. The governing principles upon which the provisions rest are equality between the sexes, respect for the status of women and improvement in the conditions of children. Despite the common goal, the measures prescribed for improving the rights of women vary and at times even contradict each other. This is due to the fact that the drafts are premised on two different concepts of equality, the formal and the substantive.[1]

The formal approach to equality is based on equal treatment doctrine, viz. treating likes alike. As per this premise those who are the same or similarly situated must be treated in the same manner. When matrimonial reliefs are based on this approach, a gender neutral term 'spouse' is used while determining the rights of the parties within the matrimonial relationships. This doctrine equalizes the responsibilities and obligations of the husband and the wife who, within the prevailing socio-cultural and economic structures are unequally situated. This approach of treating the unequal partners of a marriage contract, with the mantle of equality will only serve to widen the gender divide.

Conversely, the doctrine of substantive equality directs attention to the question of historic and systemic disadvantage and the actual impact of reform upon the disadvantaged group. The objective of substantive equality is the elimination of the root structure of inequality in society.[2] This approach is not based on equal treatment of the law but addresses the actual impact of the law upon the concerned group. The two approaches to equality would inadvertently result in two different sets of rights and obligations within marriage.

11.1 Drafts by Legal Scholars

The two drafts discussed in this section were formulated during the period immediately following the Shah Bano controversy. During the debate on the *Muslim Women's Bill*, the then Prime Minister, Rajiv Gandhi, proclaimed that the enactment was the first step towards a Uniform Civil Code. This comment seems to have provided the impetus for these formulations.[3] According to the initiators, the drafts are based on the constitutional values of equality, social justice and secularism and incorporate the doctrine of legal pluralism. There is also an assurance that the code would not interfere with the right to religion or the freedom of minorities.[4]

Draft by the Bar Council of India (1986) (Hereafter referred to as the Bar Council draft). There seems to be an immediate response from the Bar Council of India to the Prime Minister's assurance regarding enforcement of a comprehensive family code. At their behest several legal luminaries concerned themselves with the task of drafting the various sections of an entire code. The whole gamut of personal laws, marriage, divorce, maintenance, custody and guardianship of children, adoption, legitimacy, inheritance, succession, implementation machinery and procedures were addressed. The tentative draft was discussed at a three-day National Convention organized by the Bar Council of India at Delhi in October 1986. The convention was attended by judges, lawyers, jurists, law ministers, legislators, law officers and law teachers from all over the country. This seems to be the most broad-based and comprehensive attempt at drafting a code. The recommendations of the convention were submitted to the Prime Minister. But the interest of the Bar Council of India in this issue seems to be one-time, as the Convention did not lead to any public debate or other follow-up measures.

The controversy of compulsory versus optional code seems to have dominated the convention. The initial draft proposed an optional code.[5] There was considerable opposition to this proposal from a section of the participants. The final recommendations have been in favour of a compulsory code with other options built into it[6]. The possibility of exempting certain communities from the application of part of the code or the entire code for a particular period or its implementation in phases has been examined. There was a consensus that sufficient time should lapse after the enactment of the code before it is brought into force. It was also felt that it might be more feasible to introduce reforms within small and specific aspects of personal laws by generating sufficient pressure within communities. There is a note of caution that though the enforcement of a new and progressive code from above may seem as a quick solution, this kind of crude homogenization may not be the best solution[7].

A concern was expressed regarding the style of legislative drafting. The Continental style renders itself to translation more easily and facilitates effective dissemination. It was recommended that this style should be adopted if the message has to permeate to the lower strata of society, than the present British style which is formal and meant mainly for lawyers.[8] But a uniform guideline regarding drafting style was lacking and this experiment seems to have been carried out only in a small portion of the code.

The draft prescribes compulsory registration of marriages and stipulates that a marriage certificate is essential for claiming maintenance.[9] This stipulation would adversely affect the rights of women and children.

A new section, i.e. effect of marriage which could have spelt out concrete matrimonial rights, deals only with irrelevancies like change of surname after marriage, a provision which is not found in any matrimonial statute and is based only on custom and tradition with wide regional variations. As per the stipulations of the draft, a change of surname after marriage seems to be mandatory and the claim to women's liberation lies in an absurd notion of granting the spouses the freedom to use the surname of either of them.[10]

While the draft retains the conventional matrimonial reliefs, the provisions regarding permanent alimony and maintenance during litigation are absent. Instead S.125 Cr.PC has been incorporated to provide for maintenance of wives and children during the subsistence of marriage and after its dissolution. The existing ceiling of Rs 500 per month has been abolished.

The draft protects the children's interests by recognizing them as an independent party during matrimonial litigation and stipulates that unless adequate arrangements are made for protecting children's interests, the matrimonial court should not pass a decree. The property of both parents should be settled in favour of the children so that the welfare of the children is not jeopardized due to paucity of funds.[11] These are positive provisions which would safeguard children's rights.

The draft introduces the concept of joint ownership of matrimonial property.[12] Under this concept all property acquired after marriage is deemed to be the joint property of the spouses. The concept of joint ownership of property was introduced by the French Code (Continental system) and has been subsequently adopted by several legal systems based on principles of English law (Commonwealth systems). Curiously, this right is placed in the section on inheritance rather than as a matrimonial right. Upon breakdown of marriage, the spouses would be entitled to half the share each. Upon death, the surviving spouse will inherit half the property while the other half devolves by testamentary or intestate succession. Property acquired by the spouses prior to marriage is deemed to be their separate property. This includes the customary gifts received by a woman, i.e. stridhana, mehr etc. Introduction of the concept of joint ownership of matrimonial property is a significant development in the realm of women's rights.

Draft by ILS Law College, Pune (1986) (Hereafter referred to as the ILS draft). A Bill titled 'The Indian Marriage and Matrimonial Act of', was presented at a public meeting in Pune in 1986, by ILS Law College. Thereafter, it was discussed at various seminars in Pune, Bombay and other places.[13] The authors cautioned:

The Bill provides for the repeal of all existing matrimonial statutes and to this extent prescribes a compulsory code. But elsewhere the authors have examined possibilities of an optional code or reform within personal laws in keeping with the federal structure of the Indian state.[14] The authors cautioned:

> There is great danger in enforcing a compulsory code in a sudden fashion as it might result in the alienation of the minorities which is not wise from the point of view of national integration. Even the most authoritarian State would avoid doing so. Any enactment of a uniform code must be preceded by a well conceived programme of public education.[15]

Viewed in the context of this concern, the provision of repeal of all existing laws seems to be a contradiction.

In addition to the prevailing matrimonial reliefs, the draft incorporates provisions of maintenance under S. 125 Cr.PC, conviction for bigamy under Ss. 494, 495 and 496 of IPC (which deal with matrimonial offence of bigamy) and punishment for non-payment of maintenance.[16]

The draft provides for compulsory registration of marriages and invalidates non-registered marriages. Not withstanding this stipulation, it seeks to marginally protect the rights of women and children in void marriages by conferring on them the right to maintenance.[17]

Adopting the formal equality model (reflected in the *Hindu Marriage Act*) it provides for maintenance to husbands,[18] a concept which is not prevalent in other statutes, the *Indian Divorce Act*, the Muslim Personal Law and the *Special Marriage Act*) and S.125 of Cr.PC.

Regarding rights to matrimonial property, a vague and confusing provision of the *Hindu Marriage Act*, which confers on the court, jurisdiction over property presented jointly to the parties at the time of marriage is incorporated.[19] Here there is no mention of any other property acquired by the spouses during the subsistence of the marriage, customary gifts, monetary security made to the bride at the time of marriage or the property of either of the spouses acquired prior to the marriage. Perhaps the concept of joint ownership of property is included in a separate bill dealing with inheritance and succession.

11.2 A Critique of the Proposed Drafts

There is no radical departure from the reliefs under the existing matrimonial statutes, The *Hindu Marriage Act*, 1955, the *Special Marriage Act*, 1954 and the *Parsi Marriage and Divorce Act*, 1936, and hence the claim to modernity cannot be sustained. The drafts have retained the conventional matrimonial remedies which were adopted from the English family law principles including the archaic remedy of restitution of conjugal rights, although the same has now been abolished under the English matrimonial statutes.[20]

Leprosy as a matrimonial offence which is a relic of biblical Christianity is retained, despite advances in the field of medicine which have helped to reduce the stigma attached to it. Archaic remedies such as bestiality, sodomy and unnatural sex have been retained. The term 'sodomy' also carries with it a biblical flavour.

Rather surprisingly, the ILS draft has also retained conversion as a matrimonial offence, under a purely civil statute and to this extent undermined the existing provision of the *Special Marriage Act*. The stipulation of conversion as a matrimonial offence had a rationality under religious laws which provided for marriages between persons professing the same religion. Since the draft provides for the solemnization of marriages of two persons belonging to two different religions, it is difficult to comprehend how change of religion can be a matrimonial offence. In any case, grounds such as leprosy, conversion, bestiality, sodomy and unnatural sex are hardly used in the normal course as grounds of divorce and would have more academic than practical use.

The drafts do not provide for maintenance as an ancillary matrimonial relief in matrimonial proceedings and the provisions of S.125 Cr.PC seem to have been substituted for this relief. The drafts recommend the abolition of the ceiling of Rs 500 prescribed under S.125 Cr.PC. While the stipulation for abolishing the ceiling is welcome, such a recommendation has also been made by the Law Commission in its *132nd Report*.[21] But it is not clear whether the right of maintenance will be shifted to a district court from the magistrate's court, where the proceedings are of a summary nature. Also under the prevailing matrimonial statutes, the courts can order lump sum maintenance and settlements. The proposed drafts do not seem to include this very useful provision. The procedures for enforcing an order of a criminal court are more stringent that those of the civil court and hence the provisions of S.125 Cr.PC will provide a better scope for enforcing maintenance orders. But the drafts have not addressed these deeper implications.

The ILS draft has retained the clause linking maintenance to sexual purity. It would be useful to compare the existing provisions regarding this stipulation. Clause (4) of S.125 Cr.PC stipulates that if the woman is living in adultery she is not entitled to maintenance; Clause (5) stipulates that if subsequent to the order, the woman is living in adultery, the husband can move the court to vary the order. In contrast, S.17 (6) of the ILS draft modifies the position and stipulates as under:

> If the Court is satisfied that the party in whose favour an order has been made under this section has had sexual intercourse with any person other than the spouse, it may, at the instance of the other party, vary, modify or rescind any such order in such manner as it may deem just.

Under the prevailing stipulations, the courts have ruled that the words 'living in adultery' used in clauses (4) and (5) of S.125 Cr.PC indicate that isolated instances of adultery are not sufficient to deny the wife maintenance. The husband must prove that the woman is living with another man and that other man is now maintaining the wife. Even when a husband has succeeded in obtaining divorce on the ground of wife's adultery, the wife cannot be denied maintenance.[22] By substituting the words, 'sexual intercourse' to the prevailing phrase, 'living in adultery' the draft narrows the scope of maintenance and renders the situation far worse for women than the prevailing stipulation.

Although an attempt to justify this stipulation can be made by pointing out that a similar restraint is also placed upon husbands, one cannot loose sight of the social reality that the norms of sexual morality applicable to women are very different from those which apply to men. Further, the stipulation would apply only to women in the normal course, as maintenance to husbands would only be under exceptional circumstances.

The draft renders maintenance a premium to chastity not only during the subsistence of marriage but even after the marital bond is dissolved through a decree of divorce. Since this provision is often used by husbands to embarrass women in court proceedings, the Law Commission in its *132nd Report* had recommended its abolition.[23] To this extent the stipulation in the ILS draft lags far behind and is even more regressive and anti-women than the prevailing legal position.

The stipulation by the Bar Council that maintenance would be granted only on the production of a marriage certificate will also adversely affect the rights of women and children and falls below the existing stipulation under matrimonial statutes and S.125 Cr.PC. In addition, proceedings under S.125 Cr.PC are of a summary nature and a woman is not required to prove the marriage. Women approaching the courts for maintenance are protected by the presumption regarding valid marriage laid down under S.50 of the *Indian Evidence Act*.

It is rather alarming to observe that the stipulations for maintenance contained in both the drafts are inconsistent with their objective, i.e. improving the rights of women and children. The drafting authors seem to have lost sight of this objective somewhere along the way.

The claim to modernity rests on the stipulation of monogamy and compulsory registration of marriages. The provision of registration exists under the Parsi, Christian and Special Marriage Acts and also, to a limited extent, under the Muslim law (where marriages are performed through written contracts, nikahnamas, and are registered with the office of the qazi.) S. 8 of the *Hindu Marriage Act* provides for registration of Hindu Marriages. But keeping in view the plurality of Hindu society, its loose social and religious organizations and non state regulatory structures, the Act has specifically laid down that non-registration cannot invalidate an existing marriage. The stipulations of compulsory registration seek to modify the existing legal position under the Hindu law to the detriment of women's rights. The provision seems to stem from a concern to curb bigamy by providing for valid proof of marriage and to this extent is defended as beneficial to women. But in reality, the suggestion is extremely short-sighted. The fact that a far greater number of women are likely to approach the courts for maintenance than for a criminal prosecution in cases of bigamy and maintenance is of far more crucial importance to women than penal provision of bigamy is something that seem to have escaped the notice of the drafters.

The recommendations are also confusing and contradictory. For instance, the Bar Council draft provides for registration of two types of marriages, i.e. civil and traditional.[24] The recommended procedure for registering a civil marriage is a verbatim repetition of the provision under the present *Special Marriage Act*. The procedure for registering a traditional marriage is complex. After solemnization of a marriage in the traditional form, a declaration signed by the parties and three witnesses must be sent to the registrar, which is treated as a mere notice. After the expiry of one month and after the Registrar satisfies himself that the requirements of a valid marriage have been complied with, the parties will have to present themselves before the Registrar along with three witnesses for completing the formalities of registration.

The marriage becomes valid and binding only after a certificate of marriage is issued by the Registrar. Hence, a section which elaborately lays down various traditional forms of marriage under different religions and some customs (S.21) seems redundant and illusory and a mere token gesture to provide for legal plurality. This will lead to unnecessary ambiguities and legal complexities. Traditional marriage is a social event with customary rituals and ceremonies which include the ritual of consummation. It is rather absurd to presume that a mandatory refrain from consummation under a statute, will prevent a couple from consummating the marriage performed traditionally until a certificate is obtained from the Registrar after a month. The implications of consummating a marriage performed in a traditional form before a certificate is obtained from the registrar are not addressed.

In this context, the ILS draft is more direct and provides greater clarity. While civil registration is mandatory, the parties are free to perform religious ceremonies of their choice. This provision is projected as incorporating legal plurality.[25] The marriage becomes legal and binding only upon a civil registration. But the draft stipulates that the parties are free to celebrate their marriage in the traditional manner. Since in any case, social events are celebrated with traditional rituals and ceremonies and sanction of the state is not necessary for these celebrations, providing for them within a statute would still amount to a gesture of mere tokenism and may lead to ambiguities which are best avoided.

The stipulations loose sight of the fact that civil registration of marriages is an alien concept under the Hindu law. If this stipulation has to meet with a measure of success, it is essential that the procedures are simple, inexpensive and decentralized. The drafts do not provide for this. The statutory notice of one month stipulated under the *Special Marriage Act* of 1954 is mechanically retained. The fact that this has proved to be the greatest deterrent against registering marriages under the *Special Marriage Act* has not been examined. The stringent stipulations have led to the mushrooming of several *vivaha karyalayas*, where registration of marriages has become a lucrative business. In Mumbai and other cities of Maharashtra and Gujarat, forced, fraudulent and invalid marriages can be registered for a premium within a matter of minutes, by manipulating the provisions of an outdated statute, *Bombay Marriage Registration Act, 1953* (BMRA) (which provides for the registration of a mere document and not of the marriage.)[26] Unscrupulous lawyers have successfully misled naive, unassuming, young couples, who wish to marry despite parental opposition, into registering invalid marriages in this manner. This could be done only because the procedures for registering a marriage under the *Special Marriage Act* are stringent and cumbersome and information about correct procedures is scarce. Hence there is an urgent need to simplify and decentralize the procedures of registration and reduce the existing notice period of one month. The drafts do not concern themselves with these current social realities.

The ILS draft starts off with rigid stipulation regarding registration of marriages, but the rigidity is relaxed in a subsequent section which grants women in void marriages the right of maintenance. If a woman can prove a customary marriage and subsequent cohabitation, despite the fact that the marriage is bigamous, she will be entitled to maintenance. While this is a positive suggestion which will be beneficial to women who are tricked into bigamous marriages, it leads to an internal inconsistency within the draft and reduces registration to a mere facilitating measure. This in any case is the present legal position. Hence while the Bill may rake a controversy over abolition of bigamy and compulsory registration of marriage, on closer scrutiny, the Bill would not drastically change the existing situation.

While granting women in void marriages a right to maintenance is beneficial, the provision of granting husbands a similar right of maintenance under the concept of formal equality would open up new avenues of harassment in matrimonial litigation and will saddle women with unwarranted encumbrances.

The prescribed ceremony of solemnizing the marriage under both the drafts is a marriage oath, rooted in Christianity, i.e. 'I take thee (name of the spouse) as my lawful husband/wife'. Most Indian women are under cultural constraints regarding pronouncing their husband's name. It is rather ironical that while Indian Christians have, in recent years, sanskritized their marriage ceremonies and other religious rituals, the framers of the draft have not paid due attention to evolve a solemnization which would reflect the tradition and culture of a pluralistic and predominantly rural Indian society.[27]

The failure to provide for the right of residence in the matrimonial house as a right flowing from the contract of marriage and for civil injunctions restraining the dispossessing of the wife from the matrimonial home seems to be another major drawback of both the drafts. Perhaps this provision is sought to be included under the section dealing with succession and inheritance. But the right to reside in the matrimonial home and the right to a share of matrimonial assets need to be clearly stipulated as matrimonial rights flowing from the contract of marriage. Further, since there is a lot of ambiguity regarding the matrimonial home in judicial discourse there is an urgent need to define the matrimonial home within the statute. The drafts have failed to respond to this pressing need.

So overall, despite their stated objective, the primary concern of the drafts seems to be with uniformity and regulation of sexuality than a genuine concern for protecting the rights of women and children.

11.3 Recommendations by Women's Organizations

The new phase of the women's movement which gained recognition during the early eighties has focused primarily on issues of violence against women—rape, dowry harassment and domestic violence. As a response to the growing need, several women's groups set up counselling and legal aid centres. In this process the groups have had to grapple with the failure of the legal system to protect the economic rights of women in matrimonial relationships. The recommendations of the women's organizations stem from this grassroot level experience. The recommendations discussed here are not fully formulated drafts but are principles upon which a bill could eventually be formulated.

Confronted with the problems of desertion leading to destitution, dilatory and manipulative tactics adopted by husbands to evade economic responsibilities and complex, cumbersome and expensive litigation processes, the concern of the recommendations is to plug existing loopholes within the legal system. The recommendations are clearly and unambiguously based on the substantive model of equality. The two drafts discussed in this section are rooted in two different streams within the women's movement, the autonomous groups and party affiliated women's organizations.

Women's organizations had been advocating a compulsory Uniform Civil Code till 1985.[28] But the Shah Bano judgment seems to be the turning point. Due to the distinct communal tone of the demand in recent times, there has been a gradual shift within the women's movement to an optional code and reform within personal laws.[29] So while a reading of the recommendations may seem like a brief for a compulsory code, these have to be contextualized within the shift towards an optional code and other possible strategies of reform.[30]

Recommendations by Vimochana and Lawyers Collective (1988): These recommendations were evolved at a workshop organized by Vimochana, a counselling and support group based in Bangalore along with *Lawyers Collective*, in May 1988 at Bangalore.[31] Protection of economic rights of women within marriage is a major concern of this draft. The draft proposes joint ownership of property acquired after marriage and grants women the right to reside in the matrimonial home. The husband is restrained from selling the matrimonial home or relinquishing the tenancy of the house without the consent of the wife.

Departing from the outdated 'fault' theory of divorce where one spouse has to prove a matrimonial fault (adultery, cruelty, desertion, insanity etc.) against the other, the 'breakdown' theory is based on incompatibility between the spouses and is borrowed from the principles of English matrimonial statutes of recent times.[32] With this, the archaic provision of restitution of conjugal rights is automatically abolished. To grant additional protection to women, it is proposed that a divorce demanded by the husband on the ground of irretrievable breakdown of marriage, should be granted only after he makes adequate economic provision for the wife. The draft stipulates that if the wife is in possession of the matrimonial home, her right of residence should not be extinguished upon divorce.

Since enforcement of maintenance orders is one of the major hurdles faced by women, the draft suggests that the husband should be required to make a voluntary disclosure of his assets and income immediately after a petition for divorce is filed by either of the spouses. Thereafter, he must deposit three months' maintenance for the wife and children. The amount must be calculated by dividing the income in equal shares between the husband, wife and minor children. The draft also stipulates that matrimonial courts should have the power to award lump sum maintenance, property settlements and salary attachments. Criminal and civil remedies to prevent violence against women including ouster injunctions are also proposed to provide protection to women within marriage.

The concept of father as the natural guardian of the child is sought to be abolished. The draft specifically protects the mother's rights to custody by stipulating that custody should be given to the parent who has taken the responsibility of looking after the child in the past. The draft also suggests that the lack of earning capacity of the mother or the fact that she has no dwelling should not disentitle her to the custody of the children and further, factors like alcoholism, violence towards the mother or the children should be considered while determining the best interest of the child in custody petitions.

The recommendations provide for compulsory registration of marriages but grant rights to women in informal relationships. Further, it is clarified that for the purpose of conviction for bigamy, cohabitation should be deemed as marriage. It recommends abolition of the offence of adultery under S.497 IPC.

The contradiction between providing for compulsory registration of marriages, granting recognition to informal marriages and providing for the rights of cohabittees, abolishing the punishment for adultery and broadening the base of conviction for bigamy (from formal marriages to informal relationships) has not been addressed in the recommendations. This seems to be its major drawback. If the rights of cohabittees are on par with the rights of spouses then registration serves no purpose at all and there would be no compulsion to register a marriage in a society where marriages are viewed more as social functions than legal contracts. Also if marriages and informal cohabitations are granted similar weightage and are deemed as offences then the whole premise upon which conviction for bigamy is based collapses. Here the existing law makes a clear distinction between solemn marriages and illegitimate and informal alliances where the ceremony of solemnization and permanency of the relationship is of greatest relevance. The widening of the scope would render adultery an offence rather than bigamy. But in the same stroke, it is recommended that adultery ought not to be deemed as an offence. So there is an ambiguity about whether the focus of the reform is curbing sexual immorality by a penal provision or protecting women's economic rights through widening the scope of maintenance to include women in informal alliances.

The recommendations introduce the remedy of irretrievable breakdown of marriage. This was proposed by the Law Commission in its *71st Report*.[33] But due to opposition from various women's organizations, the issue was abandoned. The opposition from the women's organizations was based on the fact that the remedy may not suit the Indian cultural ethos and women will be worse affected by it. It will provide an avenue for husbands, after years of marriage, to opt out on flimsy grounds and leave the wife and children in the lurch. While the opposition is valid, it is premised on an abstract theoretic basis since at the practical level, the remedy has already made a back door entry into the matrimonial statutes. Firstly, the ground of mental cruelty is used by the parties almost on the same footing as irretrievable breakdown of marriage.[34] Further by the 1976 amendment, several new grounds of divorce have been introduced in the *Hindu Marriage Act* and the *Special Marriage Act* which amount to irretrievable breakdown of marriage.[35] So the opposition does not have a legal basis. The proposed recommendations are an improvement on the current legal position as well as the Law Commission recommendations. As far as the husbands are concerned, the remedy is linked to economic settlements in favour of wives. But if the litigations for maintenance are an indication, the husbands will find myriad ways to wriggle out of their economic responsibilities.

Recommendations by the All India Democratic Women's Association (AIDWA) (1995): The AIDWA is affiliated to CPI (M) and has been active in the campaign for women's rights in the post-independence period. Its campaign against the enactment of the Muslim Women's Bill is particularly significant.[36] While initially the group endorsed the demand for a UCC, in its more recent convention, it has opposed this demand and has suggested alternate recommendations.

While concern for strengthening women's rights is the governing principle, the focus of the recommendations is upon the strategies of reform. At its national convention held at Delhi on 9–10 December 1995 titled Equal Rights, Equal Laws, AIDWA has proposed a step by step approach to bring in reform.[37] The convention rejected implementation of a comprehensive code, whether compulsory or optional, and instead has advocated legislation on specific issues and reform within existing personal laws as dual strategies of achieving the goal of gender justice.

An umbrella legislation would require the complete overhauling of all existing laws. This may pose obstacles in the path of immediate reform. Before implementing a comprehensive code, the foundation of equality between men and women would have to be laid. Secular legislation in specific areas of crucial concern will be an important step in this direction. The three specific areas of legislative reform proposed by the convention are: (i) right to matrimonial property; (ii) protection against domestic violence; and (iii) marriage registration facilities.

A legislation on joint matrimonial property would grant recognition to women's contribution to the household by way of unpaid labour and reduce the incidents of destitution which are common to women of all communities. A Domestic Violence Act could provide for both civil and criminal remedies. The demand for a law on registration of marriages clarified that there should be no interference in the nature of rituals and ceremonies of marriages. A decentralized machinery should be provided for registering marriages at the village levels and local panchayats could be granted the power of registration. Such registration could be of great help to women by providing documentary proof of a valid marriage in the event of dispute.

The convention acknowledged that the task of reform is not easy and it cannot be achieved without a sustained and broad based political struggle, campaigns and awareness programmes. Although there have been discussions within smaller groups in recent times, lack of widespread movements for changes within personal laws have been the major constraints. The convention resolved that campaigns within communities are important strategies for reform in personal laws.

Both the drafts discussed in this section are based on ground realities of helping women in distress situations and hence are aimed at seeking practical solutions to the problem despite some minor inconsistencies. If translated into specific acts, they would provide some relief to the economic problems faced by women.

11.4 Official Drafts and Parliamentary Trends

The four drafts discussed above reflect the concern of social organizations and legal academia. But unless these concerns are reflected in official state discourse, the process of law reform will not even get off the ground. Hence it is relevant to examine the position reflected in official drafts in recent times.

The recommendations made by the Law Commission from time to time have already been mentioned during the course of the discussion. But since the setting up of the National Commission for Women in 1990, law reform for women will have to be steered through this body. Hence the drafts formulated by them are important indicators of the direction of reform. In addition, there has been some debate on women's economic rights through the Private Members Bills introduced in the Parliament. One such Bill which was discussed at length in Parliament is also examined here to assess the response of Parliamentarians, for in the ultimate analysis, the legislative power to usher in reforms rests with them exclusively.

Bills formulated by the National Commission for Women (1994): It is rather disconcerting to observe that while the recommendations by women's organizations are cautious and practical, a Bill formulated by the National Commission for Women titled, 'The Marriage Bill 1994',[38] makes sweeping and unrealistic reco-mmendations, throwing all caution to the winds.

The primary concern of the Bill seems to be abolition of

polygamy by ensuring compulsory registration of marriages. But instead of a facilitating measure (of providing proof in case of dispute), registration becomes an end in itself.[39] The Bill stipulates that a declaration of marriage must be sent to the Registrar of marriages within three days of its performance. A fine of Rs 100 per day is levied for default for a period of one month and thereafter the marriage is deemed void.[40] While prescribing such stringent measures of compulsory registration, the fact that the government has not been able to provide bare necessities like clean drinking water, primary education and basic health facilities to a large section of its people has been overlooked. The Bill does not spell out the measures through which the government will make it possible for people to register their marriages within three days of its performance.

While many countries in the south Asian region stipulate compulsory registration, no country has extended this logic so far as to invalidate an existing marriage with its adverse implications to women and children. In fact, the modern trend is towards granting rights and benefits to people in informal relationships. But the official trend in India seems to be tilting towards greater regimentation in family relationships.

The Bill abolishes the concept of restitution of conjugal rights. While this could be interpreted as a positive measure, it leaves no legal avenue for a deserted woman to apply to the courts for remedies of maintenance, custody of children, right of residence in the matrimonial home etc. unless she is willing to dissolve the marriage either by divorce or annulment. These crucial rights are incorporated only as ancillary reliefs in petitions for divorce and annulments. The Bill does not confer a statutory right of residence in the matrimonial house during the subsistence of marriage.

While stipulating stringent measures for registration of marriages, divorce is made easy by introducing the ground of incompatibility or irretrievable breakdown of marriage.[41] The statutory period of separation for a divorce by mutual consent is reduced from one year to three months.[42] The rationality behind rendering the bond of marriage so transient at one level and prescribing such stringent measures for its registration at the other are difficult to comprehend.

While the Bill deals elaborately with the issue of registration, only one section collectively deals with the economic rights of maintenance and residence, both during the subsistence of marriage and after its dissolution.[43] Here, adopting the model of formal equality, the Bill grants husbands and wives similar rights of maintenance and residence in the matrimonial home as ancillary measures.[44]

Another Bill drafted by the Women's Commission titled, The Domestic Violence to Women (Prevention) Bill (1994)[45], seems to offer a more practical solution to the problems faced by women and is based on the substantive model of equality. While the term 'domestic violence' is gender neutral, the Bill recognizes that the IPC already provides for violence of a generic category and concerns itself only with the specificity of violence faced by women in domestic situation.[46] The wide definition of violence includes not only any conduct amounting to cruelty, but also acts which violate the dignity of women. To make justice more accessible the term 'court' includes, family court, civil court and mahila court (which can consist of three women members of a gram panchayat). To avoid delays, a time frame of six months is prescribed for disposing off cases filed under its provisions. The Bill also provides for urgent *ex-parte* injunctions.

The most important aspect of this Bill is the stipulation to provide safe shelter to the woman either within the matrimonial home or alternatively, where feasible, in a separate residence. While the provision of a separate accommodation may not be viable in most cases, granting women the right to reside within the matrimonial home and securing their safety through protective orders is a very useful recommendation which will help a large number of women who are victims of domestic violence. As it is well established, the problem of domestic violence transcends class, caste and religious denominations.[47]

Private Member's Bill (1994): This bill was introduced by a Congress member, Veena Verma, in the Rajya Sabha in May 1994 and is titled, *The Married Women's (Protection of Rights) Bill 1994*.[48] It is in the nature of specific enactments like *Dowry Prohibition Act*, *Medical Termination of Pregnancy Act* and punishment for cruelty to wives (S.498(A) IPC) etc. Although these enactments altered the provisions of personal laws, they were not situated within the political controversy of Uniform Civil Code versus personal laws.

This Bill is significant for a number of reasons: (i) it provides for a new remedy which is non-existent in any matrimonial statute; (ii) it subscribes to the step by step approach; (iii) it is premised on the model of substantive equality; and (iv) the debate in Parliament provides insights into legislative responses to protecting women's economic rights.

While the drafts discussed earlier, grant women rights over property acquired after marriage (and also grant husbands reciprocatory rights over wives' property) this Bill grants rights to women over all the property of the husband and does not confer similar rights to husbands. Whether these provisions will be within the scope of protective discrimination under Art. 15 (3) of the Constitution is yet to be ascertained. But if they withstand this test, they will indeed be beneficial stipulations.

In its 'Statement of Objects and Reasons' the Bill highlights the exploitation faced by women:

> ...Although we are going to cross over to the 21st Century, our attitude towards women is still that of the feudal lords. Even today we are not prepared to grant the same liberty to women which men themselves are enjoying dauntlessly. ...The real cause of the exploitation of a woman by her husband is that she has no right in the house of her husband. ...Our laws confer the right of property on a woman only after the death of her husband. ...If a woman's right in the property of her husband is recognised she will start feeling secure and she will overcome her sense of helplessness and economic insecurity... .

The term property is defined broadly and is inclusive of movables and immovables whether ancestral or self-acquired, whether held jointly with other members of the family and includes contributions to provident fund and public saving schemes, bank deposits, shares, ornaments, land and dwelling house.[49]

The Bill grants the wife the right to live in the house of her husband, whether owned by him or by members of his joint family, the right to food, clothing and other facilities; the right to an equal share in the property of her husband and the right to be consulted in matters of family business and other financial transactions regarding the husband's property.[50]

The Bill was debated in the Rajya Sabha during three sessions, 12 August 1994, 9 December 1994 and 31 March 1995. The 23 members who commented on the Bill, barring stray adverse comments, unanimously supported the Bill. The adverse comments were made by Mr S. S. Ahluwalia (Congress) on the following presumptions: (i) In Indian society women are treated as Devis and hence would not need any such protective law based on western concepts. The Bill will cause chaos and confusion and is against the norms of Indian (read Hindu) culture and tradition. (ii) Since most people do not own property the Bill would benefit only a few educated, urban women who do not wish to fulfil their role as dutiful wives and want to while away their time in kitty parties.[51]

The Minister of State for Law, Justice and Company Affairs, Mr H.R. Bhardwaj endorsed these views and commented:

> We cannot insist that a husband must give fifty per cent of his property to his wife. The women's movement in India is different from the west. We cannot really think that women will be better only by making legal provisions. ...We will also have to see how the question of property can be settled under diverse personal laws...There was a suggestion to examine whether a flat allocated to a man under government schemes should be in joint names of husband and wife. But Income Tax regulations and other problems crop up. ...[52]

The problem of diverse personal laws was raised by the minister and not by any Muslim member of Parliament. It is also interesting to note that the reluctance to enact the Bill was not based only on diverse laws of succession but also on taxation laws. When reforms cause a dent in the economics of patriarchy, perhaps it is easier to stall them off by communalizing the issue. Due to the overwhelming support, the minister was constrained to assure the house that it will be re-introduced as a government Bill. But the government did not keep to this assurance, and after elections when the new United Front government assumed power there was no further development on this issue.

11.5 Salient Points Emerging from the Model Drafts

A summary of the salient points which emerge from the various model drafts may help to focus the debate upon the various and at times contradictory premises, examine their theoretical base and prioritize the reform measures.

1. Starting from the premise of a compulsory Uniform Civil Code, a consensus seems to be steadily, albeit gradually, emerging that the process of family law reform has to be cautious. Enforcing a compulsory Uniform Civil Code from above may not be the best solution. Campaign and education are essential strategies for initiating reform in the realm of personal law. This reality

seems to be permeating through the suggested reforms in the wake of the current political climate of majoritarianism.

2. If the goal is to improve the rights of women and children, the recommendations have to be based on the substantive model of equality. The use of the term 'spouse' while determining the rights and obligations of the parties to a marriage will result in further deterioration of women's rights. While concern for women's welfare is universal, the concern cannot be expressed in rhetorics. A greater clarity regarding the theoretical framework upon which the remedies are based needs to be evolved, particularly where the legal academia is concerned.

3. Abolishing polygamy through compulsory registration of marriages seem to form the core of the controversy over Uniform Civil Code. Although this concern is reflected in all the drafts (except the Private Member's Bill) the drafts have not been able to recommend viable solutions to resolve the issue. This is due to the two opposing concerns which are manifested in the issue (i) prescribing stringent measures (both civil and criminal) as deterrents to (male) bigamy; and (ii) providing for the rights of women in informal relationships. A tilt towards the first option will increase state control over people's lives and will drastically affect the rights of women and children. A tilt towards the second option will render inconsequential the provisions of monogamy and compulsory registration of marriages. The drafts have not paid due attention to this internal contradiction of the demand. The consensus seems to be governed more from a sense of middle-class morality and the Christian framework of marriage adopted by the liberals in India than a genuine concern for women's rights, as the recommendations seem to indicate.

4. A shift away from—marriage as a sexual contract to control/regulate sexuality—to marriage as an economic contract where weaker partners need additional statutory protection (as in labour legislations) is visible in the drafts by women's organizations. There is an increasing realization regarding the link between divorce/desertion and destitution of women in development discourse. This has led to the coinage of a new term feminization of poverty. Some of the drafts reflect an urgency regarding this issue. Women's right to shelter in their matrimonial home and the right to a share of matrimonial property upon divorce are emerging as concrete strategies of tackling the issue at hand.

5. Since women's rights are integrally linked to the political developments, at this juncture of communally vitiated political climate, a step by step approach seems to be more feasible than a comprehensive code, either compulsory or optional. Some bills which have already been formulated, i.e. the Private Member's Bill on women's right to matrimonial property, the Bill by the Women's Commission on domestic violence which provides for urgent injunction and secures women's right to shelter and the recommendations of the *132nd report* of the Law Commission (abolishing the ceiling of Rs 500 per month maintenance under s.125 Cr.PC) can be the starting points of a campaign.

6. There seems to be one lacuna which runs through all the drafts which have been examined. The drafts are based on either of the two premises: (i) Women as a class are non-working spouses and their only contribution is unpaid domestic labour; or (ii) Men and women are equal partners and hence their rights, duties and responsibilities are equal and of a similar nature. A third category of women, who are the sole providers of their families, are invisible in this debate. The recommendations do not protect these women who shoulder the double burden as wage earners and home makers. The implications of introducing the concept of joint family property and equal right to matrimonial home and maintenance etc. using a gender neutral term spouse would be detrimental to the rights of these women, most of whom belong to the marginalized sections of society. The concerns of this large category of women are not reflected in any of the drafts.

In conclusion, while there have been some concrete efforts at evolving drafts which would protect women's rights, a sustained campaign around specific issues to pressurize the government to bring in reform is lacking. The fact that despite the media publicity on women's rights, no pressure could be exerted even to remove the ceiling of Rs 500 set in 1955, as recommended by the Law Commission, is an indication of the lack of a concentrated campaign. Women's rights seem to be lost in the larger controversy around Uniform Civil Code which today, has become a political question. Only through a step by step approach to bring in small and specific reform through concentrated campaigns can the rights of women be salvaged from the political entangle within which they are currently enmeshed.

Notes

1. The substantive model of equality is governed by Art. 15 (3) of the Constitution while the formal equality is based on Art. 14 and 15 (1) of the Constitution.

2. Kapur, R. and B. Cossman, *Subversive Sites*, New Delhi: Sage Publications (1995), p.175-80.

3. *The Times of India* 17 July 1986; Also see Mishra, V.C. (ed.), 'Special Issue on Uniform Civil Code' *Indian Bar Review* XVIII/3-4 (1991), p.293-4.

4. Mishra, V.C. Ibid and also See S.P. Sathe, 'Uniform Civil Code—Why? What? and How?', in *Towards Secular India* 1/4 Bombay: Centre for Study of Society and Secularism (1995), p.31.

5. Mishra, V.C. p.65. The initial draft proposed that Muslims and scheduled tribes be exempted from its application. An individual Muslim could opt to be governed by it. The tribal communities could be governed by it only by a notification in the Government Gazette. S.1 (a) and (b) of the proposed draft.

6. Mishra, V.C. See note 3, p.iv.

7. Ibid., p.vii.

8. Ibid.

9. S. 26, Ibid., p.65.

10. Ss. 36 & 37. Ibid., p.100.

11. Ibid., p.121.

12. Ibid., p.238.

13. The presentation at the Seminar on Personal Laws and Gender Justice organized by the Centre for Study of Society and Secularism, Bombay on 19–20 February 1994.

14. Dr S.P. Sathe has emphasized that federalism is not only a geographical phenomenon but also cultural and ethnic, that the need to be different is not anti-national and that nationalism does not require regimentation. See Sathe, S.P., 'Uniform Civil Code Implications of the Supreme Court Judgement,' in *Economic and Political Weekly*, XXX/35 (1995), p.2165.

15. Ibid. Also see note 4.

16. Ss. 17 & 33 of the proposed Bill.

17. S.18 of the Act r/w S.3(a) and S.9 of the proposed Bill.

18. S.17 of the proposed Bill.

19. S.27 of the *Hindu Marriage Act*, 1955.

20. S.20 of the *Matrimonial Proceedings and Property Act, 1970*.

21. The report brought out under the Chairmanship of M.P. Thakkar was submitted to the government in April 1989.

22. *Mahalingam Pillai v Amsavalli* (1956) 2 MLJ 289 DB; *Gulab Jagduse Kakwani v Kamla Gulab Kakwani* AIR 1985 Bom 88; *Khem Chand v State & Anr* 1 (1990) DMC 38 All; *T. Raja Rao v T. Neelamma* 1990 Cri.LJ 2430 AP; *Vijay Shankar Prasad v Manika Roy* 2 (1990) DMC 457 Pat etc.

23. Point 7 of the *132nd Law Commission Report* suggested that Sub-section (4) and (5) of S.125 depriving a wife from claiming maintenance on the ground that she is living in adultery should be deleted as it is by and large invoked to embarrass and harass the wife.

24. See Chapter III, sections 15 to 24, p.86-8.
25. See note 14 and 15.
26. Agnes, F., 'In the Dock,' *Humanscape*, Bombay August 1996, p.26.
27. See Table 5 for the urban-rural distribution of the population.
28. *Report of the Committee on the Status of Women*, (1974), 'Towards Equality,' p.142. Further, at two successive national conferences of women activists held at Bombay in 1980 and 1985 passed resolutions demanding a Uniform Civil Code. See resolutions passed during the two conferences.
29. Kishwar, M., 'Pro Women or Anti Muslim; the Shah Bano Controversy,' *Manushi* VI/2 (1986), p.4. Agnes F., *State, Gender, and the Rhetoric of Law Reform* (Bombay), Research Unit on Women's Studies, S.N.D.T.University (1995), pp.204-9; Gandhi, N. & N. Shah, *Issues at Stake*, New Delhi: Kali for Women (1991), pp.252-9; The Forum Against Oppression of Women, (1995) *Views on the Uniform Civil Code* presented at a public meeting held on 22 July 1995 (unpublished document available with the group); Anveshi Law Committee, 'Is Gender Justice Only a Legal Issue— Political Stakes in UCC Debate,' *Economic and Political Weekly*, XXXII/9-10 (1997), p. 453.
30. Vimochana, The Quest for a Uniform Civil Code: Some Dilemmas', some issues (1988) (unpublished document available with the group).
31. 'Recommendations of the Lawyers Collective Bangalore Law School,' *The Lawyers* III/7 (1988), p.20.
32. The remedy is based on a similar provision under the English law under S.2 of the *Matrimonial Causes Act* 1973. See Jackson, J. (ed.), *Raydens's Law and Practice in Divorce and Family Matters*, London: Butterworths (1983), p.2499–501.
33. The report was brought out in 1980 and was circulated to various women's organizations in 1981.
34. A scrutiny of the reported cases indicates that husbands file petitions on the ground of mental cruelty making frivolous allegations like refusal to cook food, asking the husband to clear the dining table in the presence of friends, not following specific instructions about taking care of his mother, quarrelsome nature of the wife, arrogance due to higher educational qualifications, pressurizing the husband to set up a separate house etc.
35. S.13 (1A) of the *Hindu Marriage Act* and S.27 (ii) of the *Special Marriage Act* stipulate that if after one year of obtaining a decree of restitution of conjugal rights or judicial separation the cohabitation is not resumed, either of the parties can approach the courts for a divorce. In actual effect, if the wife has obtained a decree of restitution of conjugal rights and the husband thereafter has refused to comply with the decree, one year later he can obtain decree of divorce. See the decision in *Saroj Rani v Sudarshan Kumar Chaddha* AIR 1984 SC 1562 in this respect. This provision was introduced in the *Parsi Marriage and Divorce Act* in 1988 by adding S.32(A).
36. Memorandum dated 17 April 1986 to the President of India by Susheela Gopalan, General Secretary, AIDWA and *Susheela Gopalan & Ors v Union of India*, No.1055, dated 24 July 1986.

37. Karat, B., 'Uniformity vs equality: The Concept of uniform civil code *Frontline* 17 November 1995, p.82, Singh, K. 'Combating Communalism *Seminar*, n.441 (1996), p.55.

38. The draft was approved by the Expert Committee on Laws in its meeting held on 18–19 August 1994. The bill is unpublished. For various provisions of the bill see Tiwari, B., 'Marriage Laws Revamped,' in *The Lawyers*, X/5 (1995), p.28.

39. The Statement of Object and Reason declares, 'A Bill to consolidate and amend the law relating to marriages in India and to provide for their compulsory registration.'

40. S.17 proviso of the draft Bill.

41. S.7 (2) of the draft Bill.

42. S.11 (i) of the draft Bill.

43. S.10 of the draft Bill.

44. S.14 of the draft Bill.

45. This bill seems to be debated along with the Marriage Bill, see Karat, B., 'Uniformity vs equality' n.38. For text see Appendix I.

46. The problem is grave as the statistics reveal. See Table 6 for the number of women who have died in unnatural situations in the city of Mumbai.

47. See Table 7 for a religion-wise distribution of cases filed in Mumbai under S.498(A) IPC (cruelty to wives) for the period 1990-1995.

48. Bill No.XXV of 1994 introduced by Veena Verma in the Rajya Sabha on 13 May 1994. For text see Appendix II.

49. S.2 (c) of the Bill.

50. S.3 of the Bill.

51. RSD dated 12 August 1994 p. 824–6 (unpublished).

52. Ibid., p. 836–8.

12

Strategies of Reform

12.1 Implications of the Shift in the Focus of UCC from Gender Justice to National Integration

The genesis of the demand for uniform family laws is situated within the women's movement of the pre-independence era within the larger context of the nationalist struggle. The All India Women's Conference (AIWC) was an active protagonist of this demand and placed the issue of gender within the political agenda. This led to some enactments during the thirties securing women's rights within marriage.

In 1940, the National Planning Committee, while focusing upon the economic dimension of women's rights, resolved that in a planned society, women's place shall be equal to that of men and to achieve this recommended the enactment of a Uniform Civil Code.[1] During the initial phase, the UCC was to be an optional code which could gradually replace the different personal laws followed by various religious communities. This position seems to have continued till the draft for the UCC was presented at the Convention held by the Bar Council in 1986 (discussed in the preceding chapter).

Later, during the Constituent Assembly debates, the focus shifted from gender equality to national integration. The demand for UCC was seen as a corrective measure for the divisive colonial policies. Integration of communities in the modern state was sought to be achieved through uniformity of personal laws. While pressing for setting a timeframe for the enactment of a UCC M.R. Masani, Hansa Mehta and Rajkumari Amrit Kaur bemoaned the continuance of personal laws as keeping India back from advancing to nationhood.[2] The proceedings of the Constituent Assembly show a marked absence of discussion about the significance of a UCC for women. The issue of women's rights seems to have been subsumed beneath graver political concerns of building a modern state.[3] There was also a presumption that a modern state would automatically ensure gender justice.

In the years immediately following independence, the issue of Uniform Civil Code, either for reasons of ensuring gender equality or to further the cause of national integration, did not figure in any important national debate. But a passing reference to this demand was made by conservative sections while opposing the Hindu law reforms.[4] In 1974, the report of the committee on the status of women shifted the focus and situated gender justice at the centre of the core of the demand for a UCC, but did not quite distance itself from the premise of national integration.[5]

During the subsequent decades, the issue was further problemetized by judicial comments. While examining gender bias within the Muslim personal law, the courts have explicitly commented that oneness of the nation as well as loyalty to it would be at stake if different minority groups follow different family laws.[6] It is a matter of debate whether a Uniform Civil Code will ensure national integration and communal harmony.[7] But the comments have enabled the communal forces to appropriate the demand. This appropriation has posed insurmountable obstacles in the path of family law reform from the perspective of gender justice. To counter the communal propaganda, some scholars, in recent times, have differentiated between a uniform civil code and a common civil code and held that the demand for a uniform code is premised upon modernity and gender justice, whereas the common code would only ensure commonality of oppression.[8] But this differentiation between the words 'common' and 'uniform' appears to be rather stretched.

The root of the communal propaganda is centered around the growth in the Muslim population. As per this premise, non-implementation of Art. 44 of the Constitution has resulted in a growth of the Muslim population and this constitutes a danger to the majority community. The image of a polygamous Muslim has been constructed to serve this propaganda.[9] It is in this context that monogamy imposed by a compulsory code becomes the need of the hour.[10] The gains to the gender concerns by the imposition of monogamy seems to be only incidental. Muslim scholars have countered this with statistical data and focused upon sociological factors such as poor socio-economic conditions and low level of education among the Muslims which are the root causes of a slight increase in Muslim population and pointed out that a UCC will not resolve this problem.[11] But the doctrine of monogamy (which is the basic tenet of Christianity) also draws the unquestioning support of liberals moulded in the western ethos. Here bigamy is reflective of pre-modern barbarism and monogamy symbolizes civilization, enlightenment, modernity and progress.[12]

Within the context of identity politics, a support to the demand of a Uniform Civil Code is being construed almost as a betrayal of the community not only by the religious leadership but also by secular and progressive sections of the community. The shift in the trend can be gauged by the responses to the Tilhari judgment on triple talaq and the Supreme Court verdict on conversion and bigamy discussed in Chapter 8. The obvious reference to Muslims in respect of partition and two nation theory in the case concerning Hindu bigamy have also evoked critical comments. The secular Muslim response to these comments has been: 'Those who stayed in India had a right to remain here as they were citizens of this country. This does not grant the state the power to deny Muslims a right to a separate cultural identity.'[13]

It is within this restricted sphere of communalized ambience that reforms from within assume significance. This course upholds the principle imperative to a democratic polity, that culturally distinct communities must be granted a degree of autonomy to exist alongside a majority nation. The trends within non-Muslim minorities in this direction have already been discussed in the preceding chapters. But since the issue of UCC is locked within the binaries of Muslim minority and Hindu majority, the efforts by Muslim intelligentsia and pro-reform organizations become important markers in this discourse.

12.2 Scope of Reform from Within

There is unanimity among the Muslim social reform organizations regarding the need to bring in changes in the Muslim law. A rejection of the demand for UCC cannot be construed as a negation of women's rights. There is a consensus that obstinate opposition to reform will worsen the situation and substantiate the communal propaganda that Muslims are a backward community, hostile to any change that favours women. A community which is already the victim of prejudice can ill-afford to have its negative image reinforced.[14] Since the fundamentalist religious clergy and self-serving politicians are content to preserve the status quo, the mantle of reform must now fall upon the Muslim intelligentsia.

The progressive groups have identified certain specific issues which need immediate modification. Regulation of polygamy and arbitrary divorce, delegated right of the wife to divorce herself, right to matrimonial property and provision for a reasonable and fair settlement upon divorce are being listed as areas which need immediate intervention. The suggested strategies for reform range from codification/modification of the entire realm of Muslim personal law to small, specific and focused interventions.

Codification of Muslim personal law in accordance with the needs of a modern society, through community-based initiative has been suggested by several scholars as a possible strategy. Citing the experience of enacting the *Dissolution of Muslim Marriages Act*, 1939, a positive note has been expressed by many scholars that it would be possible to create a broad forum of legal scholars and ullamas to lay the ground for eventual codification.[15] Syed Shahabuddin whose reactionary stand has often been criticized by reformers, also has endorsed the need for codification.[16]

But the process of codification can be initiated only through an institutional framework. The setting up of such institutions can be facilitated by the state. Alternatively, if the interventions by the state are viewed as an encroachment upon the autonomous space of the minorities, the concerned sections would first have to create an institutional structure for rationalization and/or reform and then dialogue with the different segments of the community to work out a consensus.[17]

Another variation of the same module is the suggestion to set up a commission comprising of Muslim women, judges, lawyers and ullamas to elicit Muslim public opinion on specific issues with the view of bringing in certain modification in the Muslim law.[18] The suggestion is based on the model adopted by Pakistan to bring in reform. In 1955, the Pakistani government set up the Rashid Commission to look into the reforms within Muslim personal law in response to the demand raised by women's groups. During Ayub Khan's regime a seven member commission was appointed to frame a questionnaire to seek the referendum of the people on the issue of family law reform. Based on the recommendations, the *Family Law Ordinance* of 1961 was enacted which regulated polygamy, provided for compulsory registration of marriages, set up arbitration councils to oversee divorce proceedings and granted women the right of delegated divorce.[19]

The criticism against this suggestion has rightly been that what was possible in a Muslim majority country may not suit the socio-political conditions of minority Muslims in India. The pro-reform voice within the community is weak and the reformers lack the institutional support available to the fundamentalist religious leaders to influence public opinion.[20]

While the task is difficult, it may not be unsurmountable as the developments in Bihar indicate. A progressive forum has drafted a Bill titled, The Muslim Family Council Bill.[21] The aim is to set up a Muslim Family Council consisting of a former Muslim High Court judge and six members to regulate the process of Muslim marriage and divorce. The Bill provides for compulsory registration of marriages. The Council is granted the power to regulate polygamy and arbitrary divorce. Women are granted the right of delegated divorce (talaq-e-tafwiz). The suggested reforms have the scope of introducing significant advancement in the rights of Muslim women.

Another course is to work towards piecemeal reform of the practices which violate the provisions of the constitution on a priority basis. This could be a small beginning which could lead to the eventual codification of the entire corpus of Muslim personal law. Since arbitrary and unilateral triple talaq has been one of the most controversial issues, this practice needs to be declared un-Islamic. The practice is prevalent mainly among Sunni Hanafis. But Pakistan and Jordan which are Sunni majority countries have abolished the practice and it would not be difficult to follow this course in India.

12.3 Reform through Judicial Interventions

While the various strategies are being debated within the Muslim intellectual fora, the resentment among women who are victims of arbitrary divorce is growing. At the time of the enactment of the Muslim Women's Bill several Muslim wor en joined the campaign against the Bill, voiced their protest and endorsed the demand for a Uniform Civil Code. In this regard, the efforts by the Muslim Satyashodhak Mandal based in Maharashtra are particularly significant. The organization has been addressing the problems of women victims of arbitrary divorce and raising the demand for a UCC to safeguard the rights of Muslim women for well over a decade.[22]

The resentment of women is manifest in delegations to the government and petitions to the Supreme Court. In 1983, Shehanaz Sheikh, a 24-year-old Muslim woman divorced by her husband through oral talaq, filed a petition in the Supreme Court challenging the constitutional validity of the various provisions of the Muslim law and pleaded for the enactment of a Uniform Civil Code.[23] The petition evoked wide publicity and the support of various women's organizations in the country. But subsequently, the petition was withdrawn, due to the apprehension in the post Shah Bano phase, that it could provide fuel in the hands of communal elements.[24]

A decade later, in 1995 the Supreme Court admitted a Writ Petition filed by Zenat Fatima Rashid, a divorced Muslim woman challenging the adverse provisions of Muslim personal law. She has demanded a common civil code to ensure justice to Muslim women who are victims of triple talaq.[25]

The petition seems to have originated from individual effort. In a recent interview, Zenat has remarked that no organization has extended support to her cause.[26] Individual efforts by women cannot be sustained without adequate institutional and organizational support. The process of reform cannot be confined to a single petition as it involves issues affecting the whole community. The Supreme Court would keep this factor in view while bringing in legal reform through litigation as the process of family law reform among the Parsis and Christians indicates.

While the Petition filed by Zenat is pending, the Supreme Court gave a ruling on the interventionist role of the judiciary. A public interest petition filed by an Ahmedabad-based women's organization, the Ahmedabad Women Action Group had challenged the various discriminatory aspects of Muslim law including polygamy and triple talaq. While dismissing this petition (and other similar petitions challenging the discriminatory aspects of Hindu and Christian law) without examining the merits of the contentions, the apex court ruled that it is not within the jurisdiction of the courts to make laws for social change. The court observed that the petitions raised issues of state policy and it is the function of the legislature to lay down these policies of social change. With this ruling, the scope of reform through judicial interventions has been curtailed.[27]

12.4 Standard Nikahnama and Pre-Marriage Agreements

Since reform through legislative and litigation process has met with severe obstacles, attempts are now being directed towards mechanisms of change which are built in within the personal laws. Here, while anti-women practices of unilateral talaq, a token amount of mehr etc. have gained popularity in recent times, through a nexus between qazis, lawyers and husbands, several protective measures provided by the Islamic law have become obscure.

A powerful weapon provided by Islam to the protection of women is the right to enter into pre-marriage agreements (Kabein nama) and stipulate conditions in the marriage deed.[28] A Muslim woman also has the additional protection of mehr which forms an essential ingredient of a marriage contract (without such stipulation the formality of marriage cannot be complete) But these safety measures have been corroded and anti-women practices have become the norm. The judicial recognition granted to these anti-women practices and the media sensationalization of these events have reinforced their validity and these are now viewed as the norm, rather than aberrations of community practices.

Rather curiously, even in the 'best of all laws' theory adopted by some model drafts[29] there is no mention of the positive stipulations of the Muslim law. This is perhaps due to the fact that the basis of the reform is a comparative study of the statutory provisions of different matrimonial laws and popular misconceptions and misappropriation of the Muslim law. Hence these model drafts also subscribe to the communal presumption that Muslim personal law is least favourable to women. A scrutiny of these provisions is essential, if the 'reform from within' strategy has to yield some positive results.

From the earliest times, Islam gave due recognition to the fact that women, being weak and unequal partners in a marriage, must be provided with additional protection. Since marriages are contracts between consenting individuals, the woman has the option of laying down detailed conditions of marriage including provision of a separate house for her use and the right to abstain from cooking food or performing other domestic chores.

Conditions could be included in the nikahnama prohibiting the husband from taking a second wife or constraining him to make it subject to her consent. The wife can also spell out terms of fair and kind treatment and prescribe the terms of divorce. Through this stipulation the husband can be committed to the *ahsan* mode of talaq and also provide for a machinery for reconciliation. She can also set out the detailed terms of a divorce, including *mattan-bilmaroof*, i.e. reasonable and fair provision. The agreement can also contain a clause assigning to the wife her right of delegated divorce, i.e. talaq-e-tawfiz. The contract may also include agreement on the proportion of share of the divorced wife in the movable and immovable property acquired during the subsistence of marriage.[30]

More than half a century ago, Maulana Ashraf Ali Thanavi, the renowned Islamic, Jurist of Hanafi Sunni school, drew up a model contract called Kabein Nama providing for delegation of right of divorce to wife or any third party which may be enforced in the event of the violation of any of the terms and conditions. Even prior to this, in 1929, Iqbal, the philosopher-poet and jurist of Islam had strongly recommended that conditions including monogamy and delegated divorce are to be included in the nikahnama.[31]

Iqbal Ansari has argued that inclusion of such provisions in the marriage contract will not need any modernization of Islamic laws through ijtihad as it is already provided for in the traditional schools of Muslim jurisprudence. Courts in India have recognized and enforced the conditions in a marriage contract or a pre-marriage contract including the right of talaq-i-tawfiz.[32]

Though theoretically, the choice to enter into a marriage agreement lies with every woman (or her parents as the case may be), the social situation of Muslim women renders it extremely difficult to implement these provisions while negotiating a marriage proposal.[33] The educational backwardness of Muslims especially of Muslim women and the low status that the Indian ethos accord to women do not leave much scope for any conditions to be stipulated in a marriage contract.

The obstacle can be overcome only if the Muslim Personal Law Board issues a direction that a standard nikahnama, with all protective provisions written into it, must be used for solemnizing all Muslim marriages in India. To facilitate the process, a group of Muslims led by a few women have prepared a model nikahnama ensuring the conditions that favour women.[34] One important suggestion is that the amount of mehr must be stipulated in gold coins, valuables, bank securities or immovable property rather than in currency to meet with the inflation and currency devaluation.

The draft evolved by the group has been forwarded to the All India Muslim Personal Law Board (AIMPLB) and the group has had preliminary discussions with the members of the Board. But sustained pressure has to be maintained through community-based organizations until the AIMPLB accepts the recommendations and issues the necessary directions.

Unfortunately, the efforts of 'reform from within' have remained sporadic and the secular voice muffled, with Muslim and Hindu fundamentalists being projected as the arch players in this tug of war. The debate is located within the paradigm of politics with gender concerns, the most popular scapegoat used by all factions for their vested interests.

Notes

1. Lateef S., 'Defining Women through Legislation,' in Hasan, Z. (ed.) *Forging Identities: Gender, Communities and the State*, New Delhi: Kali for Women (1994), p.48.
2. The note of dissent attached to the Draft Report of 14 April 1947 of the sub-committee on Fundamental Rights and the note of dissent attached to the Draft Report of 17-20 April 1947. See Shiva Rao, B., *The Framing of India's Constitution*, New Delhi: The Indian Institute of Public Administration (1968), Vol.II, p.162, 177.
3. See sub-sec. 5.6. of Chapter 5.
4. The opponents of the Hindu law reform used the occasion to remind the government of the constitutional directive to enact a UCC for all communities. Some members of Parliament argued that if a constitution could be enacted on the principles of equality and equity for the entire country, then similar laws could be made for the whole country. This was a tactic adopted by the conservatives to forestall Hindu law reforms (Vidyavachaspati, 5 February 1951, pp.2387, 2389–90; Sarwate, Ibid. pp. 2374–5; Deshmukh, Ibid. p.2399).

5. The report stated that the absence of a UCC in the last quarter of the twentieth century, twenty-seven years after independence is an incongruity that cannot be justified with all the emphasis that is placed on secularism, science and modernism (p.142).

6. See Chapters 7 and 8.

7. See Kamila Tayabji quoted in Mahmood, T., *An Indian Civil Code and Islamic Law*, Bombay : N.M. Tripathi (1976), p.29 and Aggarwal, R., 'Uniform Civil Code—a formula not a solution' in Mahmood T. (ed.) *Family Law and Social Change*, Bombay : N.M. Tripathi (1975) pp. 110–44. Also see Bhattacharjee, A.M., *Matrimonial Laws and the Constitution*, Calcutta: Eastern Law House (1996), Preface [9].

8. Dhagamwar, V., *Towards the Uniform Civil Code*, Bombay: N.M. Tripathi (1989), p.71.

9. 'Since Muslims are allowed to marry four wives, the Muslim population is growing at a faster rate', is the communal propaganda. See Table 8 for the actual rate of increase in Muslim population.

10. The hastily passed Maharashtra bill on abolition of polygamy is a case in point.

11. Badshah, H., 'Uniform Civil Code—Chasing a Mirage,' *The Hindu*, 24 December 1995.

12. While not holding a brief for male bigamy, one is only questioning whether sexuality can be controlled through state regulations when the economic restraints that were rooted in European feudalism (bastardization of children from informal alliances and denying them the right of property inheritance) have broken down. The modern tendency is towards laxity in marriage contracts, conferring rights to spouses in informal relationships and dissolving the differences between legitimate and illegitimate children.

13. Zafar, J., 'Begin by Codifying Muslim Family Law,' *The Times of India*, 29 August 1995.

14. Anand, J., 'Uniform Civil Code: Case for a Supreme Court Judgment,' *The Asian Age*, 8 June 1995.

15. Ahmad, F., 'Fatwa needed to make talaq revocable,' The Pioneer, 17 May 1994; Engineer, A.A. 'Personal Law and Gender Justice,' *The Times of India*, 10 June 1995.

16. Shahabuddin, S., 'A Mountain is being made out of a molehill,' *The Hindustan Times*, 28 May 1995.

17. Ahmed, I., 'Personal Laws: Promoting Reform from Within,' *Economic and Political Weekly*, XXX/45 (1995), p. 2851.

18. Engineer, A.A., 'A Model for Change in Personal Law,' *The Times of India*, 25 July 1995.

19. *Muslim Family Law Ordinance*, 1961 (Ordinance No.VIII of 1961) S.5 of this Ordinance provides for registration of marriage; S.6 provides for regulated polygamy with the permission of the Arbitration Council; S.7 stipulates that talaq will be valid only after 90 days of its pronouncement and provides for efforts of reconciliation during this period; S.8 grants the wife delegated right of divorce and S.10 stipulates that mehr should be paid to the wife on demand. Further, Clause 18 of

the prescribed nikahnama provides for the wife's delegated right of divorce if the query is answered in the affirmative. For text see Appendix III.

20. Anand, J., 'Only hope for gender justice rests with Supreme Court *The Times of India,* 10 August 1995.

21. Engineer, A.A., 'Muslim reformists draft new legislation on marriage and divorce,' *The Times of India,* 10 April 1996.

22. Muslim Satyashodhak, an organization based in Pune has been demanding changes in law through judicial and legislative interventions. See Shikhare D., 'Talaq Mukti Morcha in Maharashtra,' *Manushi* Vol. VI n.2 (1986), p.23. A report of a recent protest march and delegation to the government to enact a UCC organized by the group appeared in *The Times of India,* 11 May 1997.

23. For details of the petition see a report titled, 'Abusing Religion to Oppress Women,' in *Manushi* IV/4 (1984), p.9.

24. Comments based on a personal interview with Shehanaz Sheikh.

25. Bhatnagar, R., 'Muslim Woman moves Court on Talaq,' report by *The Times of India,* 31 January 1995.

26. Hussain, W., 'I am a believer in Islam but can't accept discrimination,' *The Asian Age,* 13 April 1997.

27. *Ahmedabad Women Action Group (AWAG) & Ors v Union of India* JT 1997 (3) SC 171. But in this connection also see *C. Masilamani Mudaliar & Ors v Idol of Sri Swaminathaswami Thirukoil & Ors* (1996) 8 SCC 525, where the Supreme Court, held that: 'The personal laws must be consistent with the Constitution and can be struck down if they violate fundamental rights.'

28. As already discussed in Chapter 3, only a Muslim woman has the power to stipulate conditions by way of such agreements. Such agreements are void under the English law as well as all Indian matrimonial statutes which are derived from the English law.

29. For the salient features of these drafts see Chapter 11.

30. Ansari, I., 'Muslim Women's Rights: Goals and Strategy of Reform,' in *Economic and Political Weekly* XXVI/17 (1991), p.1095.

31. Ibid.

32. Ibid.

33. Translated into ground reality, this can be compared to the right of a Hindu bride not to give dowry at the time of her marriage. In both cases, the parents of the bride can exercise this choice only at the risk of marring the chances of marriage of their daughters, a risk very few parents would take in the prevailing social milieu of both urban and rural India across caste, religion and cultural divide.

34. Engineer, A.A., 'A Model for Change in Personal Law'.

Conclusions

While examining the evolution of family laws situated within a patriarchal social structure, discrimination against women is a foregone conclusion. Caste, class and clan purities are maintained through a strict sexual control. Punitive deterrent measures and denial of economic rights are the means through which this control is exercised.

This study set out to explore whether traditionally, within this constrained sphere, there were spaces through which women's rights to property could be negotiated. And also, whether the statutory interventions during colonial and post-colonial phases have led to the widening of this constrained sphere. This historical exploration was undertaken to gauge the nature and scope of law reform which is imperative to reverse the current trend of poverty and destitution among women. In this context, whether the models of a uniform code which have evolved in recent times would provide a solution to the problem at hand has also been examined.

The study reveals that the history of women's rights is not linear with the religious and customary laws forming one extreme end of the scale and the statutory reforms slowly and steadily progressing towards the other end, as it is popularly believed. The history is complex with various interactive forces constantly at play. Women's rights are not only constrained by a uniform set of patriarchal norms but are also shaped and moulded by several social, economic and political currents. So more accurately, within this complex framework, it has been a case of 'gain some, lose some'.

While examining the patriarchy located within the parameters of Indian feudalism of the smriti and post-smriti period, it is evident that despite the negative dictates, there were certain protective measures built into laws and customs, which granted women certain significant rights over property. While these rights do not meet the modern concept of equality, they were governed by a notion of equity. The Hindu woman's rights over ornaments, valuables and movable and immovable property under a specific category called stridhana are indicative of this protectionist approach. These measures were meant to provide some respite to women who were outside the sphere of coparcenary rights bestowed upon a Hindu male.

A social structure determined by caste hierarchies, necessitates relocation of women's rights within this hierarchy. The women situated in the higher strata of the caste structure were governed by a strict code of sexual control to maintain caste purity and secure property devolution through legitimate children. The women of the lower castes were out of the varna system prescribed by Manu and hence, the smriti code of sexual morality did not apply to them. As wage earners women contributed to the household. The patriarchal control of men in matrimonial relationships was lax and women had greater freedom of divorce and remarriage. The labour powers and sexuality of these women, as well as the labour powers of their men, were at the disposal of the higher castes and the seat of oppression was located within this structure. Most marginalized communities did not own property and hence the issue of being maintained from the family property and resources was not relevant. The concept of maintenance envisages a non-working dependent woman. The working class woman did not fit this description.

The Islamic jurisprudence of the pre-colonial period sought to protect women's economic rights within the concept of contractual marriages. Since the Arabs were primarily traders, they regulated all economic and social transactions through the concept of contracts. The marriage alliance was also defined in a similar fashion with certain additional measures built into the contract for the protection of women, the weaker partners. The women were granted the power to enter into pre-marriage agreements and lay down conditions within the marriage contract. In addition, the stipulation of a fixed amount which could provide future security to the wife was an essential ingredient of a Muslim marriage. Since marriage was a dissoluble contract, stipulation of high mehr amounts was meant to act as an economic deterrent upon the husband's power of arbitrary divorce.

While this was the textual position of Hindu and Islamic

jurisprudence, the colonial interventions must be contextualized within the customary, caste based, non-state arbitration fora prevalent at the advent of the colonial rule. As already mentioned, all legal systems, i.e. the Hindu, Islamic, as well as the Roman, contained several discriminatory provisions. During the colonial and post-colonial period, the discriminatory measures within the Hindu and Islamic legal systems were highlighted with a political motive. While the portrayal of a barbaric Hindu provided the justification for the colonial interventions in the pre-independence period, the image of a backward, pre-modern and polygamous Muslim served the Hindu communal forces in the post-independence period. The negative aspects of these systems were reinforced through judicial decisions and sensationalized media reportage. The protective measures built into these systems were allowed to become obscure and redundant. Stripped off the balancing counter measures, the traditional systems became severe and harsh towards women.

It is generally believed that the interventions by the colonial state in the realm of family law were meant primarily for the liberation of Indian woman from the barbaric customs of sati, female infanticide and marital rape of infant brides. It is also believed that women's right to property is a western concept introduced by the British during its modernizing mission. But this premise overlooks the fact that the Roman law, as well as the English common law contained several stringent anti-women biases. These biases crept into India through the Anglo-Saxon jurisprudence and subverted the traditional legal systems which provided women with a certain measure of economic security. The traditional systems were remoulded into linear, formal and stringent structures, which exercised greater patriarchal control over women and their right to property.

The colonial interventions also facilitated the construction of distinct and mutually hostile religious communities of Hindus and Muslims, to be governed by their respective personal laws along the model of the canon law. The basis of the legal system were the ancient scriptures translated with a western mind set. These scriptures were never meant to be used as rigid legal principles of an adversarial legal system. The translated texts drastically changed the nature and character of the customary and scriptural Hindu law and the Hindu woman's right to property suffered a severe set back. In the process of streamlining the pluralistic society several customary rights of women were crushed as they could not meet the legal requirement set by the British courts to prove a custom. Ironically, in this process the character of the communities was fixed and the mutually exclusive communities of Hindus and Muslims were constructed through litigation over property disputes.

The restructuring of the easily accessible non-state judicial fora dispensing quick redressals through community-based interventions, into an alien model of English courts rendered justice adversarial, expensive and dilatory. Within a system of hierarchy of courts, the decisions of the Privy Council became binding principles of law and the process of evolving laws at the local level to suit the needs of local communities was arrested. Concepts of justice, equity and good conscience became the direct channels of introducing English laws, principles and puritanical notions of morality into India.

During the nationalistic struggle, there were attempts to restore women's rights. The primary aim of the two legislations enacted in 1937, The *Hindu Married Women's Right to Property* and the *Application of Shariat Act* was to restore the property rights subverted through the legal precedents set by the Privy Council. But within a changed socio-economic and political context these legislations brought in only marginal respite.

The Constitution with its mandate of equality brought in visions of gender justice. Restructuring of the feudal family laws to suit the needs of women within a modern democracy was the challenge before the newly independent state. But the much trumpeted Hindu law reforms of the post-independence period were concerned more with homogenizing the culturally diverse Hindu community through a uniform set of state regulated enactments than widening the sphere of women's rights. Hence crucial women's rights located within customary laws were compromised. The enactments turned out to be a curious mixture of the English law and the shastric law with the worst biases of both written into them.

To cite one example, although the *Hindu Marriage Act* introduced divorce, the Act did not provide for any economic security for divorced women except the right of meagre maintenance. The concept of maintenance could provide safety only within a feudal property structure where property is inalienable and marriages are indissoluble. The large-scale destitution of Hindu women after divorce in the post-reform phase seemed as though Hindu women had bartered the right of residence and economic security, to the right of divorce and consequent destitution.

Traditionally, the Hindu woman had a distinct economic right called stridhana. The definition of stridhana, its changing character during various phases of a woman's life, the woman's power of disposal over it etc. had been the subject of elaborate discussion under the smriti law. The commentators of the post-smriti period were engaged in widening its scope and strengthening its base. And yet, while restructuring the traditional sacramental form of marriage into a dissoluble contract and bestowing upon the Hindu woman a new status of a divorcee, the character of her stridhana and control over it during this new phase of life did not find a mention in the *Hindu Marriage Act*. This is perhaps due to the fact that most nationalist leaders were advocates trained in English law which they held as a model for reform and had imbibed the colonial contempt for the traditional system of law. So the *Hindu Marriage Act* turned out to be a poor imitation of the *English Matrimonial Causes Act*. Based on the concept of formal equality, the Hindu law was stripped of all its protective measures. Even the traditional right of maintenance was now extended to husbands, a concept unheard of under either the scriptural or customary Hindu law.

The principle of monogamy, which was modelled on the western and Christian doctrine was not suited to the cultural conditions of a custom-ridden, pluralistic Hindu society. So at one level the law was ineffective in curbing monogamy, but conversely it strengthened the patriarchal base by depriving women in informal relationships of their customary rights.

The much proclaimed right of inheritance was subverted by surreptitiously granting Hindu men the right to will away the property. The protective restraint against bequests under the Islamic law to safeguard women's rights, did not find a place in the codified Hindu law, since the Hindu law was remoulded on the English model of exclusive and absolute rights to the individual. To facilitate the transformation of the economic system from feudalism to capitalism, it was crucial that property be alienable in the hands of individual men. The inalienable and immovable property could now be converted into liquid and negotiable capital. Within this new economic structure, women's rights of maintenance and inheritance became transient and illusory.

Despite these limitations, the enactments were projected as proof of India's claim to modernity. During the following decades, the discourse on family law reform, targeted the Muslim personal law as the object. This criticism can be extended not only to Hindu communal forces but also to the judiciary, legal academia and the media. Polygamy and arbitrary divorce were projected as the major problems affecting women. Although at one level, statistics for wife murder and suicide by young brides signalled a phenomenal increase in family violence among Hindus and the soaring number of the destitute reflected the inadequacy of the reformed Hindu law, the discourse on the Uniform Civil Code continued to project the codified Hindu law as a model for women's liberation and empowerment. The correlation between increasing rates of suicides, murder and destitution of Hindu women and the reformed Hindu laws was not examined by the protagonists of the UCC. This led to the demand for this code acquiring a distinct communal hue.

Although uniformity was the aspiration, during the decades that followed, inroads were made into uniform laws to protect the patriarchal interests of Hindu and Muslim men. The Hinduization of the *Special Marriage Act* in 1976 and the denial of rights to divorced Muslim women through the enactment of the *Muslim Women's Act* in 1986, following the Shah Bano controversy are two concrete examples of this trend. But while the *Muslim Women's Act* has been projected as the worst instance of communal appeasement by the ruling government, the Hinduization of the *Special Marriage Act*, a decade prior to this enactment went unnoticed by scholars and the media except for a few stray protests.

The adverse comments by the judiciary while deciding issues of gender during the last decade reinforced popular communal misconceptions and served to widen the communal gulf. These comments and the adverse publicity that followed led to the alienation of even progressive segments within the Muslim community. Within the communalized politics of the post-Babri Masjid phase, support to the demand of a Uniform Civil Code came to be construed as a betrayal of the cause of identity politics and minority rights. These developments have rendered the task of family law reform extremely complex.

The issue of women's rights is also ridden with other complexities. Located within an adversarial, dilatory, formidable and expensive court structure, even the limited rights granted by the statutes have become illusory and beyond the reach of most women. Hence they could not provide any respite or tilt the balance in women's favour. In the clamour for reforms, the impact of existing legal provisions upon individual women at a micro level or on the broad category of women at a macro level has not been adequately assessed. The adversarial system modelled on the notion of formal equality has become ineffective. Unless the statutory measures are re-located within informal, inexpensive and easily accessible legal systems which are governed by an interventionist approach, the most ideal and gender just statutes will, in effect, be redundant.

The new economic order ushered in during the nineties which resulted in opening of the Indian markets has led to a widening of the gap between the rich and the poor, the urban and rural, the haves and the have nots. It is logical that in this era of increasing inequalities, the gender gulf would also widen. If the joint family structure was the norm of a feudal society and the nuclear family, the norm of a capitalist society, single women families are fast becoming the norm of the post-capitalist society. Statistics reveal that one-third of all Indian households are women headed and a large segment of these live below the poverty line.

Any suggestion for reform in family laws which sets out to redefine gender relations within marriage and the family, would have to take into consideration the above social, political, legal and economic realities. But the drafts for the enactment of a Uniform Civil Code framed by the legal academia, do not seem to have contextualized women's rights within these diverse complexities. The model for reform is the *Hindu Marriage Act* which in turn is based on archaic English principles. Since all statutory matrimonial laws in India, except the Muslim law, are based on English laws of marriage, the primary aim of the suggested reforms seems to be to streamline the 'pre-modern' or 'medieval' Islamic family law along 'modern' principles. Since a medieval Christian remedy of restitution of conjugal rights located within European feudalism is retained in these drafts, the attempt to modernize the family law appears to be confined only to the Muslim law.

Although gender justice is the stated goal of these reforms, the predominant concern seems to be with uniformity. In judicial decisions, as well as in popular projections, the demand for uniformity is linked to national integration and homogenization of religious communities through a common family law. While the demand is raised primarily in the context of Muslim personal law, there have been no attempts to examine whether such uniformity would suit the culturally diverse and unevenly modernized Hindu society. The fact that the *Hindu Marriage Act* has validated diverse customary forms of marriage and divorce, seems to have been overlooked by the zealous reformers. Although the *Hindu Marriage Act* set out to 'reform' Hindu law and bring it under the state control and regulations, sufficient scope was provided for Hindu customs and practices. Hence under the present statute, a Hindu need never approach a state functionary or a religious institution either for solemnization of his/her marriage or for its dissolution.

The *Hindu Succession Act* also contains ample examples of regional diversities. The central statute enacted in 1956, retained Hindu male coparcenaries or joint family property holdings. This concept deprived women of the right of inheritance in ancestral property. Their right to equal inheritance was limited only to self-acquired property of a Hindu male. In 1976, in the state of Kerala under the leftist scheme of land reforms, the concept of joint family holdings was abolished. In 1984, women in Andhra Pradesh were granted the right of coparcenary through a state amendment. The states of Tamil Nadu and Karnataka introduced the provisions of the Andhra Pradesh amendments in 1990 and 1994, respectively. Under a women's policy introduced in Maharashtra in 1994, women in Maharashtra were granted the right to be recognized as coparcenars.

Since the southern states had a culture of granting women rights to property under customary law, the state amendments did not cause a major stir. In contrast, none of the northern states have enacted such a provision nor has there been a central amendment to this effect. At the other extreme, the state of Haryana unanimously passed an amendment in 1987 for the abolition of Hindu women's rights in the self-acquired property of a Hindu male under the plea that it leads to fragmentation of agricultural land. The bill could not be enacted because it did not receive the President's assent. This is just one example of the cultural diversity reflected within the codified Hindu law. Once the state acquired the power to legislate for its Hindu citizens and established its superiority to the religious heads, the diversity reflected in the Hindu family law did not seem to have caused any concern to the state.

The Indian Constitution contains an internal inconsistency regarding family laws. While Art. 44 directs the state to enact a Uniform Civil Code, the power to legislate in the realm of family law is situated in the concurrent list (Entry 5, List III of the Seventh Schedule) which indicates that the power is granted to both central and state legislatures. Since the constitution provides for a federal structure with clearly defined legislative powers, depriving the states of this power through the enactment of one set of rigid and uniform family laws would lead to the dominance of the centre over the states. While this would affect the centre-state relationships in all the states, it would cause a serious dent in relationships with the north-eastern states which are further protected through specific constitutional guarantees.

The scheme of this study has been to place women's rights within the political developments of the nation. The study reflects that women's rights is not a primary concern of the dominant forces but the rhetoric can conveniently be brought into the public arena in support of other hidden political objectives. In this context, it is necessary to emphasize that when a previously colonized state achieves independence, and sets out to redefine its authority over other prevailing power structures through statutory reforms, in the fervour of constituting the infrastructure of a new state, it is relatively easy to push the agenda of women's rights and enact a comprehensive family code. But the Indian independence was marked by a bloody partition. Hence within the new democracy, it became imperative to assure the minorities of their right to a cultural identity, to ensure political stability. The continuance of the personal laws was a marker of this assurance. Hence the family law reforms undertaken by the independent Indian nation in the fervour of the newly acquired independence were confined to the majority community. Even this limited task was undertaken only after the ruling Congress party, under the leadership of Pundit Nehru, the most popular prime minister of independent India, was returned to power with an overwhelming majority in the first elections held in 1952.

Regarding law reform for minorities, it was hoped that in the years that followed, the ruffled feathers would smoothen and the political stability would facilitate the enactment of a uniform family law. But the decades that followed witnessed not only the widening of the communal gulf but formations of precariously perched minority and coalition governments. In this climate of increasing electoral insecurity, no government would risk forcing a uniform code upon unwilling constituencies or rake up controversies which could become politically costly. The government's approach towards Christian law reforms is an indication of this political apathy.

In this vitiated atmosphere, the process of reform would have to be carefully carved out and systematically followed up through sustained campaigns. Within a democratic political structure with an assurance of the protection of the cultural identity of the minorities, the law reform for minorities would essentially have to be initiated from within the communities and endorsed by its leaders. The efforts of non-Muslim minorities in this direction have been discussed in detail. The strategies adopted by the Parsi community are particularly relevant. The community has been able to preserve its specific cultural identity while modernizing the family laws. The attempts by the Christian community have been more laborious and are marked by tensions between liberal Protestants and conservative Catholics at one end and the Catholic clergy and the laity at the other, with the government's posture of inaction supporting the status-quoists. It is only through a balancing act that the community has been able to inch its way towards reform.

Community-based initiatives are particularly lacking among the Muslims. Although the progressive Muslim intelligentsia has expressed concern over the discriminatory provisions within the personal laws, the suggestions for reform lack the institutional support which is essential to organize sustained campaigns. One concrete suggestion which could lead to redefining gender equations within the framework of Islamic jurisprudence is the formulation of a standard nikahnama and the setting up of arbitration councils to regulate marriages and divorces. The standard nikahnama could contain provisions of monogamy, curtail the power of arbitrary and unilateral divorce, grant the wife delegated power of divorce and provide for the future security of the wife by stipulating securities, conceding valuable or immovable property as mehr in lieu of token cash amounts, in accordance with the economic status of the parties. If the

Muslim Personal Law Board acts upon the suggestions made by progressive groups, the Muslim personal law would be more equitable towards women while retaining its specific characteristics without invoking a major political controversy. But this can be achieved only when the progressive elements within the community are able to exert pressure on the Muslim Personal Law Board which is not the case at present.

Another important political strategy at this juncture is to disassociate concerns of gender from the context of identity politics within which the demand for a Uniform Civil Code is currently located. The legislative history of last fifty years reveals that it is possible to enact uniform legislations in specific areas of family law without invoking the controversy of majority-minority politics. *The Dowry Prohibition Act*, 1961, the Medical *Termination of Pregnancy Act*, 1971, introduction of new offence of cruelty to wives under S.498(A) *IPC* in 1983 and the *Family Courts Act*, 1984 are indicative of this possibility. In a phased out scheme of reform, least controversial aspects could be prioritized. Concrete suggestions for specific enactments made by some women's organizations have already been discussed. In this context the Private Member's Bill to secure the rights of married women is of special significance.

The suggestions for widening the base of women's economic rights would have to be backed by campaigns. During the eighties, women's organizations were successful in bringing about changes in laws concerning rape and dowry after sustained, nationwide campaigns. But in the realm of economic rights such campaigns are particularly lacking. Even the recommendations by the Law Commission in its *132nd Report* in 1989 to abolish the ceiling of Rs 500 maintenance under S.125 of the Cr.PC has not been backed by a public campaign. Similarly although there has been a demand for the enactment of a Domestic Violence Act with powers of granting restraining injunctions and the Law Commission has also formulated a Bill in this regard, so far a Bill on this issue has not been introduced in Parliament. Focused and sustained campaigns around specific issues might prove more effective than following the mirage of an all-encompassing, ideal Uniform Civil Code.

The suggestions by women's organizations which bring economic rights at the centre of matrimonial reforms are indicative of a shift in the women's rights discourse. While this is positive, a theoretical framework regarding the nature of matrimonial rights under different economic systems has not yet evolved.

Currently, the matrimonial statutes revolve around the concept of marital conjugality and exclusive sexual access/control. The reformist concept of contractual marriages with the right to terminate the contract of conjugality was ushered in as a liberating and empowering weapon which would relieve women of the sacramental bond of sexual servitude. But this definition of marriage as primarily a sexual or conjugal contract overlooks a historical reality of marriage as an institution of economic regulation of property relationships. Sexual control within marriage served primarily to regulate property relationships. If this is the basic framework, then the sexual liberation ushered in through the concept of contractual and dissoluble marriages would be a hollow relief if it is not simultaneously linked to a redefinition of property relationships. This intrinsic link between the right of divorce and access to property is apparent in the evolution of English matrimonial statutes but is sadly lacking in the Indian statutes. Although based on English principles, Indian matrimonial statutes have failed to incorporate the more recent developments regarding matrimonial property under the English law on a perfunctory premise that marriage is a holy and sacrosanct union under the Indian setting and hence it cannot be reduced to a contract of property regulations.

Since the institution of marriage is integrally linked to the institution of property, then any change in the character of property under different economic systems would necessarily bring in changes in the nature of matrimonial property and its access. The economic rights which flow from a marriage contract under the Indian matrimonial statutes are presently defined within archaic laws which originated in a feudal society of agrarian landholdings which were inalienable and immovable. The concepts of the permanency of marriage and inalienability of land were coordinate. The members of the joint family were maintained by the produce of the land. In the event of lapses, the property could be charged for maintenance of its members and this right could be traced to the subsequent buyer. It is within this economic structure that the right to maintenance had evolved and had a specific significance for women. When the economic structure changed from feudalism to capitalism and the organization of the society changed from agrarian-rural to industrialized-urban the land became alienable and property was rendered movable and transient. Simultaneously, the western woman's rights to property also underwent a change. Concepts such as married women's right to separate property, joint matrimonial property with equal rights to both spouses, right of residence in the matrimonial home after the dissolution of the marriage, the spousal claim to a share of matrimonial property in the event of it being willed away depriving her/him of her/his rights etc. have become important principles of matrimonial law.

But in India the rights of married women and divorcees have continued to be confined to a right of maintenance. The implication of this right to women from propertyless, wage earning sections of societies has not been examined. The right is also defined in the context of a dependent woman who is treated under the matrimonial statutes as a ward of her husband. The concept of maintenance also envisages a sexually pure woman, both within marriage and after divorce and renders maintenance a premium to sexual purity.

These are complex questions which need to be addressed in the discourse on family law reform. Unless a theoretical framework is evolved which situates marriages centrally within the context of economic structures, women's right to economic security in matrimonial relationships will continue to be illusive.

In this study, while discussing the political context of women's rights, a passing reference to the economic systems under which these rights evolved, has been made. But the issue of property was not the central focus of this study. There is a need to locate property at the centre of matrimonial law reform, if adequate solutions to the trend of poverty and destitution of women have to be evolved. Since patriarchy is reinforced through economic structures, be they of feudalism, capitalism or post-capitalism, a solution to the oppression and destitution of women would have to be found primarily in the context of the economic structures and the state responsibility towards women within these structures. It is towards these directions that efforts of family law reform need to be forged.

Appendix I

THE DOMESTIC VIOLENCE TO WOMEN (PREVENTION) BILL, 1994*

A BILL to provide for the prevention of domestic violence to women and for matters connected therewith or incidental thereto BE it enacted by Parliament in the Forty-fifth Year of the Republic of India as follows:

1. Short title, extent and commencement

    (1) This Act may be called the *Domestic Violence to Women (Prevention) Act*, 1994.

    (2) It extends to the whole of India.

    (3) It shall come into force on the 1st day of January, 1995.

2. Definitions

In this Act, unless the context otherwise requires:-

(a) 'Court' means, in any area for which there is a Family Court established under the provisions of the *Family Courts Act*, 1984, that Court, and in any other area, the principal civil court of original jurisdiction, and includes any civil court or a Mahila Panchayat consisting of three women members of a Gram Panchayat which the State Government may, by notification, specify as the court competent to deal with all or any of the matters specified in this Act.

(b) 'Domestic violence' means any of the following acts committed on a woman by her husband or any of his or her relatives, namely;

    (i) any willful conduct which,

        • is of such a nature as is likely to drive the woman out

*As Approved by the Expert Committee on laws in its meeting held on 18-19 August 1994

of the house or to commit suicide or to injure herself, or

- causes injury or danger to the life, limb or health (whether mental or physical) of the woman; or

(ii) harassment which causes distress to a woman; or

(iii) any act which compels the woman to have sexual intercourse against her will either with the husband or any of his relatives or with any other person; or

(iv) any act which is unbecoming of the dignity of the woman; or

(v) any other act of omission or commission which is likely to cause mental torture or mental agony to the woman.

(c) 'Notification' means a notification published in the Official Gazette.

(d) 'Prescribed' means prescribed by rules made under this act.

(e) 'Protection Officer' means an officer appointed by the State Government in relation to or for the purposes of this Act and includes any institution or organization designated by the Government to perform the functions of a Protection Officer under this Act, in relation to an area.

(f) 'Protection Order' means an order made under this Act for the protection of a woman subject to domestic violence and for such other provisions like separate stay, maintenance and the prevention of further domestic violence.

(g) 'Relative' includes any person related by blood, marriage or adoption.

3. Act Not in Derogation of Any Other Law

The provisions of this Act shall be in addition to, and not in derogation of the provisions of any other law, for the time being in force.

4. Presentation of Petition to Court

(1) Any woman subject to domestic violence or any other person on her behalf or a Protection Officer may, without prejudice to the provisions of this Act, or of any other law for the time being in force, present a petition to the court for the passing of a Protection Order.

(2) A petition presented under sub-section (1) shall, among other things, contain the following particulars, namely:

(a) the name and particulars of the woman subject to domestic violence or if the petition is presented by any other person, the particulars also of such other person;

(b) the name and address of the husband or the relative who has committed domestic violence;

(c) the nature of domestic violence;

(d) all other particulars which would be necessary for the issue of a Protection Order.

(3) On receipt of a petition under sub-section (1), and on consideration of the statements made therein, and the evidence produced, if the Court is satisfied that a Protection Order may properly be made forthwith, it may make such order *ex-parte*, and shall fix a date for further consideration of the petition.

(4) If, on consideration of the petition under sub-section (3) the Court is not so satisfied, it shall fix a date for further consideration of the petition without making any Protection Order.

(5) The notice of the date fixed under sub-section (3) or sub-section (4), which shall not be more than seven days from the date of issue of such notice, shall be given to the petitioner, or if the petitioner is not the woman subject to violence, to the woman and the Protection Officer, her husband or the relative who has been committing domestic violence and to any other person to whom, in the opinion of the Court, such notice shall be given.

(6) A notice given under sub-section (3) or sub-section (4), shall be served on all the persons to whom it is intended, sufficiently in advance of the date of hearing, and if it is not possible for any reason to serve such notice on any of the parties, it shall be pasted on the main door of the premises in which the person to whom the notice is intended is known to have last resided or worked for gain, in accordance with the provisions specified in the *Code of Civil Procedure*, 1908 for such service, and any notice so served shall be deemed to have been validly served on the party, to whom it is intended to be served and shall not be called in question in any court on the ground that the notice had not been validly served.

(7) On the date fixed under sub-section (3) or sub-section (4) or on such date or dates to which the hearing may be adjourned and after hearing the parties, the Court is satisfied that the woman is subjected to domestic violence, it may pass a Protection Order, and if it is not so satisfied, it shall dismiss the petition setting forth the reasons for such dismissal:

Provided that the Court may extend any Protection Order issued under sub-section (3) with or without any alteration or modification or where no such order is issued, it may issue such order, pending disposal of the petition.

(8) Every endeavour shall be made by the Court hearing the petition under this Act to dispose off it expeditiously and in any case not later than three months from the date of presentation of the petition.

(9) Where any of the parties to the petition so desire, the Court shall on an application made by such party, conduct the proceedings in camera.

(10) A copy of the Protection Order shall be forwarded to the Protection Office and to all the parties concerned.

(11) A Protection Order made under this section shall be in force for such period not exceeding four years as the Court may fix.

5. Contents of Protection Order

The Protection Order shall contain, among other things, the following matters, namely:

(a) directing the husband or the relative to desist from committing any domestic violence;

(b) directing in all cases that the wife live separately from her husband, along with the children, if any, and the matrimonial home be given to the wife for her separate living.

Explanation: For the purpose of this clause, 'matrimonial home' means the accommodation in which the husband and the wife lived together immediately before the presentation of the petition, and if such accommodation happens to be rented or belonging to a joint family in which the husband is a member, that house or part of the house.

(c) Where the women subject to domestic violence is unmarried, widow, divorcee or deserted, directing that separate accommodation be provided for her living along with the children, if any;

(d) directing that the expenses of such separate living be borne by the husband or relative;

(e) directing the husband or relative to pay such maintenance to the wife or any children staying with her;

(f) such other matters as may be considered necessary.

Explanation: For the removal of doubts, it is hereby declared that in the cases covered under clause (e), no maintenance will be provided under any other law for the time being in force.

6. Duties of the Protection Officer

(1) It shall be the duty of the Protection Officer to make himself aware of all the domestic violence being committed in the area for which he is appointed and try to settle it peacefully and amicably between the parties.

(2) Without prejudice to sub-section (1), it shall be within the competence of the Protection Officer,

On an application presented to him by the woman subject to domestic violence or any other person on her behalf to arrive at a mutual settlement or on the failure of the parties to arrive at any settlement, to file a petition to the Court under this Act.

(3) It shall also be the duty of the Protection Officer to see that the provisions of the Protection Order are complied with.

7. Protection Officer to be a Public Servant

The Protection Officer shall be deemed to be a public servant within the meaning of Section 21 of the *Indian Penal Code.*

8. Power to Call for Information or Document

The Protection Officer may, for the purposes of efficient performance of his duties specified in Section 6, require any person or authority to furnish any information or document and it shall be the duty of such person or authority to furnish such information or document.

9. Consequential Amendment to the *Indian Penal Code* and the *Code of Criminal Procedure* 1973

(1) In Chapter XX-A of the Indian Penal Code, 1860, after section 498-A, the following section shall be inserted, namely:

498-B. Husband or relative of husband or of the woman subjecting her to domestic violence: Whoever, being the husband or the relative of the husband or of the woman, subjects such woman to domestic violence shall be punished with imprisonment for a term which may extend to three years and shall also be liable to fine.

Explanation: For the purposes of this section, 'relative' and 'domestic' violence shall have the same meanings as in the *Domestic Violence to Women (Prevention) Act*, 1994.

(2) In the *First Schedule to the Code of Criminal Procedure* 1973, in the entries relating to 'Chapter xx-A—Of cruelty by husband or relative of husband', after the entries relating to section 498-A, the following entries shall be inserted, namely:-

498 (B) Punishment for subjecting a woman to domestic violence.	Imprisonment for three years and fine.	Cognizable if information relating to the commission of the offence is given to an officer incharge of a police station by any person aggrieved by the offence or by any person related to her by blood, marriage or adoption, or if there is no such relative, the Protection Officer appointed under the Domestic Violence to Women (Prevention) Act, 1994, or such other officer as may be notified by the State Government in this behalf.	Non-bailable.	Magistrate 1st Class

10. Power to Make Rules

The State Government may by notification make rules to carry out the provisions of this Act.

Background

The Committee of Experts considered aspects pertaining to domestic violence with a view to providing legal remedies to the distressed victims, taking note of the Indian conditions. It recommends the accompanying Draft Bill, titled 'The *Domestic Violence of Women (Prevention) Bill*' for adoption. The background relating to domestic violence and the salient features of the Draft Bill are given below:

The term domestic violence is wide and encompasses in its scope all types of violence resorted to within the precincts of a home whether by male or female members of a family. But the overwhelming majority of victims of domestic violence are women. To be sure all such acts are punishable under the provisions of the *Indian Penal Code*, 1861. Nonetheless resort to the general law of the land is very seldom made by the women-victims of domestic violence owing to a variety of factors. Some of these factors are : a) close familial relationship; b) dependency, financial or otherwise; c) lack of legal literacy; and d) helplessness of the victims. Most of these cases go unreported and give rise to serious human problem.

Studies have pointed out that family violence is cyclic and is apt to pass from one generation to another; that children who had experienced violence are more likely to be violent towards wife and children in their adult life, and that in order to reduce societal violence, it is necessary to reduce violence within the family.

A prominent type of domestic violence in India is dowry-related domestic violence. In recent years considerable number of legislations were enacted and amendments to legislation were made to curb the evil. The *Criminal Law (Second Amendment) Act,* 1983 introduced the new offence of cruelty under Section 498-A; Section 174 of the *Criminal Procedure Code* was amended to secure post-mortem in case of death or suicide of a married girl; section 113-A was inserted in the *Indian Evidence Act;* and new Section 304-B relating to 'Dowry death' was incorporated in the *Indian Penal Code.* In view of these specific legislative provisions, the Draft Bill limits itself to other forms of domestic violence against women.

Domestic violence has been given a wide definition. It includes not only conduct which amounts to cruelty but also includes any act which is unbecoming of the dignity of the woman. Clause 3 of the Draft Bill states that the provisions of the *Domestic Violence to Women (Prevention) Act* are in addition to and not in derogation of any other law.

The Committee considered the 'Model Law Against Domestic Violence' of the *Lawyers Collective* sent by Ms. Indira Jaising. The Draft sent by her is heavily based on Lisa G. Lerman's 'A Model State Act: Remedies for Domestic Abuse' published in *Harvard Journal of Legislation*. This Model State Act. does not at all take into consideration the social milieu and conditions in India. For this reason the Model State Law was found to be unsuitable.

The other foreign legislation noticed by the Committee was the *Domestic Violence and Matrimonial Proceedings Act*, 1976 of the U.K. Under this, a party to a marriage is entitled to get an injunction from a Country court restraining the other party from molesting the applicant or a child living with the applicant. Their injunction may also contain a provision excluding the other party from the matrimonial home or any part of it. Further, if the judge is satisfied that actual bodily harm has been caused to the party to a marriage or a child of the spouse, it may attach a power of arrest to the injunction for its breach; thereby a constable is empowered to arrest a person committing the breach of the injunction without a warrant.

Some of the factors which inhibit or discourage women-victims from seeking the available legal remedies have been mentioned before. The approach of the Draft Bill to meet these problems may be pointed out.

One of the major difficulties faced by victims of domestic violence is their inability to approach the courts for relief as they (courts) are located in urban centres. This is specially so in case of victims drawn from rural areas. The Draft defines a 'court' in wide terms as including a Family Court, a Civil Court and a Mahila Panchayat consisting of three women members of a Gram Panchayat, if so declared by a State Government. The creation of Mahila Panchayats as courts takes note of the socio-cultural context that prevails in rural areas and will help in rendering speedy justice in cases of domestic violence.

The existing delays in getting a legal remedy in cases of domestic violence discourage a victim, or a relation of the victim or a social worker who wants to aid the victim from seeking relief. Therefore, Clause 4 of the Draft Bill proposes a time-frame in the matter of disposal of the petitions. First, if the court is satisfied on a consideration of the statement made in the petition, it can forthwith make a Protection Order, even *ex-parte*, and fix a date for further consideration of the petition. Second, in case it is not satisfied with the statement made in the petition, it will fix a date without making an order; but the date so fixed should not be more than seven days from the date of issue of notice to the concerned persons. Sub clause 8 of Clause 4 of the Draft envisages that the court should dispose of the petition expeditiously and not later than 3 months from the date of filing of the petition.

Experience shows that lack of living accommodation primarily makes a woman suffer silently the battering given by the husband or other male relative. To meet this difficulty Clause 5 of the Draft Bill says that the Protection Order direct that the woman shall live separately from her husband and the matrimonial home be given to the wife for her separate living. The term 'matrimonial home' includes accommodation that is rented as well as belonging to the joint family. The Draft also envisages that in case the battered woman is unmarried or widow or divorcee, the Protection Order will direct separate living accommodation be provided for her living. Lack of financial support and fear of losing the custody of children force victims of violence to lead a captive existence. To overcome this the Clause 5 empowers the court to grant maintenance to the wife and children living with her, and give directions with respect to 'such other matters as may be considered necessary'.

The Draft envisages a key-role to Protection Officers. The term Protection Officer covers not only an officer appointed by the State Government but also any institution or organization designated by the State Government to perform the function of a Protection Officer in relation to an area. Thus it envisages a role to non-governmental organizations in combating the problem of domestic violence. If the helpless condition of a woman does not permit her to file a petition for Protection Order, any person on her behalf or a Protection Officer can file a petition for securing the remedies.

Sd/-
Professor B. Sivaramayya

Appendix II

The Married Women (Protection of Rights) Bill 1994 (Bill No. XXV of 1994) (R.S. 13-5-94)

A BILL to protect the rights of a married woman and for matters connected therewith.

BE it enacted by Parliament in the Forty-fifth Year of the Republic of India as follows:

1. Short Title

This Act may be called the *Married Women (Protection of Rights) Act, 1994.*

2. Definition

In this Act unless the context otherwise requires:

(a) 'appropriate government' means the Central or the State Government under whose employment the husband of the widow was at the time of his death;

(b) 'prescribed' means prescribed by rules made under this Act;

(c) 'property' means movable and immovable property whether ancestral or not, or whether acquired jointly with other members of the family or by way of accretion to any ancestral property of the husband of a married woman, and includes deposits of the husband in provident fund, banks, shares, any public saving schemes, ornaments, land and house.

3. Rights of a Married Woman

A married woman shall be entitled to the following rights, namely:-

(1) she shall have a right to live in the house of her husband whether owned by him or by his joint family without seeking

judicial separation or divorce from her husband;

(2) she shall without seeking judicial separation be entitled to have food, clothing and other facilities and maintenance and support for herself form her husband;

(3) she shall be entitled to have an equal share in the property of her husband from the date of her marriage and shall also be entitled to dispose off her share in the property by way of sale, gift, mortgage, will or in any other manner whatsoever;

(4) she shall have a right of free access till her life to the children born out of the wedlock if they remain in the custody of her husband irrespective of the dissolution of marriage;

(5) she shall have an option to bring up the children separately, have their custody, maintenance and education consistently by remaining in the family of her husband;

(6) she shall be consulted by her husband in matters of family business and other financial transactions made out of the property of her husband or of the joint family.

4. Rights of a Widow

A widow shall be entitled to the following rights, namely:

(1) she shall, if eligible, be entitled to get suitable employment in the event of the death of her husband who happened to be an employee in a given Department;

(2) she shall be entitled to pension at such rates and on such conditions as the appropriate Government may have prescribed;

(3) she shall have the first claim and absolute right on the property of her deceased husband.

5. Enforceability of Rights

(1) The rights conferred by this Act shall be enforceable in a court of law or in a Lok Adalat.

(2) Any transaction or business entered into in violation of subsection (6) of Section 3 shall be null and void.

6. Act to Have Overriding Effect

The provisions of this Act shall have effect notwithstanding anything inconsistent therewith contained in any other law for the time being in force or in any instrument having effect by virtue of any law other than this Act or in any decree or order of any court, tribunal or other authority.

7. Power to Make Rules

The appropriate Government may, by notification, make rules for carrying out the provisions of this Act.

Statements of Objects and Reasons

In the wake of independence, the Indian woman has not only been able to recognize her status but has also made man recognize it. Nevertheless, the status of a woman is still far from being dignified and safe in the Indian society. Although we are going to cross over to the twenty-first century from the twentieth century, our attitude towards women is still that of the middle-aged feudal lords. Even today we are not prepared to grant the same liberty to women which men themselves are enjoying dauntlessly.

Today, the real cause of the exploitation of a woman by her husband is that she has got no right in the house of her husband; she has got no right on the property of the husband. Even our laws confer the right of property on a woman only after the death of her husband and not during her coverture.

If a woman's right in the property of her husband is recognized the moment she marries, she will start feeling secure and will overcome her sense of helplessness and economic insecurity. This will minimize if not eliminate to a great extent the cases of separation and divorce whose basic reason is economic in many cases. What she will get on divorce, society should grant her during the subsistence of marriage. It is the most glaring injustice and indignity to woman that while she is a partner of the husband, the latter does not even think it necessary to inform her about his financial and family transactions, leave alone consultation with her.

The Bill seeks to achieve the above objectives by granting women certain rights.

VEENA VERMA

Appendix III

A: The Muslim Family Law Ordinance, 1961
[Ordinance No. VIII of 1961]

[15th July, 1961]

Preamble, WHEREAS it is expedient to give effect to certain recommendations of the Commission on Marriage and Family Laws:

NOW, THEREFORE, in pursuance of the Proclamation of the seventh day of October 1958, and in exercise of all powers enabling him in that behalf, the President is pleased to make and promulgate the following Ordinance:

1. Short Title, Extent, Application and Commencement

(1) This Ordinance may be called the *Muslim Family Laws Ordinance*, 1961.

(2) It extends to the whole of Pakistan, and applies to all Muslim citizens of Pakistan, wherever they may be.

(3) It shall come into force on such date as the Central Government may, by notification in the official Gazette, appoint in this behalf.

2. Definitions

In this Ordinance, unless there is anything repugnant in the subject or context:

(a) 'Arbitration Council' means a body consisting of the Chairman and a representative of each of the parties to a matter dealt with in this Ordinance:

Provided that where any party fails to nominate a representative within the prescribed time, the body formed without such representative shall be the Arbitration Council;

(b) 'Chairman' means the Chairman of the Union Council or a person appointed by the [Central Government in the Cantonment areas or by the Provincial Government in other areas] or by an officer authorized in that behalf by any such Government, to discharge the functions of Chairman under this Ordinance:
Provided that where the Chairman of the Union Council is a non-Muslim or he himself wished to make an application to the Arbitration Council, or is owing to illness or any other reason, unable to discharge the functions of Chairman, the Council shall elect one of its Muslim members as Chairman for the purpose of this Ordinance;
(c) 'Prescribed' means prescribed by rules made under section 11;
(d) 'Union Council' means the Union Council or the Town Union Committee constituted under the Basic Democracies Order, 1959 (P.O. No. 18 of 1959), and having jurisdiction in the matter as prescribed,
(e) 'Ward' means a ward within a Union or Town as defined in the aforesaid Order.

3. Ordinance to Override Other Laws, etc.

(1) The provisions of this Ordinance shall have effect notwithstanding any law, custom or usage, and the registration of Muslim marriages shall take place only in accordance with these provisions.
(2) For the removal of doubt, it is hereby declared that the provisions of the *Arbitration Act*, 1940 (X of 1940), the *Code of Civil Procedures* 1908 (Act V of 1908), and any other law regulating the procedures of Courts shall not apply to any Arbitration Council.

4. Succession

In the event of the death of any son or daughter of the propositus before the opening of succession, the children of such son or daughter, if any, living at the time the succession opens, shall per stripes receive a share equivalent to the share which such son or daughter, as the case may be, would have received if alive.

5. Registration of Marriages

(1) Every marriage solemnized under Muslim Law shall be

registered in accordance with the prevision of this Ordinance.

(2) For the purpose of registration of marriages under this Ordinance, the Union Council shall grant licenses to one or more persons, to be called Nikah Registrars, but in no case shall more than one Nikah Registrar be licensed for any one Ward.

(3) Every marriage not solemnized by the Nikah Registrar shall, for the purpose of registration under this Ordinance be reported to him by the person who has solemnized such marriage.

(4) Whoever contravenes the provision of sub-section (3) shall be punishable with simple imprisonment for a term which may extend to three months, or with fine which may extend to one thousand rupees, or with both.

(5) The form of nikahnama, the registers to be maintained by Nikah Registrars, the records to be preserved by Union Councils, the manner in which marriages shall be registered and copies of nikahnama shall be supplied to the parties, and the fees to be charged thereof, shall be such as may be prescribed.

(6) Any person may, on payment of the prescribed fee, if any, inspect at the office of the Union Council the record prescribed under sub-section (5), or obtain a copy of any entry therein.

6. Polygamy

(1) No man, during the subsistence of an existing marriage, shall except with the previous permission in writing of the Arbitration Council, contract another marriage, nor shall any such marriage contracted without such permission be registered under this Ordinance.

(2) An application for permission under sub-section (1) shall be submitted to the Chairman in the prescribed manner together with the prescribed fee, and shall state reasons for the proposed marriage, and whether the consent of existing wife or wives has been obtained thereto.

(3) On receipt of the application under sub-section (3), Chairman shall ask the applicant and his existing wife or wives each to nominate a representative, and the Arbitration Council so constituted may, if satisfied that the proposed marriage is necessary and just, grant, subject to such condition if any, as may be deemed fit, the permission applied for.

(4) In deciding the application the Arbitration Council shall record its reasons for the decision and any party may, in the prescribed

manner, within the prescribed period, and on payment of the prescribed fee, prefer an application for revision, in the case of West Pakistan to the Collector and, in the case of East Pakistan, to the Sub-Divisional Officer concerned and his decision shall be final and shall not be called in question in any Court.

(5) Any man who contracts another marriage without the permission of the Arbitration Council shall:

(a) pay immediately the entire amount of the dower whether prompt or deferred, due to the existing wife or wives, which amount, if not so paid, shall be recoverable as arrears of land revenue; and

(b) on conviction upon complaint be punishable with simple imprisonment which may extend to one year, or with fine which may extend to five thousand rupees, or with both.

7. Talaq

(1) Any man who wishes to divorce his wife, shall, as soon as may be after the pronouncement of talaq in any form whatsoever, give the Chairman a notice in writing of his having done so, and shall supply a copy thereof to the wife.

(2) Whoever contravenes the provision of sub-section (1) shall be punishable with simple imprisonment for a term which may extend to one year, or with fine which may extend to five thousand rupees, or with both.

(3) Save as provided in sub-section (5) talaq, unless revoked earlier, expressly or otherwise, shall not be effective until the expiration of ninety days from the day on which notice under sub-section (1) is delivered to the Chairman.

(4) Within thirty days of the receipt of notice under sub-section (1), the Chairman shall constitute an Arbitration Council for the purpose of bringing about a reconciliation between the parties, and the Arbitration Council shall take all steps necessary to bring about such reconciliation.

(5) If the wife be pregnant at the time talaq is pronounced, talaq shall not be effective until the period mentioned in sub-section (3) or the pregnancy, whichever later, ends.

(6) Nothing shall debar a wife whose marriage has been terminated by talaq effective under this Section from remarrying the same husband, without an intervening marriage with a third person, unless such termination is for the third time so effective.

8. Dissolution of Marriage Otherwise Than by Talaq

Where the right to divorce has been duly delegated to the wife and she wishes to exercise that right, or where any of the parties to a marriage wishes to dissolve the marriage otherwise than by talaq the provisions of section 7 shall, mutatis mutandis and so far as applicable, apply.

9. Maintenance

(1) If any husband fails to maintain his wife adequately, or where there are more wives than one, fails to maintain them equitably, the wife, or all or any of the wives, may in addition to seeking any other legal remedy available, apply to the Chairman who shall constitute an Arbitration Council to determine the matter, and the Arbitration Council may issue a certificate specifying the amount which shall be paid as maintenance by the husband.
(2) A husband or wife may, in the prescribed manner, within the prescribed period, and on payment of the prescribed fee, prefer an application for revision of the certificate, in the case of West Pakistan to the Collector and, in the case of East Pakistan to the Sub-Divisional Officer concerned and his decision shall be final and shall not be called in question in any Court.[1]
(3) Any amount payable under sub-section (1) or, (2) if not paid in the due time, shall be recoverable as arrears of land revenue.

10. Dower

When no details about the mode of payment of dower are specified in the nikahnama or the marriage contract, the entire amount of the dower shall be presumed to be payable on demand.

---

1. Under the *Punjab Amendment Punjab Act* XI of 1975 Section 9 of Ordinance VIII of 1961 was amended thus: In Section 9, sub-section (2), the full stop occurring at the end shall be replaced by a colon and thereafter the following provision shall be added, namely:-
   'Provided that the Commissioner of a Division may, on an application made in this behalf and for reasons to be recorded, transfer an application for revision of the certificate from a Collector to any other Collector, or to a Director, Local Government, or to an Additional Commissioner in his Division.'

11. Power to Make Rules

(1) [The Central Government[2] in respect of cantonment areas and the provincial Government in respect of other areas] may make rules to carry into effect the purposes of this Ordinance.

(2) In making rules under this section such Government may provide that a breach of any of the rules shall be punishable with simple imprisonment which may extend to one month, or with fine which may extend to two hundred rupees, or with both.

(3) Rules made under this section shall be published in the Official Gazette and shall thereupon have effect as if enacted in this Ordinance.

12. Amendment of Child Marriage Restraint Act, 1929 (XIX of 1929).[3]

13. Amendment of the *Dissolution of Muslim Marriages Act*, 1939 (VIII of 1939)[4].

2. Substituted by PO No.1 of 1964.
3. Omitted by Ordinance XXVII of 1981.
4. Omitted by Ordinance XXVII of 1981.

Bibliography

BOOKS

Agnes, F., *State, Gender, and the Rhetoric of Law Reform*, Bombay: Research Unit on Women's Studies, S.N.D.T. University (1995).

Ahmad, F., *Triple Talaq: An Analytical Study*, New Delhi: Regency Publications (1994)

Alladi, K., (ed.), *Mayne's Treatise on Hindu Law & Usage*, New Delhi: Bharat Law House (1993) (13th edn.).

Balchin, C. (ed.), *A Handbook on Family Law in Pakistan*, Lahore: Shirkat Gah (1994) (2nd edn.).

Banerjee, G., *Hindu Law of Marriage and Stridhana* (TLLS-1878), Calcutta: S.K. Lahiri & Co. (1923) (5th edn.).

Basu, A. & B. Rai B., *A History of the AIWC 1927–1990*, Delhi: Manohar (1992).

Basu, T. *et al.*, *Khaki Shorts Saffron Flags*, New Delhi: Orient Longman (1993).

Bhattacharjee, A.M., *Hindu Law and the Constitution*, Calcutta: Eastern Law House (1994) (2nd edn.).

——————, *Muslim Law and the Constitution*, Calcutta: Eastern Law House (1994) (2nd edn.).

——————, *Matrimonial Laws and the Constitution* Calcutta: Eastern Law House (1996).

Bhattacharji, S., *Women and Society in Ancient India*, Calcutta: Sasumati Corporation Ltd. (1994).

Borradaile's, *Report of Civil Cases 1820 - 1824*, Bombay Sudder Adaulat Folio 1825 Bombay: Education Society's Press (1825) (Rpt. 1862).

Bromley, P.M., *Family Law*, London: Butterworths (1976) (5th edn.).

Cabinetmaker, P.H., 'Parsis and Marriage,' Pune: International Institute of Population Studies (Mimeograph) (1991).

Cassandra, B. (ed.), *Muslim Law in Modern India*, Allahabad:

Allahabad Law Agency (1993) (6th edn.) p.62.

Dadachanji, F.K., *Parsis—Ancient and Modern*, Karachi: (1980).

Desai, S.T., *Mulla's Principles of Hindu Law*, Bombay: N.M. Tripathi (1994) (16th edn.).

Diwan, P., *Law of Marriage and Divorce*, Allahabad: Wadhwa & Company (1988).

————, *Muslim Law in Modern India*, Allahabad: Allahabad Law Agency (1993) (6th edn.).

————, *Hindu Law*, Allahabad: Wadhwa & Company (1995).

Derrett, D.J.M., *Hindu Law Past and Present*, Calcutta: Mukherjee & Co. (1957).

————, *Religion Law and the State in India*, New York: The Free Press (1968).

Davis, E.G., *The First Sex*, New York: Putnam (1971).

Desika Char, S.V., *Readings in the Constitutional History of India 1757–1947*, Delhi: Oxford University Press (1983).

Dhagamwar, V., *Towards the Uniform Civil Code*, Bombay: N.M. Tripathi (1989).

Dube, L., *Matriliny and Islam Religion and Society in the Laccadives*, Delhi: National Publishing House (1969).

Framjee, D., *The Parsees, Their History, Manners, Custom and Religion*, London: Smith Elder & Co. (1858).

Fyzee, A.A.A., *Outlines of Mohammadan Law*, 4th Edn. New Delhi: Oxford University Press (1974).

Gandhi, N. & N. Shah, *Issues at Stake*, New Delhi: Kali for Women (1991).

Gill, K., *Hindu Women's Right to Property in India*, Delhi: Deep & Deep Publications (1986).

Grafe, H., *History of Christianity in India—Tamil-Nadu in the Nineteenth and Twentieth Centuries*, Bangalore: The Church History Association of India (1982), Vol.IV (Part 2).

Hasan, Z. (ed.), *Forging Identities: Gender, Communities and the State*, New Delhi: Kali for Women (1994).

Hidayatullah, M. & A. Hidaytulla *Mulla's Principles of Mahomedan Law*, Bombay: N.M. Tripathi (1990) (19th edn.).

Jackson, J. (ed.), *Raydens's Law and Practice in Divorce and Family Matters*, London: Butterworths (1983).

Jain, M.P., *Outlines of Indian Legal History*, Bombay: N.M. Tripathi (1966) (2nd edn.).

Jolly, J., *Hindu Law*, Tagore Law Lecture Series (TLLS) (1883).

Kapur, R. and B. Cossman, *Subversive Sites,* New Delhi: Sage Publications (1995).

Kumar, R., *The History of Doing An Illustrated Account of Movements for Women's Rights and Feminism in India 1800–1990.* New Delhi: Kali for Women (1993).

Mahmood, T., *Family Law Reform in the Muslim World*, Bombay: N.M. Tripathi. (1972).

—————, *An Indian Civil Code and Islamic Law,* Bombay: N.M. Tripathi (1976).

—————, *Civil Marriage Law,* Bombay: N.M. Tripathi (1978).

Manchanda, S., *Parsi Law in India,* Allahabad: The Law Book Co. (1991) (V edn.).

Martin, D., *Battered Wives,* New York: Pocket Books (1976).

Mishra, V.C., (ed.), 'Special Issue on Uniform Civil Code', *Indian Bar Review,* XVIII/3-4 (1991).

Mullati, L., *The Bhakti Movement and the Status of Women: A case study of Virasaivism,* Abhinav Publications (1989).

Mundadan, A.M., *History of Christianity in India Upto Sixteenth Century,* Bangalore: The Church History Association of India (1982) Vol.I.

Parashar, A., *Women and Family Law Reform in India,* New Delhi: Sage Publications (1992).

Raghavachariar, N.R., *Hindu Law: Principles and Precedents,* Madras: The Madras Law Journal Office (1980) (7th edn.) Vol I & II.

Rankin, G.C., *Background to India Law*, Cambridge: Cambridge University Press (1946).

Roy Chowdhury, S.K. and H.D. Saharay (ed.), *Paruck's The Indian Succession Act,* Bombay: N.M. Tripathi (1988) (7th edn.).

Sachs, A. and J. H. Wilson, *Sexism and the Law—A Study of Male Beliefs and Judicial Bias,* Oxford: Law in Society Series, Martine Robertson (1978).

Sangari, K. & S. Vaid (ed.), *Recasting Women, Essays in Colonial History,* New Delhi : Kali for Women (1989).

Sarkar Shastri, G.C., *A Treatise on Hindu Law,* Calcutta (1933) (7th edn.).

Schacht, J., *An Introduction to Islamic Law,* Delhi: Oxford University Press (1964) (Rpt. 1975).

Sarkar, S., *Modern India 1885–1947,* Madras: Macmillan India Ltd. (1983).

Sharma, R.S., *Material Culture & Social Formations in Ancient India,* Madras: Macmillan India Ltd. (1983).

Shiva Rao, B., *The Framing of India's Constitution* New Delhi: The Indian Institute of Public Administration (1968) Vol.I & II.

Shodhan, A., *Legal Representations of Khojas and Pushtimarga Vaishnavas : The Aga Khan Case and the Maharaj Libel Case in Mid-nineteenth Century Bombay'* (unpublished Doctorate Dissertation submitted to the faculty of the Division of the Humanities), Department of South Asian Languages and Civilizations. Chicago, Illinois (1995).

Srinivas, M.N., *Caste in Modern India And Other Essays,* Bombay: Media Promoters & Publishers (1962) (Rpt. 1986).

—————, *Some Reflections on Dowry.* New Delhi: Oxford University Press (1984).

Steele, A., *Hindu Caste, Their Law, Religion and Customs,* Bombay: Courier Press (1827).

Talim, M., *Women in Early Buddhist Literature,* Bombay: Popular Prakashan (1972)

Thapar, R.. *A History of India,* Delhi: Penguin (1992) Vol. I.

Thekkedath, J., *History of Christianity in India 1542–1700,* Bangalore: The Church History Association of India (1982) Vol.II.

Usgaocar, M.S., *Family Laws of Goa, Daman and Diu,* Vaso Da Gama: Devi Shreevani Education Society (1980) Vol I.

—————, *Family Laws of Goa, Daman and Diu,* Panaji: Vela Associates (1988), Vol. II.

ARTICLES

'Abusing Religion to Oppress Women', in *Manushi* IV/4 (1984), p.9.

'Recommendations of the Lawyers Collective Bangalore Law School', in *The Lawyers,* III/7 (1988), p.20.

'A Christian Woman Demands Equal Succession Rights', in *Manushi* No.25 (V/1) (1984), p.7.

'Hazir Hai—Mary Roy', in *The Lawyers* I/11–12 (1986), pp.33-5.

Agnes, F., 'Protecting Women Against Violence—Review of Decade of Legislation', in *Economic and Political Weekly,* XXVII/17 (1992), p.WS-19.

—————, 'Triple Talaq Judgment Do Women Really Benefit', in *Economic and Political Weekly.* XXIX/20 (1994), p. 1169.

—————, 'Hindu Men, Monogamy and the Uniform Civil Code', in *Economic and Political Weekly*, XXX/50 (1995), p.3238.

—————, 'Economic Rights of Muslim Women', in *Economic and Political Weekly*, XXXI/41–42 (1996), p.2832.

—————, 'The Politics of Women's Rights', *Seminar* no.441 (1996), p. 62.

—————, 'In the Dock', in *Humanscape* August 1996, p.26.

Aggarwal, R., 'Uniform Civil Code—a formula not a solution', in *Family Law and Social Change* (ed.) Mahmood T. Bombay : N.M. Tripathi (1975), pp. 110–44.

Ahmed, I., 'Personal Laws: Promoting Reform from Within', in *Economic and Political Weekly*, XXX/45 (1995), p. 2851.

Ansari, I., 'Muslim Women's Rights: Goals and Strategy of Reform', *Economic and Political Weekly*, XXVI/17 (1991), p.1095.

Anweshi Law Committee 'Is Gender Justice Only a Legal Issue—Political Stakes in UCC Debate', in *Economic and Political Weekly*, XXXII/9–10 (1997), p. 453.

Banerjee, S., 'Marginalization of Women's Popular Culture in Nineteenth Century Bengal', in Sangari, K. & S. Vaid (ed.), *Recasting Women, Essays in Colonial History*, New Delhi : Kali for Women (1989), p.127.

Bindra, A., 'Child Custody for Hindus only', *The Lawyers* IX/2 (1994), p.11.

Carroll, L., 'Law, Custom and Statutory Social Reform: The Hindu Widow's Remarriage Act of 1856', *Indian Economic and Social History Review*, Vol. XX/4 (Oct–Dec) (1983), pp. 363-88.

—————, 'Law, Custom and Statutory Social Reforms The Hindu Widow Remarriage Act, 1856', J Krishnamurthi (ed.), *Women in Colonial India : Essays on Survival Work and State*, Delhi: Oxford University Press (1989).

Chandra, S., 'Rukmabai: Debate over Woman's Right to Her Person', in *Economic and Political Weekly*, XXXI/44 (1996), p.2927.

Chhachhi, A., 'Identity Politics, Secularism and Women: A South Asian perspective', (1994) in Zoya Hasan (ed.), *Forging Identities: Gender, Communities and the State*, New Delhi: Kali for Women (1994) p.82.

Circular from the Catholic Bishops' Conference of India (CBCI) 90/ckir-17, Sub-Christian Marriage Law II, 6 June 1990.

Cohn, B.S., 'Anthropological Note on Disputes and Law in India', in L Nader (ed.), *The Ethnography of Law* (American Anthropological Association) (1965), p.112.

Dube, L., 'Conflict and Compromise Devolution and Disposal of Property in Matrilineal Muslim Society', in *Economic and Political Weekly*, XXIX/21 (1994), p. 1273.

Fazalbuoy, N., 'The Debate on Muslim Personal Law', Paper presented at the Third National Conference on Women's Studies, Chandigarh (1986).

Fyzee, A.A.A., 'The Muslim Wife's Right of Dissolving her Marriage', in (1936) 38 Bom.LR, p. 113.

Gangoli, G., 'Anti-Bigamy Bill in Maharashtra', in *Economic and Political Weekly*, XXXI/29 (1996), p. 1919.

Hasan, M., 'Indian Muslims since Independence: In search of Integration and Identity', in *Third World Quarterly*, April, 1988.

Hasan, Z., 'Minority Identity, State Policy and the Political Process' (1994), in Hasan, Z. (ed.), *Forging Identities: Gender, Communities and the State*, New Delhi: Kali for Women (1994), p.59.

Karat, B., 'Step by Step Approach: Equal Rights, Equal laws', in *Women's Equality* V/1 (1993), p.5.

Khanna, S., 'Padmasini's Quest for Justice', in *The Lawyers* VII/2 (1992), p.25.

Kannabiran, K.G., 'Outlawing Oral Divorce' in *Economic and Political Weekly*, XXIX/25 (1994), p. 1509.

Kishwar, M., 'Pro-Women or Anti Minority? the Shahbano Controversy', in *Manushi* VI/2 (1986), p.4.

————, 'Codified Hindu Law: Myth and Reality', in *Economic and Political Weekly*, XXIX/33 (1994), p. 2145.

Lateef, S., 'Defining Women through Legislation' (1994), in Hasan, Z. (ed.), *Forging Identities: Gender, Communities and the State*, New Delhi: Kali for Women (1994), p.38.

Mani, L., 'Contentious Traditions: The Debate on Sati in Colonial India' (1989), in Sangari K. & S. Vaid (ed.), *Recasting Women, Essays in Colonial History*, New Delhi : Kali for Women (1989), p. 88.

Monterio, R., 'Belief, Law, and Justice for Women', in *Economical and Political Weekly*, XVII/43& 44 (1992), WS-74.

Mukhopadhyay, M., 'Between Community and State: The question of women's right and personal laws' (1994), in Hasan, Z. (ed.), *Forging Identities: Gender, Communities and the*

State, New Delhi: Kali for Women (1994), p.109.

Mukund, K. 'Turmeric Land—Women's Property Rights in Tamil Society since Medieval Times', in *Economic & Political Weekly*, XXVII/17 (1992), p.WS-2.

Nag, A., 'The Many faces of Sati in the Early Nineteenth Century', *Manushi* 42–3 (1987), p.26.

Navlakha, G., 'Triple talaq: Posturing at Women's Expense', in *Economic and Political Weekly*, XXIX/21 (1994), p. 1264.

Pathak, Z. and R.S. Rajan, 'Shah Bano', *Signs*, Vol. 14, n.3 (1989).

Sarkar, T., 'Rhetoric Against Age of Consent', *Economic and Political Weekly*, XXVIII/36, (1993) p.1869.

Sathe, S.P., 'Uniform Civil Code Why? What? and How?' (1995), in *Towards Secular India*, I/4, Bombay: Centre for Study of Society and Secularism (1995), p.31.

—————, 'Uniform Civil Code Implications of the Supreme Court Judgement', *Economic and Political Weekly*, XXX/35, (1995), p.2165.

Shikhare D. , 'Talaq Mukti Morcha in Maharashtra', in *Manushi*, VI/2 (1986), p.23.

Singh, K., 'The Constitution and the Muslim Personal Law' (1994), in Hasan, Z. (ed.), *Forging Identities: Gender, Communities and the State*, New Delhi: Kali for Women (1994), p.96.

—————, 'Combating Communalism', *Seminar*, N.441 (1996), p.55.

Sivaramayya, B., 'The Special Marriage Act, 1954 Goes Awry', in V. Bagga (ed.), *Studies in the Hindu Marriage and the Special Marriage Acts*, Bombay: N.M. Tripathi (1978), p.310.

Tiwari, B., 'Marriage Laws Revamped', *The Lawyers* X/5 (1995), p.28.

The Forum Against Oppression of Women Views on the Uniform Civil Code' (1995), unpublished document available with the group.

Upadhya, C., 'Dowry and women's property in coastal Andhra Pradesh' (1990), in *Contributions to Indian Sociology*, Delhi: Sage Publications (n.s.) 24, 1 (1990) p.29.

Vargo, N. and R. Goldfaden, 'The Goa Uniform Civil Code—Alive and Kicking', in *The Lawyers* X/7 (1995), p.21.

Vimochana, 'The Quest for a Uniform Civil Code: Some Dilemmas, some issues' (1988), unpublished document available with the group.

NEWSPAPER REPORTS/ARTICLES

'Muslims resent talaq verdict', *The Times of India*, 18 April 1994.
'Triple Talaq Again', *The Times of India*, 19 April 1994.
'Muslim women welcome court verdict on talaq', *The Statesman*, 22 April 1994.
'Divorced From Reality', *The Pioneer*, 25 April 1994.
'The practice is contrary to the spirit of Islam', *Indian Express*, 25 April 1994.
'Another Shah Bano in the Making', *The Times of India*, 25 April 1994.
'One Nation, One Law', *Sunday* 1-7 May 1994.
'Beyond the law—The Strange Case of Justice Tilhari', *Frontline*, 20 May 1994.
'Fear Behind the Purdah', *Blitz*, 21 May 1994.
'Avadh Bar to Suspend Advocate General', *The Times of India*, 19 May 1994.
'No change in Muslim personal law, says P.M.', *The Times of India*, 28 July 1995.
'Suggestion on civil code not binding says Court', *The Asian Age*, 12 August 1995.
The Times of India, 11 May 1997.
Ahmed, F., 'Fatwa needed to make talaq revocable', *The Pioneer*, 17 May 1994.
Anand, J., 'Uniform Civil Code: Case for a Supreme Judgment', *The Asian Age*, 8 June 1995.
—————, 'Only hope for gender justice rests with Supreme Court', *The Times of India*, 10 August 1995.
Ashraf, A., 'A cap and a beard: Is that all to Muslims', *The Pioneer*, 1 May 1994.
Badshah, H., 'Uniform Civil Code—Chasing a Mirage', *The Hindu*, 24 December 1995.
Basu, A., 'Behind the Four Walls The Veil', *The Statesman*, 30 April 1994.
Bhatnagar, R., 'Muslim Woman moves Court on Talaq', *The Times of India*, 31 January 1995.
Chadha, K., 'The Law that breaks the Constitution', *The Hindustan Times*, 8 August 1993.
Engineer, A.A., 'Personal Law and Gender Justice', *The Times of India*, 10 June 1995.

——————, 'Muslim reformists draft new legislation on marriage and divorce', *The Times of India*, 10 April 1996.

——————, 'A Model for Change in Personal Law', *The Times of India*, 25 July 1995.

Hussain, W., 'I am a believer in Islam but can't accept discriminination', *The Asian Age*, 13 April 1997.

Jung, Z., 'Begin by Codifying Muslim Family Law', *The Times of India*, 29 July 1995.

Karat, B., 'Uniformity vs Equality: The Concept of uniform civil code', *Frontline* 17 November 1995.

Latifi, D., 'Verdict on talaq', *The Hindustan Times*, 5 May 1994.

Mali, A., 'Uniformity among equals', *The Hindustan Times*, 8 May 1994.

Punwani, J., 'Women veto a common civil code', *The Sunday Review*, 23 July 1995.

Seervai, H.M., 'Judiciary oversteps its Brief', *The Times of India*, 5 July 1995.

Shahabuddin, S., 'A Mountain is being made out of a molehill', *The Hindustan Times*, 28 May 1995.

Venkataramanan, S., 'Devaluation of rupee: Past and present', *The Sunday Times of India*, 10 August 1997.

Vyas, N., 'Much more at stake than triple talaq', *The Hindu*, 1 May 1994.

OFFICIAL DOCUMENTS

Constituent Assembly Debates
Gazette of India, (Extraordinary, Part II, S. 2, 22 June 1962)
Joint Select Committee Report *Evidence on Adoption Bill*
Law Commission Reports
Parliamentary Debates
Rajya Sabha Debates
Report of the Commmittee on Status of Women
Towards Equality (1974)

Tables

Table 1: Caste-wise Composition of the Population

A:	SCHEDULED CASTES AND TRIBES:	22.65
	SCHEDULED CASTES	15.05
	SCHEDULED TRIBES	7.51
B:	NON HINDU COMMUNITIES AND RELIGIOUS GROUPS:	16.16*
	MUSLIMS	11.19
	CHRISTIANS	2.16
	SIKHS	1.67
	BUDDHISTS (OTHER THAN SC)	0.47
C:	FORWARD HINDU CASTES AND COMMUNITIES:	17.58
	BRAHMINS	5.52
	RAJPUTS	3.90
	JATS	1.00
	MARATHAS	2.21
	VAISHNAVAS	1.58
	KAYASTHA	1.02
	OTHER FORWARD CASTES	2.00
D.	OTHER BACKWARD CASTES (OBC) (DERIVED):	43.70
	100 - (A+B+C)	
	*AN ESTIMATED 52% UNDER B ARE ALSO OBC:	8.40
	TOTAL OTHER BACKWARD CASTES	52.10
	(43.70 + 8.40)	

Note : Cast-wise ennumeration of population began in 1881, stopped in 1931, therefore culled out from 1931 by the Mandal Commission.

Source : Report of the Backward Class Commission, 1980, Government of India.

Table 2A: Marriages Registered Under the Special Marriage Act
(SMA) in Mumbai. 1968–72

MARRIAGES REGISTERED UNDER SMA AND THOSE PERFORMED
IN OTHER FORMS AND SUBSEQUENTLY REGISTERED UNDER SMA

Year	Org. Reg.	Sub. Reg
1968	601	19
1969	621	18
1970	766	43
1971	705	36
1972	816	26

Source: Towards Equality, p.114.

Table 2B: Marriages Registered under the Special Marriage Act
(SMA) in Mumbai. 1986–96

	City		Suburbs		Total	
Year	BMRA	SMA	BMRA	SMA	BMRA	SMA
1986	14,300	755	5,885	787	20,185	1,542
1987	16,460	777	6,625	929	23,085	1,706
1988	15,572	693	7,005	790	22,577	1,483
1989	19,133	773	7,126	956	26,259	1,729
1990	18,200	719	9,657	901	27,857	1,620
1991	15,100	764	10,697	958	25,797	1,722
1992	12,423	634	16,075	937	28,498	1,571
1993	11,316	672	16,415	962	27,731	1,634
1994	11,581	606	17,962	1,113	29,543	1,719
1995	12,516	602	19,925	1,101	32,441	1,703
1996	11,380	577	18,264	1,325	29,644	1,902

SMA   - *Special Marriage Act*, 1954
BMRA   - *Bombay Marriage Registration Act*, 1953

Source: Office of the Registrar of Marriages Bombay City and Suburbs.

Table 3: Community-wise Incidences of Polygamous Marriages

A: INCIDENCES OF POLYGAMOUS MARRIAGES 1951+1960

Tribal	-	17.98%
Hindus	-	5.06%
Muslim	-	4.31%

Source: Towards Equality, p.67

B: INCIDENCES OF POLYGAMY

Tribals	-	15.25%,
Buddhists	-	7.97%,
Jains	-	6.72%,
Hindus	-	5.8%
Muslims	-	5.7%.

Source : Towards Equality, p.104.

Note : Since Buddhists and Jains are also governed by Hindu law, the statistics for Hindus collectively would be 6.83% as compared to 5.7% for Muslims.

Table 4: Parsi Population in India 1901–1961

1901	—	94, 190
1911	—	100, 096
1921	—	101, 778
1931	—	101, 778
1941	—	109, 752
1951	—	114, 890
1961	—	100, 772

Source : Cabinetmaker, P.H. (1991), Parsis and Marriage, Pune: International Institute of Population Studies, p.1-2.

Table 5: Population of India : Urban–Rural Distribution

Total Population of India	:	843,930,861
Urban Population of India	:	25.7%
Rural Population of India	:	74.3%

Source : Census Report—1991.

Table 6: Reported Cases of Unnatural Deaths of Married
Women in Mumbai

Year	1990	1991	1992	1993	1994	1995	1996
Dowry Murder	7	3	12	8	9	43	11
Dowry Death	14	21	13	8	21	-	16
Dowry Suicide	21	8	18	21	34	18	59
Total	42	42	43	37	64	61	86

Source : Commissioner of Police, Bombay.

Table 7: Religion-wise Distribution of Cases Filed under
S. 498(A) IPC 1990–95

	No.	Percentage
Hindus	737	69.1%
Sikhs	28	2.6%
Buddhists	63	5.9%
Jains	2	0.2%
Total Hindus governed by Hindu law	**830**	**77.8%**
Muslims	204	19.2%
Christians	25	2.3%
Parsis	4	0.4%
Religion not Known	3	0.3%
Total	1066	100%

Source : Research conducted by Tata Institute of Social Science, 1996 (unpublished).

Table 8: Population of India—Religion-wise Distribution
1961–91

RELIG ION	PERCENTAGE TO THE TOTAL			
	1961	1971	1981	1991
Hindus	83.5	82.7	82.6	82.41
Sikhs	1.4	1.9	2.0	1.99
Buddhists	0.7	0.7	0.7	0.77
Jains	0.5	0.5	0.5	0.41
Total Hindus governed by Hindu law	**86.1**	**85.8**	**85.8**	**85.58**
Muslims	10.7	11.2	11.4	11.67
Christians	2.4	2.6	2.4	2.32
Others	0.4	0.4	0.4	0.43

Source : Census Reports.

Index